WOMAN IN THE NINETEENTH CENTURY
AND OTHER WRITINGS

MARGARET FULLER was born in Cambridge, Massachusetts, in 1810, the eldest child in a family of nine. Her father Timothy educated her as a prodigy, giving her a classical education of the sort usually reserved for boys. With Ralph Waldo Emerson she edited *The Dial*, the Transcendentalist journal which set the canon of early nineteenth-century American literature, publishing such writers as Thoreau for the first time. After travels among pioneer and Native American women in the West and work with prostitutes in Sing Sing Prison, she became the political and literary editor of Horace Greeley's *New York Daily Tribune* in 1844. Reporting the city's ills made her increasingly socialist; she was already a feminist, and her book on the Woman Question, *Woman in the Nineteenth Century* (1845), was enormously popular and influential. Susan B. Anthony judged that Fuller had a greater influence on the nascent women's movement than any other writer of her time.

In 1846 Fuller sailed for Europe as the *Tribune*'s foreign correspondent. Interviews with Thomas Carlyle, William Wordsworth, George Sand, Chopin, Adam Mickiewicz and Giuseppe Mazzini established her reputation, which was consolidated by her reports from Rome during the Revolution of 1848–9, when she ran a hospital for injured republican soldiers. Her son Angelo, by a marquis in the Roman civic guard, Giovanni Ossoli, was born in September 1848. In late 1849 the Ossolis were forced to become refugees in Florence after the fall of Rome; there they became friendly with Robert and Elizabeth Barrett Browning. Returning to America in July 1850, Margaret Fuller, her husband, and their 1-year-old child were drowned fifty yards off shore in a hurricane.

DONNA DICKENSON is a Lecturer at the Open University and the author of a critical biography applying modern feminist literary and political theory to Fuller's life and work: *Margaret Fuller: Writing a Woman's Life* (1993). She has also written feminist biographies of Emily Dickinson (1985) and George Sand (1988).

THE WORLD'S CLASSICS

MARGARET FULLER

Woman in the Nineteenth Century
and Other Writings

Edited with an Introduction by
DONNA DICKENSON

Oxford   New York

OXFORD UNIVERSITY PRESS

1994

Oxford University Press, Walton Street, Oxford OX2 6DP

Oxford New York Toronto
Delhi Bombay Calcutta Madras Karachi
Kuala Lumpur Singapore Hong Kong Tokyo
Nairobi Dar es Salaam Cape Town
Melbourne Auckland Madrid
and associated companies in
Berlin Ibadan

Oxford is a trade mark of Oxford University Press

Editorial material © Donna Dickenson 1994

First published as a World's Classics paperback 1994

British Library Cataloguing in Publication Data
Data available

Library of Congress Cataloging in Publication Data
Fuller, Margaret, 1810–1850.
Woman in the nineteenth century and other writings/Margaret
Fuller; edited with an introduction by Donna Dickenson.
p. cm.—(The World's Classics)
Includes bibliographical references.
1. Women—History—Modern period, 1660–   . I. Dickenson, Donna.
II. Title. III. Series.
HQ1154.F87 1994 305.4'09034—dc20 93–11097
ISBN 0–19–283085–6

1 3 5 7 9 10 8 6 4 2

Typeset by Best-set Typesetter Ltd., Hong Kong
Printed in Great Britain by
BPCC Paperbacks Ltd.
Aylesbury, Bucks

CONTENTS

INTRODUCTION

> 'My dear Sir,' I exclaimed, 'if you'd not been afraid
> Of Margaret Fuller's success, you'd have stayed
> Your hand in her case and more justly have rated her.'
> Here he murmured morosely, 'My God, how I hated her!'[1]

Margaret Fuller was privileged in her lifetime—as a woman editor, essayist, political journalist, and arts critic in an otherwise largely male domain—because she was one of the first of her kind. When women began entering the literary lists in greater numbers, after Fuller's death and partly through her inspiration, she became a greater threat, to be excoriated and exorcised. Yet throughout her life she herself was ambivalent about her critical and creative abilities, saying of herself, 'I have no art'. Such diffidence was further ammunition against her after her death: she was taken at her own modest word by male successors who 'came to praise but also, perhaps unconsciously, to bury her'.[2]

Fuller was the emblematic woman of her time. The American critic Norman Podhoretz has suggested that at most only one woman of her generation and place is allowed to be the 'Dark Lady', the intellectual superstar of her sex. This female lead in the mid-twentieth-century United States was taken first by Mary McCarthy, and then by Susan Sontag. Elaine Showalter has identified Margaret Fuller as the Dark Lady of the American Renaissance. Showalter also suggests that the Dark Lady is inevitably punished for accepting the eminence thrust upon her, citing recent harsh criticism of Sontag's previously influential work. Could this also help to explain the volte-face in Fuller's reputation?

What befell Fuller's reputation has happened to that of many other women writers, in the manner documented for a later

---

[1] Amy Lowell, 'A Critical Fable' (1922), in *Complete Poetical Works* (Boston: Houghton Mifflin, 1955), 409.

[2] Bell Gale Chevigny, *The Woman and the Myth: Margaret Fuller's Life and Writings* (Old Westbury, NY: Feminist Press, 1976), 9.

period by Sandra M. Gilbert and Susan Gubar;[3] but it happened to her first. Fuller wrote her own life by living it. She wove it into a tapestry of epic proportions, a new *Aeneid* of Rome's refounding by an outsider. But after her early death alterations were made: the garment of her life was refashioned by male tailors—primarily Emerson and Hawthorne—to suit the prevailing female fashion. The mode which they chose was less than flattering: the styles on which they modelled her garb were the female invalid, the cerebral spinster, the vestal devotee.

Yet Fuller's life and death were heroic. She made her life not into the Gothic tale which women's novels of the time portrayed, but into a Latin epic: beginning from a youth steeped in the Latin texts from which most girls were barred, she spent the three last and most vital years of her life supporting the Roman revolution and running a hospital for the wounded during the siege of Rome. Earlier, she had edited the magazine which was to epitomize the Transcendentalist movement (*The Dial*), written criticism and social-policy articles for the *New York Daily Tribune*, worked with prostitutes at Sing Sing Prison in Ossining, New York, and visited the Native American women on Mackinac Island in the Great Lakes.

Fuller's most influential publication, *Woman in the Nineteenth Century* (1845), sold out within a week. *Woman* was based on Fuller's earlier work on the Woman Question, 'The Great Lawsuit: Man *versus* Men. Woman *versus* Women' (*The Dial* (July 1843), 4: 1–48), but the book was much more politically minded than the earlier essay. Bringing to the fore such issues as prostitution, employment, and marriage reform, *Woman* helped to set the tone, if not the precise agenda, for the Seneca Falls convention of 1848 and the American women's movement. (Fuller did not explicitly advocate women's suffrage, which did become a focus of the movement: the *Tribune* editor Horace Greeley, who sponsored the publication of *Woman*, was an inveterate foe of votes for women.) After her death

---

[3] Sandra M. Gilbert and Susan Gubar, *No Man's Land: The Place of the Woman Writer in the Twentieth Century*, vol. 1, *The War of the Words* (New Haven, Conn. and London: Yale University Press, 1988).

'Margaret Fuller Clubs' sprang up all over America. Elizabeth Cady Stanton and Susan B. Anthony judged that Fuller 'possessed more influence upon the thought of American women than any woman previous to her time'.[4]

Fuller's personal life, too, was heroic in the best woman's way: caring for her mother and seven younger siblings, then later enduring her own first childbirth without family support in Italy, and with no one who could so much as speak her language. Even her death—in a hurricane, fifty yards off the coast of Fire Island, returning to America from Italy with her Italian husband and 22-month-old son—was tragic rather than merely poignant.

It was Ralph Waldo Emerson who began the process of mythologizing Fuller into obscurity after her death. As one of three editors of her posthumous *Memoirs*, together with James Freeman Clarke and William Henry Channing, friends of Fuller's youth, he rewrote the heroic epic which she had lived as a minor novelette. The three editors' names did not even appear on the title-page of the *Memoirs* which re-invented Fuller in their preferred image. Nevertheless, Emerson sold more copies of Fuller's *Memoirs* than of any work of his own: his *Nature* (1836) took seven years to clear an edition of 500 copies. Fuller's *Woman in the Nineteenth Century* sold out an edition twice that size in one week.

The 'best possible motives' with which Emerson and his fellow editors were generally acknowledged to have acted— saving Fuller's sexual reputation—absolved them of any blame for finishing the 'autobiography' which her premature death had stopped short. They rewrote her life, apparently with her own posthumous permission.

Added to the editors' prurience about Fuller's Italian years— when she had a baby by Marchese Giovanni Angelo Ossoli, to whom she may or may not have been married at the time of their son Nino's birth in 1848—was their fear of what might be revealed about their own idiosyncrasies when Fuller's correspondence with them was printed. Fuller had a talent for

[4] Quoted in Eleanor Flexner, *A Century of Struggle* (Cambridge, Mass.: Belknap Press, 1959), 68.

inspiring confidences. Very soon after her death Emerson wrote in his journal: 'When I heard that a trunk of her correspondence had been found and opened, I felt what a panic would strike all her friends, for it was as if a clever reporter had got underneath a confessional and agreed to report all that transpired there in Wall street.'[5] What he had to fear appears to have been less any sort of sexual innuendo than the embarrassing revelation that Fuller could actually make the august sage of Concord laugh. He recorded of their first meeting in July 1835:

She had a dangerous reputation for satire, in addition to her great scholarship ... her talk was a comedy in which dramatic justice was done to everybody's foibles. I remember that she made me laugh more than I liked ... She had an incredible variety of anecdotes, and the readiest wit to give an absurd turn to whatever passed; and the eyes, which were so plain at first, soon swam with fun and drolleries, and the very tides of joy and superabundant life.[6]

Emerson also lays great stress on Fuller's alleged ugliness— accepted as fact by subsequent critics, though feminists have pointed out that Thoreau's horsey nose and Emerson's fishy eyes have never been held against *them*. The abiding image of Fuller has been the one Emerson paints: bulging eyes, half-closed in perpetual sibylline contemplation; dishwater-blond locks; and a stooped posture. 'It is to be said that Margaret made a disagreeable first impression on most persons, including those who became afterwards her best friends, to such an extent that they did not wish to be in the same room with her.'[7]

Male bitchiness about Fuller's appearance has continued. Henry James imagined her as 'glossily ringletted and monumentally breastpinned'; the modern editor and critic Perry Miller, as 'phenomenally homely', her hair 'not quite blond, stringy and thin'.[8] But the most salacious have been her admirers: 'At

[5] Ralph Waldo Emerson, *The Journals and Miscellaneous Notebooks of Ralph Waldo Emerson*, vol. XI, *1848–51*, ed. A. W. Plumstead, William H. Gilman, and Ruth H. Bennett (Cambridge, Mass.: Belknap Press, 1975), 258.

[6] *Memoirs of Margaret Fuller Ossoli* (London: Richard Bentley, 1852), i. 270.

[7] Ibid. 259.

[8] Both quoted in Marie Mitchell Olesen Urbanski, *Margaret Fuller's Woman in the Nineteenth Century: A Literary Study of Form and Content, of Sources and Influence* (Westport, Conn.: Greenwood Press, 1980), 37.

thirteen her breasts were so developed that she seemed eighteen, or twenty . . . Her hair was blond, fine and softspun, reflecting light like buckwheat honey when poured from a pottery jar. Her mouth was soft and curving . . .'[9]

A similar male prurience pervades Nathaniel Hawthorne's characterization of the Fuller-figure Zenobia in *The Blithedale Romance* (1852). Although in life Fuller counted Hawthorne more 'a brother to me, than ever . . . any man before',[10] Hawthorne fulminated after her death against 'a damned mob of scribbling women'.[11] More woundingly, he created in *The Blithedale Romance* a character widely assumed to be Fuller, with implications which were less than flattering. Throughout the novel the narrator makes openly sexual remarks about Zenobia, admitting to imagining her in 'Eve's earliest garment'.

She should have made it a point of duty, moreover, to sit endlessly to painters and sculptors, and preferably to the latter; because the cold decorum of the marble would consist with the utmost scantiness of drapery, so that the eye might chastely be gladdened with her material perfection in its entireness . . . what was visible of her full bust,—in a word, her womanliness incarnated,—compelled me sometimes to close my eyes, as if it were not quite the privilege of modesty to gaze at her.[12]

Whether or not Hawthorne intended Zenobia really to *be* Fuller, the novel ends with her drowning, and most readers took that to be more than coincidence. Most unpleasantly of all, Hawthorne wrote in his notebooks—later published by his son with great damage to Fuller's remaining reputation—that she was better off dead.

She was a great humbug; of course with much talent, and much moral reality, or else she could not have been so great a humbug . . . tragic as

[9] Joseph Jay Deiss, *The Roman Years of Margaret Fuller* (New York: Thomas Y. Crowell, 1969), 13–14.

[10] Mason Wade, *Margaret Fuller: Whetstone of Genius* (New York: Viking, 1940), 113.

[11] A comment made in 1855, quoted by Caroline Ticknor in *Hawthorne and His Publishers* (Boston: Houghton Mifflin, 1913), 142.

[12] Nathaniel Hawthorne, *The Blithedale Romance*, The World's Classics edn. (Oxford: Oxford University Press, 1991), 44.

her catastrophe was, Providence was, after all, kind in putting her and
her clownish husband, and their child, on board that fated ship.[13]

But however bitter Hawthorne's personal feelings about
Fuller, modern critical opinion has begun to explore the idea
that he was greatly influenced by *Woman in the Nineteenth
Century*. Hawthorne may have been more angered by Fuller's
disclosure of her sexuality through her affair with and marriage
to Ossoli than was Emerson, more 'disappointed' in her, because of the two men he actually shows the greater awareness of
the Woman Question. In chapter 14 of *The Blithedale Romance*,
'Eliot's Pulpit', Hawthorne demonstrates quite a sophisticated
understanding of the conflicting pressures on Zenobia. Though
the eloquent advocate of her sex, she can only win the orator
Hollingsworth's heart by letting him monopolize her speech and
belief. Hawthorne parodies Hollingsworth's tired arguments
about male superiority: woman is made to be protected by man,
Hollingsworth asserts, and if she doesn't recognize that, by
God, she should be beaten into it. It is worth noting that
Hollingsworth is often taken to be Emerson.

Some critics also see in Hawthorne's *Scarlet Letter* the influence of Fuller's 'apocalyptic feminism', particularly in this
passage from the novel's conclusion:

Women . . . in the continually recurring trials of wounded, wasted,
wronged, misplaced, or erring and sinful passion,—or with the dreary
burden of a heart unyielded, because unvalued and unsought,—came
to Hester's cottage demanding why they were so wretched, and what
the remedy . . . She assured them of her firm belief, that, at some
brighter period, when the world should have grown ripe for it, in
Heaven's own time, a new truth would be revealed, in order to establish
the whole relation between man and woman on a surer ground of
mutual happiness. Earlier in life, Hester had vainly imagined that she
herself might be the destined prophetess, but had long since recognized
the impossibility that any mission of divine and mysterious truth should
be confided to a woman stained with sin, bowed down with shame, or
even burdened with a lifelong sorrow. The angel and apostle of the
coming revelation must be a woman, indeed, but lofty, pure and beautiful; and wise, moreover, not through dusky grief, but the ethereal

[13] From Hawthorne's French and Italian notebooks, published by Julian
Hawthorne in *Nathaniel Hawthorne and His Wife* (Boston, 1884).

medium of joy; and showing how sacred love should make us happy, by the truest test of a life successful to such an end![14]

In *Woman* Fuller anticipates Hawthorne's belief that the female Messiah must herself be pure (though not his extraneous assumption that she must also be beautiful), remarking, in an otherwise adulatory passage about George Sand: 'Those who would reform the world must show that they do not speak in the heat of wild impulse; their lives must be unstained by passionate error; they must be severe lawgivers to themselves' (p. 48).

Underlying this sentiment was the political need for Fuller to placate the devotees of the then dominant discourse, what has since been termed the 'Cult of True Womanhood'. Earlier, in the late eighteenth and early nineteenth centuries, American thought on the woman question was actually more progressive than in Fuller's period. What the feminist historian Jane Rendall calls 'the rhetoric of republican motherhood' had elevated educational aspirations for women, though without challenging their confinement to the domestic sphere. In that realm—through boycotting tea, producing cloth for the revolutionary army's uniforms, and bearing the burden of billeting troops—American women had shown themselves worthy. The popular heroines 'Molly Pitcher' (Mary Hays), who carried water to American troops at the Battle of Monmouth, and Betsy Ross, who sewed the new republic's flag, epitomized this combination of patriotism and domesticity during the War of American Independence.

Some women, like the poet and playwright Mercy Otis Warren (1728–1824), had also used their pens to denounce the corruption of the old order and proclaim the glories of the new republic. These women writers of the late eighteenth and early nineteenth centuries saw no contradiction between female independence of spirit and domestic harmony. The successful novelist and poet Susanna Rowson (1762–1824) urged husbands to treat their wives as intelligent and free beings if they wanted peace at home. Her patriotic comedy, *The Slaves in Algiers, or, a Struggle for Freedom*, centres on a group of American women held for ransom by Barbary Coast pirates. A parable of

---

[14] Nathaniel Hawthorne, *The Scarlet Letter*, The World's Classics edn. (Oxford: Oxford University Press, 1990), 263.

liberty from the former colonial oppressor whose privateers still ravaged American shipping on the seas, Rowson's text has one of the women say: 'I feel that I was born free, and while I have life, I will struggle to remain so.'

In an essay, 'On the Equality of the Sexes', written in 1779 and published in 1790 in the *Massachusetts Magazine*, Judith Sargent Murray had urged her fellow Americans to instil republican virtues into new generations of women. Coincidentally Murray's essay described the education given to a girl called 'Margaretta' by 'Mrs Vigilius'. Timothy Fuller, Margaret's father, likewise chose to indoctrinate his daughter in the republican virtues of Rome as well as those of America. Margaret's first extant essay, written at the age of about 12 for her father, showed that the cult of republican virtue had a new convert. 'Resolved, united hearts freed America ... [I]t is not in the power of circumstance to prevent the earnest will from shaping round itself the character of a great, a wise, or a good man.'[15]

From an early age Margaret learned Latin, French, logic, rhetoric, and a little Greek. One of her first letters to her father, written at 7, shows that she was being fed on a diet of warrior kings:

I have been reviewing Valpy's Chronology [of ancient and English history]. We have not been able to procure any books [on] either Charles 12th of Sweden or Philip IId of Spain but Mama intends to send to Uncle Henry. I hope to make greater proficuncy [*sic*] in my Studies I have learned all the rules of Musick but one.[16]

By 9 she was writing letters to Timothy in Latin and working her way through the fifth book of Virgil, whom she had begun memorizing at 6, along with passages from Plutarch and Ovid. She had ingested not only the language but also its agonistic spirit, smarting inwardly because one Mary Elliot had finished *her* Virgil in thirty days. The ambition which she expressed openly all her life was already alive in a letter to her father of 3 February 1820. There she reiterated her determination to best

[15] Quoted in Thomas Wentworth Higginson, *Margaret Fuller Ossoli* (Boston: Houghton Mifflin, American Men of Letters Series, 1884), 47.

[16] *The Letters of Margaret Fuller*, ed. Robert N. Hudspeth (Ithaca, NY: Cornell University Press, 1983), i. 81 (13 Jan. 1818).

Mary Elliot's record and sealed her resolve with the Lord's Prayer in Latin. In reply, Timothy wrote: 'I would not discourage you, my girl, by being too critical and yet I am anxious to have you admit to one *fault*, which you will remember I have often mentioned, as the source, the very fountain of others—carelessness.'[17]

In *Woman* Fuller still shows her father's influence: when she is overly pedantic, when her recital of historical evidence becomes interminable, it is as if she is still trying to forestall any possible accusations of carelessness or lack of scholarship. Timothy Fuller, who took sole charge of his daughter's early education, had been adamant:

You must not speak, unless you can make your meaning perfectly intelligible to the person addressed; must not express a thought, unless you can give a reason for it, if required; must not make statements, unless sure of all particulars—such were his rules. 'But', 'if', 'unless', 'I am mistaken', and 'it may be so', were words and phrases excluded from the provinces where he held sway.[18]

Fuller was taught to talk like a man. This alone would account for why many men found her so insufferable, and her erudition so dismaying, as this English comment makes pungently plain:

Margaret Fuller was one of those he-women, who, thank Heaven! for the most part figure and flourish, and have their fame on the other side of the Atlantic. She was an intellectual Bloomer of the largest calibre. She understood Socrates better than Plato did, Faust better than Goethe did, Kant Philosophy [*sic*] better than Kant did . . . but alack the difference between an encyclopaedia bound in calf and an encyclopaedia moving in blue stockings. Every fact, word, thought, idea, theory, notion, line, verse, that crowded in the cranium of Margaret Fuller was a weapon. They shot from her like pellets from a steam gun. She bristled all over with transcendentalism, assaulted you with metaphysics, suffocated you with mythology, peppered you with ethics, and struck you down with heavy history . . .[19]

---

[17] Letter from Timothy to Margaret Fuller, 22 Feb. 1820, in *Letters*, i. 97, fn. 7.

[18] *Memoirs*, i. 12–13.

[19] Quoted in Frances M. Barbour, 'Margaret Fuller and the British Reviewers', *New England Quarterly*, 9 (Dec. 1936), 622–3.

But between Fuller's assault-course education in girlhood, and her maturity, there had been a 'backlash'. The Roman constancy of will and purpose which the young Fuller so much admired played no part in the increasingly dominant cult of the True Woman, which celebrated submissiveness, piety, and passivity as the 'genius' of the female. The Cult of Republican Motherhood had allowed women a sturdy independence: but that of True Womanhood saw her as fully absorbed in her vocation, purifying and restoring fallen Man. Selfishness of any kind was the prime sin for women, and independence was a kind of selfishness. In return for abjuring all autonomy of thought and action, the 'True Woman'—the epitaph on the tombstone of Margaret's mother, Margarett Crane Fuller—could expect worship. As an article of 1830 in the *Ladies' Magazine* put it: 'A halo of glory encircles her, and illumines her whole orbit. With her, man not only feels safe, but is actually renovated. For he approaches her with an awe, a reverence, and an affection which before he knew not that he possessed.'[20]

This conservative backlash began at the turn of the nineteenth century—with the victory of the Federalist party in 1796 and the puritanical American reaction to the publication of the frank *Memoirs of Mary Wollstonecraft* by her husband, William Godwin, after her death in 1797. (The damage done to Wollstonecraft by Godwin—who was her rival as well as her survivor—neatly parallels that done to Fuller by Emerson and the other editors.) Although conservative reaction to women's advancement was initially less pronounced in America than in England or France, it drew extra strength from the rise of religious evangelicalism, the narrowing of female employment opportunities outside the home, and concern for family cohesion on the Western frontier. True Womanhood was now held to be largely incompatible with the virtues of self-reliance and critical thought, though a partial exception would be made for female moral education.

In the political sphere, too, the early nineteenth century was a period of retreat for women. During the American Revolution

[20] Quoted in Ann Douglas, *The Feminization of American Culture* (New York: Knopf, 1977), 46.

enthusiasm for the logical consequences of the idea that all *men* are created equal had undermined the common-law position inherited from England, that married women had no legal, economic, or political existence. Women married to Tories who had been exiled, and their property confiscated, were sometimes able to regain their own share if they swore loyalty to the new republic. This implied that married women's property rights were not entirely subsumed in those of their husbands, and that women's political commitment could have some meaning, even if they were not full citizens. In 1790 the state of New Jersey even went so far as to adopt a franchise statute referring to voters as 'he or she'. In the aftermath of the Revolution divorce, overruled by the Privy Council in 1773 as contrary to the law of England, also became a right for those women in the New England and mid-Atlantic seaboard states whose legislatures had legalized it.

With the end of the Revolution and no further need for female support in the war effort, and the rise of an entrepreneurial capitalism which confined women's economic activity more closely to the home, these political and economic gains were generally short-lived. By the 1830s and 1840s, ironically the high tide of individualistic liberalism, the political and economic rights of American women had never been fewer. At the same time that white American men had gained near-total control over their wives' property, they were benefiting from the abolition in almost all states of property requirements for the franchise. Rhode Island, for example, one of the few states which still limited white male suffrage to freeholders, extended the vote to all native-born men after the Dorr rebellion of 1842. The contrast between the sexes was sharper in America than in England, where the 1832 Reform Act still left lower middle-class and working-class men disenfranchised. (There, too, however, the forces of misogyny were in the ascendant: the 1832 Act specified for the first time in statute form that the voter must be male.)

For women Jacksonian America was not the land of opportunity: rather the land of *shrinking* opportunity. Early revivalists of the Great Awakenings had allowed women to take a key part in meetings and to lead prayers; but by 1823 they were forbidden to do either in a pamphlet on 'Female Influence', published by the Presbyterian Utica Tract Society and typical of the changes in the hotbed of evangelicalism, the Burnt-Over District of western New York State. In the repressive 1820s and 1830s even maternal and moral-reform societies were beginning to be thought suspect. To step outside the domestic sphere, hardliners argued, would sully the purity which alone gave women the right to call themselves morally superior to men, and capable of the other sex's moral reform.

Education was the last of the partial exemptions which remained intact—and indeed flourished—in the early 1840s. Improvement of the female intellect was acceptable as a means to an imperative end. As Fuller herself enunciated the dominant view, American daughters were exhorted to strive constantly for spiritual and intellectual perfection, not only for the sake of their own salvation, but for the good of their fathers, brothers and beaux—whose contact with the sharp world of business excused them from any such strictness with themselves. 'Improvement in the daughters will best aid the reformation of the sons of this age', she wrote in *Woman* (p. 11). (This jars oddly with Fuller's assertion that 'Not one man in the million, shall I say? no, not in the hundred million, can rise above the belief that Woman was made *for* Man . . .' (p. 19), and her complaint that 'So much is said of women being better educated, that they may become better companions and mothers *for men*' (p. 61, original emphasis).

Catharine Beecher, founder of the Hartford Female Seminary and later of the Western Female Institute in Cincinnati, had justified female education by women's aptitude as natural missionaries, spreading a civilizing influence from the holy hearth. This imperial role for women was given a patriotic force by Philo Stewart, co-founder of Oberlin, the first college to educate men and women together. 'The work of female education', wrote Stewart, 'must be carried on in some form, and in a much more efficient manner than it has been hitherto, or our country will go to destruction.'[21]

[21] Quoted in Susan Phinney Conrad, *Perish the Thought: Intellectual Women in Romantic America* (New York: Oxford University Press, 1976), 29.

In the Cult of True Womanhood a strong religious component coexisted more or less peacefully with what might appear the ideological opposite, the philosopher John Locke's doctrine of the mind as a *tabula rasa* or blank slate. Since the child's personality was entirely a reflection of what the educator put into it, mothers as principal child-rearers bore a ponderous responsibility. Both the true man and the true woman were formed by their mothers. This perilous power in women's hands had to be tamed, by educating them to be reliable propagandizers. The 'concession' made in favour of education was not so much a privilege afforded to women as a further mechanism of control. Education was certainly not intended to prepare women for the professions and public life; it was meant to make them more reliable stewards of the master's most important resources, his children.

But by operating within the constraints of the acceptable, early nineteenth-century reformers had secured some educational advancement for women. Colluding with the doctrine of separate spheres, 'domestic feminists' such as Catharine Beecher helped to breed a class of educated heretics within the Cult, women who would *not* accept separate spheres. Further, the legitimacy of evangelical fervour, and the partial exceptions made in favour of philanthropic causes and education, had allowed some women a taste of life outside the home. Ladies' societies gave women experience in drawing up regulations, electing officers, corresponding with other charitable organizations, and overseeing accounts. The rise of 'Moral Reform' (the movement against prostitution) and of the abolitionist movement presented further opportunities for public participation, though women's increased activity on the platform was met by intense and sometimes violent male resentment.

It was in this situation of simultaneous male backlash and female backlash *against* male backlash that *Woman in the Nineteenth Century* appeared. The language and conclusions of 'The Great Lawsuit'—and to a lesser degree of *Summer on the Lakes* and *Woman in the Nineteenth Century*—reflect the baleful influence of the Cult of True Womanhood. That this was so should not be surprising, or a cause for castigating Fuller, as some of her earlier feminist biographers tended to do. In order to reach her intended audience, Fuller had to speak their language, and that was the diction and discourse of the True Woman. The 'hegemony' of a cultural discourse, in the term used by the Italian social philosopher Antonio Gramsci, affects not only the woman writer's audience, but also her own opinions.

A similar set of Gramscian ideas has been applied to the English Victorians by Deirdre David,[22] who judges that Elizabeth Barrett Browning, George Eliot, and Harriet Martineau were 'neither ideological slaves to patriarchal thought, nor distinctly separate from patriarchal culture. They were both collaborateurs and saboteurs in the world that enabled their very existence as women intellectuals.'[23] Is this also true of Margaret Fuller? Is it the price a woman writer must pay for being allowed to play the Dark Lady?

It would be unfair, I think, to say that Fuller was partly colluding in her own oppression, as David implies of Barrett Browning, Eliot, and Martineau. Her attitudes towards women *were* considerably more radical than those of any of these three, though she is closest to Eliot. But it is certainly true that Fuller must be judged against the background of her time as well as that of her own personal development.

It is also perfectly true that Fuller's high abstraction and individualistic, self-reliant solutions to women's social disadvantage are still cast in the Emersonian mould. 'As his disciple, Fuller used all the arguments that Emerson promulgated about the individual and applied them to women.'[24] 'The Great Lawsuit', and the first two-thirds of *Woman* (which largely reproduces 'Lawsuit') are hymns to women's equal powers of self-reliance with men.

Indeed, self-reliance was the story of Fuller's life, and of her death. Fuller had to be economically independent—and to provide for her father's children from the limited means available from a woman's profession, teaching. It did her health no good, and probably caused her death. The boat on which she went down, the *Elizabeth*, was an old-fashioned wooden-bottomed

[22] Deirdre David, *Intellectual Women and Victorian Patriarchy: Harriet Martineau, Elizabeth Barrett Browning, George Eliot* (Basingstoke: Macmillan, 1987), 3–6.

[23] Ibid. 230.

[24] Urbanski, *Fuller's Woman*, 109.

merchantman; Fuller could not afford a modern steamer or packet ship. When the *Elizabeth* foundered on a sand-bar off Fire Island, the bottom ruptured under the cargo of Italian marble and a statue of John Calhoun—that advocate of nullification, states' rights to self-reliance.

In her dispatches written during the Roman Revolution of 1849, when she ran a hospital and her husband Ossoli served in the Civic Guard, Fuller became much more practical, more communitarian, and quite radically socialist. But 'The Great Lawsuit' is marred by the Transcendentalist tendency to see reality through the lens of symbols. Although it contains striking and powerful statements, it also carries a heavy freight of vagueness and conceptual sloppiness.

Similarly, *Woman in the Nineteenth Century* reflects not only Timothy Fuller's educational influence and the spell of the Cult of True Womanhood, but also the ideals of the New England Transcendentalist movement. Transcendentalist literary theory consciously rejected syllogistic reasoning and systematic analysis. In accord with these dictates which she had helped to set as editor of the movement's canon-forming journal, *The Dial*, Fuller conceived *Woman* as an organic, subjective composition, a free association of ideas.

Although Fuller's writing could be quite pungent and down-to-earth—as in much of *Summer on the Lakes*—*Woman* is often high-blown in the Transcendentalist style, which was characterized by 'inchoate structure, prodigal imagery, wit, paradox, symbolism . . . and a manifesto-like tone'.[25] Part of the difficulty was that 'the Transcendentalists were exceedingly weak in the genres most in favor today (poetry, drama, prose fiction)',[26] but were attempting to revive styles little known at present, and to create new genres. In *Woman* Fuller welds sermon and conversation into such a form, one which may seem archaic to modern readers but which struck her contemporaries as powerful and new. Even Henry David Thoreau, who 'never liked anything', according to Emerson, considered 'The Great Lawsuit', the earlier essay which Fuller drew on in compiling the book-

[25] Lawrence Buell, *Literary Transcendentalism: Style and Vision in the American Renaissance* (Ithaca, NY: Cornell University Press), 18.
[26] Ibid. 16.

length *Woman*, to be 'rich extempore writing ... talking with pen in hand'.

The Transcendentalist, consciously literary manner departs about two-thirds of the way through *Woman*, however—the point (marked in the Explanatory Notes to this edition) at which the recycled 'Lawsuit' essay ends and the pages penned exclusively for the book begin. Between the publication of 'Lawsuit' in July 1843 and the final editing of *Woman* in November 1844, Fuller's thought had become more concrete and more radical, particularly on the subjects of slavery, Native American women, and prostitution. In all three cases she now saw, as she put it in *Summer on the Lakes*, 'the aversion of the injurer for him he has degraded'.[27]

'[T]here exists in the minds of men a tone of feeling toward women as toward slaves', she wrote in *Woman* (p. 17). Indeed, slavery is more honest: 'In slavery, *acknowledged* slavery, women are on a par with men' (p. 38, emphasis added). Fuller was not the first to make this uncomfortable comparison. Drawing on ideas first advanced by the Irish feminist Anna Wheeler (b. 1785), William Thompson's *Appeal of One-Half the Human Race* (1825) likewise remarks:

As little as slaves have had to do in any part of the world in the enacting of slave-codes, have women in any part of the world had to do with the partial codes of selfishness and ignorance, which everywhere dispose of their right over their own actions and all their other enjoyments, in favour of those who made the regulations; particularly that most unequal and debasing code, absurdly called the contract of marriage ... From regulating the terms of this pretended contract, women have been as completely excluded as bullocks, or sheep, or any other animals subjugated to man, have been from determining the regulations of commons or slaughter-houses.[28]

Earlier still, Charles Brockden Brown, writing in the 1790s, had identified marriage as a 'compact of slavery'.[29] But there is

---

[27] Margaret Fuller Ossoli, *Summer on the Lakes in 1843: With Autobiography and Memoir by Ralph Waldo Emerson, W. H. Channing and Others* (London: Ward and Lock, 1861, reprint of the 1844 edition with selections from the *Memoirs*), 110.

[28] William Thompson, *Appeal of One-Half the Human Race, Women, against the Pretensions of the Other Half, Men, to Retain Them in Political, and thence in Civil and Domestic, Slavery* (London: Virago, 1983, repr. of 1825 edn.), 56–7.

[29] Charles Brockden Brown, *Alcuin: A Dialogue*, ed. Lee R. Edwards (New York, 1970).

no firm indication that Fuller had read Thompson or Brown by the time she wrote her texts on women's position; and in the climate of the 1840s, such sentiments were much more shocking—particularly when they came from a woman. Even more controversial was Fuller's scepticism about the arguments put forward by white men to justify their political and economic dominance: that women, or slaves, are incapable of fiscal wisdom or political *nous*. These, she judged, are only psychological mechanisms which the dominant sex, or race, must use in order to justify its own arbitrary power to itself.

Fuller was not an active abolitionist at this time, but the examples of slaves and Native Americans had galvanized her thought on women. In 1843 she had made a journey to Niagara Falls and the Great Lakes with her friends Caroline Sturgis, Sarah Ann Clarke, and Clarke's brother William. The book which resulted, *Summer on the Lakes in 1843* (1844), represents a forward hop, if not a leap, in both style and thought. Although the book lacks what Fuller admired—'the Spartan brevity and sinewy grasp of Indian speech' (p. 156)—it is liberally sprinkled with Thoreauvian salt:

[At Niagara] what I liked best was to sit on Table Rock, close to the great fall. There all power of observing details, all separate consciousness, was quite lost. Once, just as I had seated myself there, a man came up to take his first look. He walked close up to the fall, and, after looking at it for a moment, with an air of thinking how he could best appropriate it to his own use—he spat into it. (p. 152)

The range of Fuller's thought on women was stretched by the example of the squaws of Mackinac Island, among whom she was able to wander freely. Unlike the Enlightenment, which explored various constellations of domestic power relations—matrilineal Iroquois society, polyandry among the Nairs of Malabar, collective marriage in eastern Iran—the early nineteenth century lumped together all 'uncivilized' women's positions as barbarous. Fuller agreed that Native American women were lumbered with drudgery: their 'peculiarly awkward gait, and forms bent by burthens . . . so different from the steady and noble step of the men, [mark] the inferior position they occupy' (p. 193). But she also observed more tenderness towards children among Native American braves than among white men, and considerable respect for matrons who were mothers of warriors. Native American children were called by the mother's name, and divorce was easy, more advantageous to women than men. On the boat for Sault St Marie, Fuller met a Native American woman (with whom she quite markedly did *not* identify, since she says that she was the only lady on board the ship). The woman had left her husband because he drank and wasted their earnings; she earned a living for herself and her child as a chambermaid. 'Now and again, she said, her husband called on her, and asked if he might live with her again, but she always answered, no. Here she was far freer than she would have been in civilized life' (p. 201).

But if *white* western women were not freer than eastern, Fuller thought it was probably their own fault. Still unable to see women's position as socially conditioned, in *Summer* Fuller remains within the True Woman tradition by looking to western women for their own salvation.

It is ... evident that ... the women have great power at home. It can never be otherwise, men being dependent upon them for the comfort of their lives. Just so among ourselves, wives who are neither esteemed nor loved by their husbands, have great power over their conduct by the friction of every day, and over the formation of their opinions ... This power is good for nothing, unless the woman be wise to use it aright. Has the Indian, has the white woman, as noble a feeling of life and its uses, as religious a self-respect, as worthy a field of thought and action as man? If not, the white woman, the Indian woman, occupies an inferior position to that of man. It is not so much a question of power, as of privilege. (p. 198)

Individual before social reform remains Fuller's creed in *Woman*, even though she is considerably more aware of social ills than she showed herself to be in 'Lawsuit'. The particular target on which she expends most fire-power is prostitution, with marriage a close second. The remaining selections in this volume, particularly the review of George Sand's novel *Consuelo* (1843) and the excerpt from Fuller's story 'Aglauron and Laurie', often bear witness to Fuller's concerns about sexual politics. It was the politics of sexuality which roused Fuller's interest in the politics of politics. In 'The Great Lawsuit' Fuller had preached the Emersonian creed of self-reliance. But when 'we women have no profession except marriage, mantua-making and school-keeping',[30] to be *economically* self-reliant without following one of these three 'trades', or the working-class equivalents of service and factory work, could only mean one possibility: the enter-prise which the women of Sing Sing had pursued. Realization of this anomaly in her own thought combined with Fuller's detes-tation of hypocrisy—'Give me truth, cheat me by no illusion'—to ignite her fiery denunciation of the double standard.

It was prostitution which emblematized all other social ills, and which propelled Fuller into her increasing public concern and sympathy for socialism. Evangelical writers conflated pros-titution with other forms of social chaos, including socialist radicalism; conversely, Owenite socialists saw prostitution as the paradigm of exploitation in industrial capitalism.

Fuller's concern about prostitution was by no means unique, nor was her analysis as systematic or programmatic as that of existing activists. The New York Female Moral Reform Society, founded in 1834 to convert prostitutes to evangelical Prot-estantism, had proposed to keep vigil at brothels and to publish a list of clients in the society's journal, the *Advocate of Moral Reform*. By the 1840s the American Female Moral Reform Society, as it became, had over 500 branches, providing cannon fodder for intensive political lobbying of the legislature to make seduction imprisonable—and succeeding in their demands by 1848. The Society also pilloried the male monopoly of the professions and claimed that low wages for women caused pros-titution. (Many working-class girls used casual prostitution to eke out low earnings or get through periods of unemployment.)

What made the double standard particularly pernicious in the nineteenth century was the decline of the New England communitarian ideal in favour of the deracinated, deregulated market-place. Among the Puritans each member of the com-munity, man or woman, had been responsible for the moral health of the group as a whole. This legitimized prying into what the more private-minded nineteenth century would regard as nobody else's business. Such institutionalized nosiness had

[30] Letter to George T. Davis, 1 Feb. 1836, forthcoming in *Letters*, vol. VI, as no. 120a.

meant that Puritan men's misdeeds were as likely to be un-
covered as women's, even if they might be less strictly punished.
But disestablishment of the Protestant churches after the Revolution lessened the religious imperative to uncover a neighbour's
nakedness. Ironically, the nineteenth-century ideology of domesticity, retreating into the sanctity of the private home, also
covered up male mis-steps *outside* the home. The wife's blissful
domestic ignorance would be threatened if a husband's wrong-
doing were revealed, it could be argued.

A new ideal of female 'passionlessness' emerged in Anglo-
American culture in the late eighteenth century. The *natural*
woman was sexless; prostitutes were unnatural. Both male and
female writers began to stress female chastity as protection
for both the individual woman and society as a whole, and
evangelical fervour heightened the imperative. Vestiges of the
older joy in sexuality remained: Peter Gay has documented, at
least in private sources such as diaries, that eroticism between
loving partners was as great in the nineteenth century as ever or
as now.[31] But at least formally the ideology *did* change. As the
early nineteenth century came to reject the Ideal of Republican
Motherhood in favour of the Cult of True Womanhood, it replaced more egalitarian notions about male and female sexuality
with what Bram Dijkstra calls 'the cult of the Household Nun'.[32]
The purity of the Angel in the House required a demon outside
to service male sexuality. This accentuated the divide between
good and 'fallen' women, but also legitimized male libido. Prostitution was a boon to society, and the whore the upholder of
the wife's chastity.

Further, the dominant discourse only applied to native-born
white middle-class women; women of colour, immigrants, and
working-class women were not regarded as passionless, but as
fair sexual game. Native American women were also thought
debased: the heroic figures of Pocahontas and Sacajawea, both of
whom saved men, were replaced by accounts in mid-nineteenth-

[31] Peter Gay, *The Bourgeois Experience: Victoria to Freud*, vol. 1, *Education of the Senses* (Oxford and New York: Oxford University Press, 1984).
[32] Bram Dijkstra, *Idols of Perversity: Fantasies of Feminine Evil in Fin-de-Siècle Culture* (New York and Oxford: Oxford University Press, 1986), 3.

century travel journals of 'dirty little squaws' leading male adventurers astray.

Fuller's view, never conditioned by prejudice against immigrant or Native American women, travels far beyond this dominant discourse, yet also begins from a starting-point in the Cult of the True Woman. Prostitution posed a particular problem for anyone who accepted, as Fuller did, that women were different from men in nature: a basic premiss of the Cult as well. Fuller writes in *Woman*:

The especial genius of Woman I believe to be electrical in movement, intuitive in function, spiritual in tendency. She excels not so easily in classification, or recreation, as in an instinctive seizure of causes, and a simple breathing out of what she receives that has the singleness of life, rather than the selecting and energizing of art. (p. 75)

Men's especial nature apparently included being more *immoral*. In the Cult of True Womanhood: 'Passionlessness was on the other side of the coin which paid, so to speak, for women's admission to moral equality.'[33] But prostitutes were sexual women. Either Fuller could accept that prostitutes were passionless victims of male predatory sexuality—or she could prove the rule by the exceptions, denigrating prostitutes as false to all that True Womanhood stood for. Both strategies would have confirmed the Cult by ratifying asexuality in the 'normal' female. Instead, Fuller asks: 'Why can't a man be more like a woman?' She extends the True Womanly ideal of chastity to men: 'We shall not decline celibacy as the great fact of our age.'

In the end Fuller stands the Cult of the True Woman on its head: female moral nature, rightly reconstituted in the case of aberrant specimens such as prostitutes, can and should instruct male. It follows the Cult to its own logical conclusions, uncomfortable for men though they may actually turn out to be.

This aspect of Fuller's thought was *not* typical of her time, but it can be seen in later feminists. English campaigners against the Contagious Diseases Acts of 1864, 1866, and 1869 likewise rejected the mere regulation of prostitution as benefiting men only. They, too, called for an abolition of the sexual double

[33] Nancy F. Cott, 'Passionlessness: An Interpretation of Victorian Sexual Ideology, 1790–1850', *Signs*, 4 (1978), 234–5.

standard and the establishment of a single joint code of sexual behaviour. If the prostitute was the unwitting guardian of the domestic hearth, this root-and-branch stance—which Fuller shares—means a radical willingness to see conventional marriage die the death. In contrast, Emerson wrote: 'We cannot rectify marriage because it would introduce such carnage in our social relations.'[34]

In her 1875 lecture 'Social Purity', Susan B. Anthony argued: 'There is no escape from the conclusion that, while woman's want of bread induces her to pursue this vice [prostitution], man's love of the vice leads him there. For every abandoned woman, there is always *one* abandoned man and oftener many more.'[35] This is pure Fuller.

In our own century, Fuller's relational feminism, her belief in separate male and female natures, prefigures an important strand in women's studies. Unlike Mary Wollstonecraft, whose 'rationalist' feminism is primarily rights-orientated and education-minded, Fuller's 'romantic' feminism seeks liberation mainly through psychological means. Second-wave feminism embodied this striving in consciousness-raising groups. Further, much modern feminist writing, particularly in psychology and educational theory, has confirmed the idea of 'a different voice',[36] the concept—central to Fuller—that male and female moral personalities are not the same.

Fuller is a romantic feminist in contending that the content of girls' education should be *affirmatively* different, not merely a watered-down version of the classic texts fed to boys. Having been privileged to learn the father speech, Latin, she need not worship the priestly tongue mindlessly. Romanticism values diversity and assigns positive value to gender differences. It does not define female nature solely in contrast to male. This is

[34] Emerson, *Journals*, viii. 95.

[35] Susan B. Anthony, 'Social Purity', quoted in John D'Emilio and Estelle B. Freedman, *Intimate Matters: A History of Sexuality in America* (New York: Harper and Row, 1988), 149.

[36] As in Carol Gilligan's influential work *In a Different Voice: Psychological Theory and Women's Development* (Cambridge, Mass.: Harvard University Press, 1982). See also Nel Noddings, *Caring: A Feminine Approach to Ethics and Moral Education* and *Women and Evil* (Berkeley, Calif.: University of California Press, 1984 and 1989).

the impetus behind Fuller's description of female nature as electrical, vital, magnetic, full of life. It is intended as the most affirmative of descriptions, nõt the mere negative of masculine identity. *Life* is what Fuller writes into her definition of woman.

Fuller's feminism is romantic in another sense: it emphasizes self-help and self-assertion, another strand in modern feminism. *Woman* is ambivalent as to whether women will achieve freedom through each other's support or their own individual striving, but it is clear that they will not achieve it in league with men. 'Men do *not* look at both sides, and women must leave off asking them.' This is another reason why political lobbying—of an all-male legislature—can have little effect, to Fuller's way of thinking. But although Fuller is not primarily remembered as a political activist, she targeted most of the inequities that would preoccupy later feminists: marriage as slavery, sex and sexuality, and women's poverty.

Fuller's attempt to state a vibrant and positive ideal of female-ness borrows from the Cult of True Womanhood, but ultimately transcends it. The qualities which Fuller claims for women by nature and right are too dynamic to sit comfortably in the hands-in-lap posture of the True Woman.

NOTE ON THE TEXT

The text of *Woman in the Nineteenth Century* is that of the first edition (February 1845), with minor emendations of printers' errors. The first two-thirds of the text (to the point signalled in the Explanatory Notes) roughly parallels Fuller's earlier essay 'The Great Lawsuit' (1843), though Fuller added a considerable number of further examples, altered some phrasings, and amended her punctuation to suit the style of Horace Greeley's printer. The excerpts from *Summer on the Lakes in 1843* are reprinted from the first edition (1844), with minor emendations of spelling. The selections from Fuller's writings in the *New York Daily Tribune* and the excerpts from her short story 'Aglauron and Laurie' are from originals in the Houghton Library, Harvard University; grateful acknowledgement is made for permission to reprint.

SELECT BIBLIOGRAPHY

PRIMARY SOURCES

BROWNING, ELIZABETH BARRETT, *Letters*, ed. F. G. Kenyon (London: Macmillan, 1897).

CHEVIGNY, BELL GALE, *The Woman and the Myth: Margaret Fuller's Life and Writings* (Old Westbury, NY: Feminist Press, 1976).

ELIOT, GEORGE, 'Margaret Fuller and Mary Wollstonecraft', *The Leader*, 13 Oct. 1855, in *The Essays of George Eliot*, ed. Thomas Pinney (London: Routledge & Kegan Paul, 1983).

EMERSON, RALPH WALDO, *Collected Works*, ed. Joseph Slater (Cambridge, Mass.: Belknap Press, 1983).

FULLER, SARAH MARGARET, *Writings*, ed, Mason Wade (Clifton, NJ: Augustus M. Kelley, 1973, repr. of 1941 Viking edn.).

—— 'The Great Lawsuit' (excerpts), in Perry Miller (ed.), *The Transcendentalists: An Anthology* (Cambridge, Mass.: Harvard University Press, 1950).

—— *Letters*, ed. Robert N. Hudspeth, 6 vols. (Ithaca, NY: Cornell University Press, 1983–94).

—— *Papers on Literature and Art* (London: Wiley & Putnam, 1846).

—— *Summer on the Lakes in 1843: with Autobiography and Memoir by Ralph Waldo Emerson, W. H. Channing and Others* (London: Ward and Lock, 1861, repr. of 1844 edn. with excerpts from *Memoirs* added).

—— 'These Sad but Glorious Days': Dispatches from Europe, 1846–1850, eds. Larry J. Reynolds and Susan Belasco Smith (New Haven, Conn.: Yale University Press, 1991).

—— *Woman in the Nineteenth Century* (New York: Greenwood Press, 1968, repr. of 1845 edn.).

HAWTHORNE, NATHANIEL, *The Blithedale Romance*, The World's Classics (Oxford: Oxford University Press, 1991).

LOWELL, JAMES RUSSELL, 'A Fable for Critics', in *Poetical Works* (Boston: Houghton Mifflin, 1904).

Memoirs of Margaret Fuller Ossoli, ed. Ralph Waldo Emerson, James Freeman Clarke, and William Henry Channing (London: Richard Bentley, 1852).

SECONDARY SOURCES

ALLEN, MARGARET VANDERHAAR, *The Achievement of Margaret Fuller* (University Park, Penn.: Pennsylvania State University Press, 1979).

BAYM, NINA, *Woman's Fiction: A Guide to Novels by and about Women in America, 1820–1870* (Ithaca, NY: Cornell University Press, 1978).

BERG, BARBARA, *The Remembered Gate: Origins of American Feminism, The Woman and the City 1800–1860* (Oxford: Oxford University Press, 1978).

BLANCHARD, PAULA, *Margaret Fuller: From Transcendentalism to Revolution* (New York: Delacorte Press/Seymour Lawrence, 1978, repr. 1987 by Addison-Wesley, Reading, Mass., with foreword by Carolyn G. Heilbrun).

BUELL, LAWRENCE, *Literary Transcendentalism: Style and Vision in the American Renaissance* (Ithaca, NY: Cornell University Press).

CAPPER, CHARLES and HOLLINGER, DAVID A., *The American Intellectual Tradition* (New York: Oxford University Press, 1993), vol. 1.

CHAPMAN, JOHN JAY, 'Emerson', in *The Shock of Recognition: The Development of Literature in the United States Recorded by the Men who Made It*, ed. Edmund Wilson (New York: Doubleday, 1943).

CHEYFITZ, ERIC, *The Trans-Parent: Sexual Politics in the Language of Emerson* (Baltimore: Johns Hopkins, 1981).

CONRAD, SUSAN PHINNEY, *Perish the Thought: Intellectual Women in Romantic America 1830–1860* (New York: Oxford University Press, 1976).

COTT, NANCY F., *The Bonds of Womanhood: 'Woman's Sphere' in New England 1780–1835* (New Haven, Conn.: Yale University Press, 1977).

D'EMILIO, JOHN and FREEDMAN, ESTELLE B., *Intimate Matters: A History of Sexuality in America* (New York: Harper & Row, 1988).

DICKENSON, DONNA, *Margaret Fuller: Writing a Woman's Life* (Basingstoke: Macmillan, 1993).

DOUGLAS, ANN, *The Feminization of American Culture* (New York: Alfred Knopf, 1977).

DURNING, RUSSELL E., *Margaret Fuller, Citizen of the World* (Heidelberg: Carl Winter, Universitätsverlag, 1969).

FLEXNER, ELEANOR, *A Century of Struggle* (Cambridge, Mass.: Belknap Press, 1959).

GILBERT, SANDRA M. and GUBAR, SUSAN, *No Man's Land: The Place of the Woman Writer in the Twentieth Century*, vol. 1, *The War of the Words* (New Haven, Conn. and London: Yale University Press, 1988).

—— *The Madwoman in the Attic* (New Haven, Conn.: Yale University Press, 1979).

HAWTHORNE, JULIAN, *Nathaniel Hawthorne and His Wife* (Boston, 1884).

HEILBRUN, CAROLYN G., *Writing a Woman's Life* (New York and London: W. W. Norton, 1988).

HELSINGER, ELIZABETH K., SHEETS, ROBIN LAUTERBACH, and VEEDER, WILLIAM, *The Woman Question: Society and Literature in Britain and America 1837–1883*, vol. 1, *Defining Voices* (Chicago: University of Chicago Press, 1989).

HIGGINSON, THOMAS WENTWORTH, *Margaret Fuller Ossoli* (Boston: Houghton Mifflin, American Men of Letters Series, 1884).

HOWE, JULIA WARD, *Margaret Fuller (Marchesa Ossoli)* (London: W. H. Allen, Eminent Women Series, 1883).

JAMES, HENRY, *William Wetmore Story and His Friends* (Boston: Houghton Mifflin, 1903).

MYERSON, JOEL (ed.), *Critical Essays on Margaret Fuller* (Boston: G. K. Hall, 1980).

RENDALL, JANE, *The Origins of Modern Feminism: Women in Britain, France and the United States 1780–1860* (London: Macmillan, 1985).

SMITH, PAGE, *Daughters of the Promised Land: Women in American History* (Boston: Little, Brown, 1970).

SWANN, CHARLES, *Nathaniel Hawthorne: Tradition and Revolution* (Oxford: Oxford University Press, 1991).

URBANSKI, MARIE MITCHELL OLESEN, *Margaret Fuller's Woman in the Nineteenth Century: A Literary Study of Form and Content, of Sources and Influence* (Westport, Conn.: Greenwood Press, 1980).

VON FRANK, ALBERT, *The Sacred Game: Provincialism and Frontier Consciousness in American Literature, 1630–1860* (New York: Cambridge University Press, 1985).

WELTER, BARBARA, *Dimity Convictions: The American Woman in the Nineteenth Century* (Athens, Ohio: Ohio University Press, 1976).

A CHRONOLOGY OF
MARGARET FULLER

1778   Birth of Timothy Fuller (Margaret's father), fourth of eleven children of Revd Timothy Fuller (1739–1805) and Sarah Williams (d. 1822).

1789   Birth of Margarett Crane (Margaret's mother), second of four children of Peter Crane (1752–1821) and Elizabeth Jones Weiser (1755–1845).

1801   Timothy Fuller graduates from Harvard.

1809   Marriage of Timothy Fuller and Margarett Crane.

1810   Birth of Sarah Margaret Fuller, 23 May.

1812   Birth of Julia Adelaide Fuller.

1814   Death of Julia Adelaide: Margaret does not remember 'insisting, with loud cries, that they should not put the body in the ground', but so she did.

1815   Birth of Eugene Fuller. Timothy is now educating Margaret at home in Latin, French, logic, rhetoric, and a little Greek. She begins memorizing all of Virgil the following year.

1817   Timothy Fuller elected to Congress. Birth of William Henry Fuller.

1820   Birth of Ellen Kilshaw Fuller.

1822   Birth of Arthur Buckminster Fuller.

1824   Birth of Richard Frederick Fuller, Margaret's favourite brother. Due to her father's belated realization that she is not developing social graces, Margaret is sent away to Miss Prescott's finishing school in Groton, Massachusetts, where she feels herself 'rather degraded from Cicero's Oratory to One and two are how many' (*Letters*, i. 138).

1825   Timothy Fuller retires from Congress and returns to his law practice in Cambridge.

1826   Birth of James Lloyd Fuller, who subsequently manifests mental illness and learning difficulties which will require Margaret to spend much time trying to find a placement for him.

1828   Edward Breck Fuller born on Margaret's eighteenth birthday.

1829   Edward dies on 15 September. 'He was some weeks wasting away, and I took care of him always half the night. He was a beautiful child, and became very dear to me then' (*Letters*, ii. 187).

1832 Publication of George Sand's *Indiana*.

1833 After re-election of Andrew Jackson as president ends all hope of his return to politics, as an opponent of Jackson, Timothy Fuller moves his family to a farm in Groton, where Margaret is isolated and miserable. She spends her days doing heavy house-work, sewing for a family of eight, and tutoring her younger siblings.

1835 Death of Timothy Fuller, who leaves no will. Family's affairs in financial chaos; Margaret forced to seek outside employment.

1836 Fuller teaches in Bronson Alcott's school in Boston, but re-ceives no pay.

1837 Ralph Waldo Emerson delivers 'American Scholar' address to Harvard graduating class. Fuller teaches in Greene Street School, Providence, for $1,000 per year, of which she gives $300 to her brother Eugene to establish his career.

1839 Return to Groton. Sells house there in spring, then moves with mother and younger brothers to Jamaica Plain, Boston. Publication of translation of Eckermann's *Conversations with Goethe*. Begins Boston 'Conversations', university-level seminars for women.

1840 July: first issue of *The Dial*, under Fuller's editorship.

1841 Henry Wadsworth Longfellow publishes 'Hesperus'; Emerson writes his essay on 'Heroism'.

1842 Unpaid and overstressed, Fuller transfers *The Dial* to Emerson's editorship; he closes it down within the year. Nathaniel Hawthorne publishes *Mosses from an Old Manse*; Henry David Thoreau, *Natural History of Massachusetts*. Fuller publishes her translations of Bettina Brentano von Arnim's correspondence with Karoline von Gunderode.

1843 Publication of 'The Great Lawsuit' (*The Dial*, July 1843). May–August: trip to Niagara, Chicago, Illinois prairies, Milwaukee, and Great Lakes.

1844 Publication of *Summer on the Lakes in 1843*. Birth on Fuller's own birthday in May of niece Margaret Fuller Channing, daughter of sister Ellen and her husband Ellery Channing, the poet. Fuller offered post as literary editor on Horace Greeley's *New York Daily Tribune*, which she takes up in December. Late summer–autumn: finishing *Woman in the Nineteenth Century* at Fishkill Landing, on the Hudson River, where she stays with Caroline Sturgis; makes visits to prostitutes in Sing Sing Prison.

1845 Publication of *Woman in the Nineteenth Century* (March). Intense relationship with German businessman James Nathan; he leaves New York in June. Fuller publishes some 250 essays in the

Tribune during this year and next, becoming first woman to earn her living by journalism. Edgar Allen Poe publishes 'The Raven' and *Tales*; Herman Melville, *Typee*.

1846   Fuller leaves for Europe in spring. Travels in north of England and Scotland, meeting William Wordsworth and staying in Harriet Martineau's cottage; arrives in London in October, meets Thomas Carlyle and Giuseppe Mazzini; leaves for Paris in November. Publication of *Papers on Literature and Art*. French Chamber of Deputies dissolved. Election of initially progressive Pope Pius IX.

1847   Meets George Sand, Frédéric Chopin, Adam Mickiewicz, Abbé Félicité Robert de Lamennais, Pierre Leroux. Departs for Italy in late February; meets Marchese Giovanni Angelo Ossoli in April. Travels on with her American companions to northern Italy and Switzerland, but decides to return to Italy in autumn while they journey on to Germany.

1848   Revolutions in Sicily, Paris, Budapest, Berlin, and Vienna. Fuller, pregnant by Ossoli, leaves Rome in May for mountains. September: birth of son, Angelo Eugene Philip Ossoli (Nino). November: flight of Pope Pius IX from Rome. December: Fuller returns to Rome, leaving baby behind with nurse.

1849   Roman republic proclaimed in February; siege of Rome by French troops; Fuller runs hospital of Bene Fratelli, Ossoli serves as captain in Civic Guard. Rome falls on 1 July. The Ossolis, reunited with Nino, flee to Florence. Friendship with Robert and Elizabeth Barrett Browning.

1850   May: the Ossolis embark on the *Elizabeth* for America. June: Captain Hasty of the *Elizabeth* dies of smallpox off Gibraltar; mate takes over vessel. 19 July: the *Elizabeth* breaks up on sand-bar off Fire Island in storm. Margaret Fuller, Giovanni Ossoli, Nino, and four others drown; five survive. Fuller's last and longest work, her manuscript history of the Roman revolution, is lost, despite efforts by Thoreau to track it down at the scene of the wreck. Body of Nino washed up on shore, but corpses of Fuller and Ossoli never found.

1852   Publication of *Memoirs of Margaret Fuller Ossoli*, edited by Clarke, Channing, and Emerson.

1855   Death from consumption of Ellen Fuller Channing.

1859   Deaths of Margarett Crane Fuller and Eugene Fuller (the latter by drowning, like his sister).

1869   Death of Richard Frederick Fuller puts paid to family's project, which he had devised, for alternative biography of Fuller, intended to right wrongs done by *Memoirs*.

1884   Publication of Julian Hawthorne's biography of his father, con-
        taining scurrilous gossip about Fuller which receives great
        publicity.

1903   Publication of Henry James's *William Wetmore Story and his
        Friends*, recollections of other Americans in Fuller's Roman
        circle. James's portrayal of Fuller as 'the somewhat angular
        Boston spinster' and 'the unquestionably haunting Margaret-
        wraith' gives final shape to what James himself calls 'the
        Margaret myth'.

Woman in the
Nineteenth Century
and Other Writings

WOMAN IN THE NINETEENTH CENTURY

PREFACE

The following essay is a reproduction, modified and expanded, of an article published in 'The Dial, Boston, July, 1843', under the title of 'The Great Lawsuit'.—Man *versus* Men; Woman *versus* Women.'

This article excited a good deal of sympathy, and still more interest. It is in compliance with wishes expressed from many quarters that it is prepared for publication in its present form.

Objections having been made to the former title, as not sufficiently easy to be understood, the present has been substituted as expressive of the main purpose of the essay; though, by myself, the other is preferred, partly for the reason others do not like it,—that is, that it requires some thought to see what it means, and might thus prepare the reader to meet me on my own ground. Besides, it offers a larger scope, and is, in that way, more just to my desire. I meant by that title to intimate the fact that, while it is the destiny of Man, in the course of the ages, to ascertain and fulfil the law of his being, so that his life shall be seen, as a whole, to be that of an angel or messenger, the action of prejudices and passions which attend, in the day, the growth of the individual, is continually obstructing the holy work that is to make the earth a part of heaven. By Man I mean both man and woman; these are the two halves of one thought. I lay no especial stress on the welfare of either. I believe that the development of one cannot be effected without that of the other. My highest wish is that this truth should be distinctly and rationally apprehended, and the conditions of life and freedom recognized as the same for the daughters and the sons of time; twin exponents of a divine thought.

I solicit a sincere and patient attention from those who open the following pages at all. I solicit of women that they will lay it to heart to ascertain what is for them the liberty of law. It is for this, and not for any, the largest, extension of partial privileges that I seek. I ask them if interested by these suggestions, to search their own experience and intuitions for better, and fill up with fit materials the trenches that hedge them in. From men I ask a noble and earnest attention to anything that can be offered on this great and still obscure subject, such as I have met from many with whom I stand in private relations.

And may truth, unpolluted by prejudice, vanity or selfishness, be granted daily more and more as the due of inheritance, and only valuable conquest for us all!

November, 1844

WOMAN IN THE
NINETEENTH CENTURY

'Frailty, thy name is WOMAN.'
'The Earth waits for her Queen.'*

The connection between these quotations may not be obvious, but it is strict. Yet would any contradict us, if we made them applicable to the other side, and began also

Frailty, thy name is MAN.
The Earth waits for its King.

Yet man, if not yet fully installed in his powers, has given much earnest of his claims. Frail he is indeed, how frail! how impure! Yet often has the vein of gold displayed itself amid the baser ores, and Man has appeared before us in princely promise worthy of his future.

If, oftentimes, we see the prodigal son feeding on the husks in the fair field no more his own, anon, we raise the eyelids, heavy from bitter tears, to behold in him the radiant apparition of genius and love, demanding not less than the all of goodness, power and beauty. We see that in him the largest claim finds a due foundation. That claim is for no partial sway, no exclusive possession. He cannot be satisfied with any one gift of life, any one department of knowledge or telescopic peep at the heavens. He feels himself called to understand and aid nature, that she may, through his intelligence, be raised and interpreted; to be a student of, and servant to, the universe-spirit; and king of his planet, that as an angelic minister, he may bring it into conscious harmony with the law of that spirit.

In clear triumphant moments, many times, has rung through the spheres the prophecy of his jubilee, and those moments, though past in time, have been translated into eternity by thought; the bright signs they left hang in the heavens, as single stars or constellations, and, already, a thickly sown radiance consoles the wanderer in the darkest night. Other heroes since Hercules have fulfilled the zodiac of beneficent labors, and then given up their mortal part to the fire without a murmur; while no God dared deny that they should have their reward.

Siquis tamen, Hercule, siquis
Forte Deo doliturus erit, data præmia nollet,
Sed meruise dari sciet, invitus que probabit,
Assensere Dei.*

Sages and lawgivers have bent their whole nature to the search for truth, and thought themselves happy if they could buy, with the sacrifice of all temporal ease and pleasure, one seed for the future Eden. Poets and priests have strung the lyre with the heart-strings, poured out their best blood upon the altar, which, reared anew from age to age shall at last sustain the flame pure enough to rise to highest heaven. Shall we not name with as deep a benediction those who, if not so immediately, or so consciously, in connection with the eternal truth, yet, led and fashioned by a divine instinct, serve no less to develop and interpret the open secret of love passing into life, energy creating for the purpose of happiness; the artist whose hand, drawn by a pre-existent harmony to a certain medium, moulds it to forms of life more highly and completely organized than are seen elsewhere, and, by carrying out the intention of nature, reveals her meaning to those who are not yet wise enough to divine it; the philosopher who listens steadily for laws and causes, and from those obvious, infers those yet unknown; the historian who, in faith that all events must have their reason and their aim, records them, and thus fills archives from which the youth of prophets may be fed. The man of science dissects the statements, tests the facts, and demonstrates order, even where he cannot its purpose.

Lives, too, which bear none of these names, have yielded tones of no less significance. The candlestick set in a low place has given light as faithfully, where it was needed, as that upon the hill.* In close alleys, in dismal nooks, the Word has been read as distinctly, as when shown by angels to holy men in the dark prison. Those who till a spot of earth scarcely larger than is wanted for a grave, have deserved that the sun should shine upon its sod till violets answer.

So great has been, from time to time, the promise, that, in all ages, men have said the gods themselves came down to dwell with them; that the All-Creating wandered on the earth to taste, in a limited nature, the sweetness of virtue; that the All-

Sustaining incarnated himself to guard, in space and time, the destinies of this world; that heavenly genius dwelt among the shepherds, to sing to them and teach them how to sing. Indeed

'Der stets den Hirten gnadig sich bewies.'

'He has constantly shown himself favorable to shepherds.'

And the dwellers in green pastures and natural students of the stars were selected to hail, first among men, the holy child, whose life and death were to present the type of excellence, which has sustained the heart of so large a portion of mankind in these later generations.

Such marks have been made by the footsteps of *man*, (still alas! to be spoken of as the *ideal* man,) wherever he has passed through the wilderness of *men*, and whenever the pigmies stepped in one of those they felt dilate within the breast somewhat that promised nobler stature and purer blood. They were impelled to forsake their evil ways of decrepit scepticism, and covetousness of corruptible possessions. Conviction flowed in upon them. They, too, raised the cry; God is living, now, to-day; and all beings are brothers, for they are his children. Simple words enough, yet which only angelic nature, can use or hear in their full free sense.

These were the triumphant moments, but soon the lower nature took its turn, and the era of a truly human life was postponed.

Thus is man still a stranger to his inheritance, still a pleader, still a pilgrim. Yet his happiness is secure in the end. And now, no more a glimmering consciousness, but assurance begins to be felt and spoken, that the highest ideal man can form of his own powers, is that which he is destined to attain. Whatever the soul knows how to seek, it cannot fail to obtain. This is the law and the prophets. Knock and it shall be opened, seek and ye shall find. It is demonstrated; it is a maxim. Man no longer paints his proper nature in some form and says, 'Prometheus* had it; it is God-like;' but 'Man must have it; it is human.' However disputed by many, however ignorantly used, or falsified by those who do receive it, the fact of an universal, unceasing revelation has been too clearly stated in words to be lost sight of in thought, and sermons preached from the text, 'Be ye perfect,'* are the only sermons of a pervasive and deep-searching influence.

But, among those who meditate upon this text, there is a great difference of view, as to the way in which perfection shall be sought.

Through the intellect, say some. Gather from every growth of life its seed of thought; look behind every symbol for its law; if thou canst *see* clearly, the rest will follow.

Through the life, say others. Do the best thou knowest to-day. Shrink not from frequent error in this gradual fragmentary state. Follow thy light for as much as it will show thee, be faithful as far as thou canst, in hope that faith presently will lead to sight. Help others, without blaming their need of thy help. Love much and be forgiven.

It needs not intellect, needs not experience, says a third. If you took the true way, your destiny would be accomplished in a purer and more natural order. You would not learn through facts of thought or action, but express through them the certainties of wisdom. In quietness yield thy soul to the causal soul. Do not disturb thy apprenticeship by premature effort; neither check the tide of instruction by methods of thy own. Be still, seek not, but wait in obedience. Thy commission will be given.

Could we indeed say what we want, could we give a description of the child that is lost, he would be found. As soon as the soul can affirm clearly that a certain demonstration is wanted, it is at hand. When the Jewish prophet described the Lamb,* as the expression of what was required by the coming era, the time drew nigh. But we say not, see not as yet, clearly, what we would. Those who call for a more triumphant expression of love, a love that cannot be crucified, show not a perfect sense of what has already been given. Love has already been expressed, that made all things new, that gave the worm its place and ministry as well as the eagle; a love to which it was alike to descend into the depths of hell, or to sit at the right hand of the Father.

Yet, no doubt, a new manifestation is at hand, a new hour in the day of man. We cannot expect to see any one sample of completed being, when the mass of men still lie engaged in the sod, or use the freedom of their limbs only with wolfish energy. The tree cannot come to flower till its root be free from the cankering worm, and its whole growth open to air and light. While any one is base, none can be entirely free and noble. Yet something new shall presently be shown of the life of man, for hearts crave, if minds do not know how to ask it.

Among the strains of prophecy, the following, by an earnest mind of a foreign land,* written some thirty years ago, is not yet outgrown; and it has the merit of being a positive appeal from the heart, instead of a critical declaration what man should *not* do.

'The ministry of man implies, that he must be filled from the divine fountains which are being engendered through all eternity, so that, at the mere name of his master, he may be able to cast all his enemies into the abyss; that he may deliver all parts of nature from the barriers that imprison them; that he may purge the terrestrial atmosphere from the poisons that infect it; that he may preserve the bodies of men from the corrupt influences that surround, and the maladies that afflict them; still more, that he may keep their souls pure from the malignant insinuations which pollute, and the gloomy images that obscure them; that he may restore its serenity to the Word, which false words of men fill with mourning and sadness; that he may satisfy the desires of the angels, who await from him the development of the marvels of nature; that, in fine, his world may be filled with God, as eternity is.'

Another attempt we will give, by an obscure observer of our own day and country, to draw some lines of the desired image. It was suggested by seeing the design of Crawford's Orpheus,* and connecting with the circumstance of the American, in his garret at Rome, making choice of this subject, that of Americans here at home, showing such ambition to represent the character, by calling their prose and verse 'Orphic sayings'—'Orphics.'* We wish we could add that they have shown that musical apprehension of the progress of nature through her ascending gradations which entitled them so to do, but their attempts are frigid, though sometimes grand; in their strain we are not warmed by the fire which fertilized the soil of Greece.

Orpheus was a law-giver by theocratic commission. He

understood nature, and made her forms move to his music. He told her secrets in the form of hymns, nature as seen in the mind of God. His soul went forth toward all beings, yet could remain sternly faithful to a chosen type of excellence. Seeking what he loved, he feared not death nor hell, neither could any shape of dread daunt his faith in the power of the celestial harmony that filled his soul.

It seemed significant of the state of things in this country, that the sculptor should have represented the seer at the moment when he was obliged with his hand to shade his eyes.

> Each Orpheus must to the depths descend,
> For only thus the Poet can be wise,
>   Must make the sad Persephone* his friend,
> And buried love to second life arise;
>   Again his love must lose through too much love,
> Must lose his life by living life too true,
>   For what he sought below is passed above,
> Already done is all that he would do;
>   Must tune all being with his single lyre,
> Must melt all rocks free from their primal pain,
>   Must search all nature with his one soul's fire,
> Must bind anew all forms in heavenly chain.
>   If he already sees what he must do,
> Well may he shade his eyes from the far-shining view.*

A better comment could not be made on what is required to perfect man, and place him in that superior position for which he was designed, than by the interpretation of Bacon* upon the legends of the Syren* coast. When the wise Ulysses passed, says he, he caused his mariners to stop their ears with wax, knowing there was in them no power to resist the lure of that voluptuous song. But he, the much experienced man, who wished to be experienced in all, and use all to the service of wisdom, desired to hear the song that he might understand its meaning. Yet, distrusting his own power to be firm in his better purpose, he caused himself to be bound to the mast, that he might be kept secure against his own weakness. But Orpheus passed unfettered, so absorbed in singing hymns to the gods that he could not even hear those sounds of degrading enchantment.

Meanwhile not a few believe, and men themselves have expressed the opinion, that the time is come when Eurydice is to call for an Orpheus, rather than Orpheus for Eurydice: that the idea of Man, however imperfectly brought out, has been far more so than that of Woman, that she, the other half of the same thought, the other chamber of the heart of life, needs now to take her turn in the full pulsation, and that improvement in the daughters will best aid in the reformation of the sons of this age.

It should be remarked that, as the principle of liberty is better understood, and more nobly interpreted, a broader protest is made in behalf of Woman. As men become aware that few men have had a fair chance, they are inclined to say that no women have had a fair chance. The French Revolution, that strangely disguised angel, bore witness in favor of woman, but interpreted her claims no less ignorantly than those of man. Its idea of happiness did not rise beyond outward enjoyment, unobstructed by the tyranny of others. The title it gave was citoyen, citoyenne, and it is not unimportant to woman that even this species of equality was awarded her. Before, she could be condemned to perish on the scaffold for treason, not as a citizen, but as a subject. The right with which this title then invested a human being, was that of bloodshed and license. The Goddess of Liberty was impure. As we read the poem addressed to her not long since, by Beranger,* we can scarcely refrain from tears as painful as the tears of blood that flowed when 'such crimes were committed in her name.' Yes! man, born to purify and animate the unintelligent and the cold, can, in his madness, degrade and pollute no less the fair and the chaste. Yet truth was prophesied in the ravings of that hideous fever, caused by long ignorance and abuse. Europe is conning a valued lesson from the blood-stained page. The same tendencies, farther unfolded, will bear good fruit in this country.

Yet, by men in this country, as by the Jews, when Moses was leading them to the promised land, every thing has been done that inherited depravity could do, to hinder the promise of heaven from its fulfilment. The cross here as elsewhere, has been planted only to be blasphemed by cruelty and fraud. The name of the Prince of Peace has been profaned by all kinds of injustice toward the Gentile whom he said he came to save. But I need not speak of what has been done towards the red man, the black man. Those deeds are the scoff of the world; and they have been accompanied by such pious words that the gentlest would not dare to intercede with 'Father, forgive them, for they know not what they do.'*

Here, as elsewhere, the gain of creation consists always in the growth of individual minds, which live and aspire, as flowers bloom and birds sing, in the midst of morasses; and in the continual development of that thought, the thought of human destiny, which is given to eternity adequately to express, and which ages of failure only seemingly impede. Only seemingly, and whatever seems to the contrary, this country is as surely destined to elucidate a great moral law, as Europe was to promote the mental culture of man.

Though the national independence be blurred by the servility of individuals, though freedom and equality have been proclaimed only to leave room for a monstrous display of slave-dealing and slave-keeping; though the free American so often feels himself free, like the Roman, only to pamper his appetites and his indolence through the misery of his fellow beings, still it is not in vain, that the verbal statement has been made, 'All men are born free and equal.' There it stands, a golden certainty wherewith to encourage the good, to shame the bad. The new world may be called clearly to perceive that it incurs the utmost penalty, if it reject or oppress the sorrowful brother. And, if men are deaf, the angels hear. But men cannot be deaf. It is inevitable that an external freedom, an independence of the encroachments of other men, such as has been achieved for the nation, should be so also for every member of it. That which has once been clearly conceived in the intelligence cannot fail sooner or later to be acted out. It has become a law as irrevocable as that of the Medes in their ancient dominion; men will privately sin against it, but the law, as expressed by a leading mind of the age,

> 'Tutti fatti a sembianza d'un Solo,
> Figli tutti d'un solo riscatto,
> In qual'ora, in qual parte del suolo
> Trascorriamo quest'aura vital,

Siam fratelli, siam stretti ad un patto:
Maladetto colui che lo infrange,
Che s'innalza sul fiacco che piange
Che contrista uno spirto immortal.'*

'All made in the likeness of the One,
  All children of one ransom,
In whatever hour, in whatever part of the soil,
  We draw this vital air,
We are brothers; we must be bound by one compact,
  Accursed he who infringes it,
Who raises himself upon the weak who weep,
  Who saddens an immortal spirit.'

This law cannot fail of universal recognition. Accursed be he who willingly saddens an immortal spirit, doomed to infamy in later, wiser ages, doomed in future stages of his own being to deadly penance, only short of death. Accursed be he who sins in ignorance, if that ignorance be caused by sloth.

We sicken no less at the pomp than the strife of words. We feel that never were lungs so puffed with the wind of declamation, on moral and religious subjects, as now. We are tempted to implore these 'word-heroes,' these word-Catos,* word-Christs, to beware of cant† above all things; to remember that hypocrisy is the most hopeless as well as the meanest of crimes, and that those must surely be polluted by it, who do not reserve a part of their morality and religion for private use. Landor* says that he cannot have a great deal of mind who cannot afford to let the larger part of it lie fallow, and what is true of genius is not less so of virtue. The tongue is a valuable member, but should appropriate but a small part of the vital juices that are needful all over the body. We feel that the mind may 'grow black and rancid in the smoke' even 'of altars.' We start up from the harangue to go into our closet and shut the

---

† Dr Johnson's one piece of advice should be written on every door: 'Clear your mind of cant.' But Byron, to whom it was so acceptable, in clearing away the noxious vine, shook down the building. Sterling's* emendation is worthy of honor:

'Realize your cant, not cast it off.'

[Fuller's note.]

door. There inquires the spirit, 'Is this rhetoric the bloom of healthy blood or a false pigment artfully laid on?' And yet again we know where is so much smoke, must be some fire; with so much talk about virtue and freedom, must be mingled some desire for them; that it cannot be in vain that such have become the common topics of conversation among men, rather than schemes for tyranny and plunder, that the very newspapers see it best to proclaim themselves Pilgrims, Puritans, Heralds of Holiness. The king that maintains so costly a retinue cannot be a mere boast, or Carabbas* fiction. We have waited here long in the dust; we are tired and hungry, but the triumphal procession must appear at last.

Of all its banners, none has been more steadily upheld, and under none have more valor and willingness for real sacrifices been shown, than that of the champions of the enslaved African. And this band it is, which, partly from a natural following out of principles, partly because many women have been prominent in that cause, makes, just now, the warmest appeal in behalf of woman.

Though there has been a growing liberality on this subject, yet society at large is not so prepared for the demands of this party, but that they are and will be for some time, coldly regarded as the Jacobins* of their day.

'Is it not enough,' cries the irritated trader, 'that you have done all you could to break up the national union, and thus destroy the prosperity of our country, but now you must be trying to break up family union, to take my wife away from the cradle and the kitchen hearth to vote at polls, and preach from a pulpit? Of course, if she does such things, she cannot attend to those of her own sphere. She is happy enough as she is. She has more leisure than I have, every means of improvement, every indulgence.'

'Have you asked her whether she was satisfied with these *indulgences?*'

'No, but I know she is. She is too amiable to wish what would make me unhappy, and too judicious to wish to step beyond the sphere of her sex. I will never consent to have our peace disturbed by any such discussions.'

' "Consent—you?" it is not consent from you that is in question, it is assent from your wife.'

'Am not I the head of my house?'

'You are not the head of your wife. God has given her a mind of her own.'

'I am the head and she the heart.'

'God grant you play true to one another then! I suppose I am to be grateful that you did not say she was only the hand. If the head represses no natural pulse of the heart, there can be no question as to your giving your consent. Both will be of one accord, and there needs but to present any question to get a full and true answer. There is no need of precaution, of indulgence, or consent. But our doubt is whether the heart does consent with the head, or only obeys its decrees with a passiveness that precludes the exercise of its natural powers, or a repugnance that turns sweet qualities to bitter, or a doubt that lays waste the fair occasions of life. It is to ascertain the truth, that we propose some liberating measures.'

Thus vaguely are these questions proposed and discussed at present. But their being proposed at all implies much thought and suggests more. Many women are considering within themselves, what they need that they have not, and what they can have, if they find they need it. Many men are considering whether women are capable of being and having more than they are and have, *and*, whether, if so, it will be best to consent to improvement in their condition.

This morning, I open the Boston 'Daily Mail,' and find in its 'poet's corner,' a translation of Schiller's 'Dignity of Woman.'* In the advertisement of a book on America, I see in the table of contents this sequence, 'Republican Institutions. American Slavery. American Ladies.'

I open the '*Deutsche Schnellpost*,'* published in New-York, and find at the head of a column, *Juden und Frauenemancipation in Ungarn*. Emancipation of Jews and Women in Hungary.

The past year has seen action in the Rhode-Island legislature, to secure married women rights over their own property, where men showed that a very little examination of the subject could teach them much; an article in the Democratic Review* on the same subject more largely considered, written by a woman, impelled, it is said, by glaring wrong to a distinguished friend having shown the defects in the existing laws, and the state of opinion from which they spring; and an answer from the revered old man, J. Q. Adams, in some respects the Phocion* of his time, to an address made him by some ladies. To this last I shall again advert in another place.

These symptoms of the times have come under my view quite accidentally: one who seeks, may, each month or week, collect more.

The numerous party, whose opinions are already labelled and adjusted too much to their mind to admit of any new light, strive, by lectures on some model-woman of bride-like beauty and gentleness, by writing and lending little treatises, intended to mark out with precision the limits of woman's sphere, and woman's mission, to prevent other than the rightful shepherd from climbing the wall, or the flock from using any chance to go astray.

Without enrolling ourselves at once on either side, let us look upon the subject from the best point of view which to-day offers. No better, it is to be feared, than a high house-top. A high hill-top, or at least a cathedral spire, would be desirable.

It may well be an Anti-Slavery party that pleads for woman, if we consider merely that she does not hold property on equal terms with men; so that, if a husband dies without making a will, the wife, instead of taking at once his place as head of the family, inherits only a part of his fortune, often brought him by herself, as if she were a child, or ward only, not an equal partner.

We will not speak of the innumerable instances in which profligate and idle men live upon the earnings of industrious wives; or if the wives leave them, and take with them the children, to perform the double duty of mother and father, follow from place to place, and threaten to rob them of the children, if deprived of the rights of a husband, as they call them, planting themselves in their poor lodgings, frightening them into paying tribute by taking from them the children, running into debt at the expense of these otherwise so over-tasked helots. Such instances count up by scores within my own memory. I have seen the husband who had stained himself by a long course of low vice, till his wife was wearied from her heroic forgiveness, by finding that his treachery made it useless, and that if she would provide bread for herself and her children, she must be separate from his ill fame. I have known this man come to instal himself in the chamber of a woman who loathed him and say she should never take food without his company. I have known these men steal their children whom they knew they had no means to maintain, take them into dissolute company, expose them to bodily danger, to frighten the poor woman, to whom, it seems, the fact that she alone had borne the pangs of their birth, and nourished their infancy, does not give an equal right to them. I do believe that this mode of kidnapping, and it is frequent enough in all classes of society, will be by the next age viewed as it is by Heaven now, and that the man who avails himself of the shelter of men's laws to steal from a mother her own children, or arrogate any superior right in them, save that of superior virtue, will bear the stigma he deserves, in common with him who steals grown men from their mother land, their hopes, and their homes.

I said, we will not speak of this now, yet I have spoken, for the subject makes me feel too much. I could give instances that would startle the most vulgar and callous, but I will not, for the public opinion of their own sex is already against such men, and where cases of extreme tyranny are made known, there is private action in the wife's favor. But she ought not to need this, nor, I think, can she long. Men must soon see that, on their own ground, that woman is the weaker party, she ought to have legal protection, which would make such oppression impossible. But I would not deal with 'atrocious instances' except in the way of illustration, neither demand from men a partial redress in some one matter, but go to the root of the whole. If principles could be established, particulars would adjust themselves aright. Ascertain the true destiny of woman, give her legitimate hopes, and a standard within herself; marriage and all other relations would by degrees be harmonized with these.

But to return to the historical progress of this matter. Knowing that there exists in the minds of men a tone of feeling towards women as towards slaves, such as is expressed in the common phrase, 'Tell that to women and children,' that the infinite soul can only work through them in already ascertained limits; that the gift of reason, man's highest prerogative, is allotted to them in much lower degree; that they must be kept from mischief and melancholy by being constantly engaged in active labor, which is to be furnished and directed by those better able to think, &c. &c.; we need not multiply instances, for who can review the experience of last week without recalling words which imply, whether in jest or earnest, these views or views like these; knowing this, can we wonder that many reformers think that measures are not likely to be taken in behalf of women, unless their wishes could be publicly represented by women?

That can never be necessary, cry the other side. All men are privately influenced by women; each has his wife, sister, or female friends, and is too much biased by these relations to fail of representing their interests, and, if this is not enough, let them propose and enforce their wishes with the pen. The beauty of home would be destroyed, the delicacy of the sex be violated, the dignity of halls of legislation degraded by an attempt to introduce them there. Such duties are inconsistent with those of a mother; and then we have ludicrous pictures of ladies in hysterics at the polls, and senate chambers filled with cradles.

But if, in reply, we admit as truth that woman seems destined by nature rather for the inner circle, we must add that the arrangements of civilized life have not been, as yet, such as to secure it to her. Her circle, if the duller, is not the quieter. If kept from 'excitement,' she is not from drudgery. Not only the Indian squaw carries the burdens of the camp, but the favorites of Louis the Fourteenth accompany him in his journeys, and the washerwoman stands at her tub and carries home her work at all seasons, and in all states of health. Those who think the physical circumstances of woman would make a part of the affairs of national government unsuitable, are by no means those who think it impossible for the negresses to endure field work, even during pregnancy, or the sempstresses to go through their killing labors.

As to the use of the pen, there was quite as much opposition to woman's possessing herself of that help to free agency, as there is now to her seizing on the rostrum or the desk; and she is likely to draw, from a permission to plead her cause that way, opposite inferences to what might be wished by those who now grant it.

As to the possibility of her filling with grace and dignity, any such position, we should think those who had seen the great actresses, and heard the Quaker preachers of modern times, would not doubt, that woman can express publicly the fulness of thought and creation, without losing any of the peculiar beauty of her sex. What can pollute and tarnish is to act thus from any motive except that something needs to be said or done. Women could take part in the processions, the songs, the dances of old religion; no one fancied their delicacy was impaired by appearing in public for such a cause.

As to her home, she is not likely to leave it more than she now does for balls, theatres, meetings for promoting missions, revival meetings, and others to which she flies, in hope of an animation for her existence, commensurate with what she sees enjoyed by men. Governors of ladies' fairs are no less engrossed by such a change, than the Governor of the state by his; presidents of Washingtonian societies no less away from home than presidents of conventions. If men look straitly to it, they will find that, unless their lives are domestic, those of the women will not be. A house is no home unless it contain food and fire for the mind as well as for the body. The female Greek, of our day, is as much in the street as the male to cry, What news? We doubt not it was the same in Athens of old. The women, shut out from the market place, made up for it at the religious festivals. For human beings are not so constituted that they can live without expansion. If they do not get it one way, they must another, or perish.

As to men's representing women fairly at present, while we hear from men who owe to their wives not only all that is comfortable or graceful, but all that is wise in the arrangement of their lives, the frequent remark, 'You cannot reason with a woman,' when from those of delicacy, nobleness, and poetic culture, the contemptuous phrase 'women and children,' and that in no light sally of the hour, but in works intended to give a permanent statement of the best experiences, when not one man, in the million, shall I say? no, not in the hundred million, can rise above the belief that woman was made *for man*, when such traits as these are daily forced upon the attention, can we feel that man will always do justice to the interests of woman? Can we think that he takes a sufficiently discerning and religious view of her office and destiny, *ever* to do her justice, except when prompted by sentiment, accidentally or transiently, that is, for the sentiment will vary according to the relations in which he is placed. The lover, the poet, the artist, are likely to view her nobly. The father and the philosopher have some chance of liberality; the man of the world, the legislator for expediency, none.

Under these circumstances, without attaching importance, in themselves, to the changes demanded by the champions of woman, we hail them as signs of the times. We would have every arbitrary barrier thrown down. We would have every path laid open to woman as freely as to man. Were this done and a slight temporary fermentation allowed to subside, we should see crystallizations more pure and of more various beauty. We believe the divine energy would pervade nature to a degree unknown in the history of former ages, and that no discordant collision, but a ravishing harmony of the spheres would ensue.

Yet, then and only then, will mankind be ripe for this, when inward and outward freedom for woman as much as for man shall be acknowledged as a right, not yielded as a concession. As the friend of the negro assumes that one man cannot by right, hold another in bondage, so should the friend of woman assume that man cannot, by right, lay even well-meant restrictions on woman. If the negro be a soul, if the woman be a soul, appareled in flesh, to one Master only are they accountable. There is but one law for souls, and if there is to be an interpreter of it, he must come not as man, or son of man, but as son of God.

Were thought and feeling once so far elevated that man should esteem himself the brother and friend, but nowise the lord and tutor of woman, were he really bound with her in equal worship, arrangements as to function and employment would be of no consequence. What woman needs is not as a woman to act or rule, but as a nature to grow, as an intellect to discern, as a soul to live freely and unimpeded, to unfold such powers as were given her when we left our common home. If fewer talents were given her, yet if allowed the free and full employment of these, so that she may render back to the giver his own with usury, she will not complain; nay I dare to say she will bless and rejoice in her earthly birth-place, her earthly lot. Let us consider what obstructions impede this good era, and what signs give reason to hope that it draws near.

I was talking on this subject with Miranda,* a woman, who, if any in the world could, might speak without heat and bitterness of the position of her sex. Her father was a man who cherished no sentimental reverence for woman, but a firm belief in the equality of the sexes. She was his eldest child, and came to him at an age when he needed a companion. From the time she could speak and go alone, he addressed her not as a plaything, but as a living mind. Among the few verses he ever wrote was a copy addressed to this child, when the first locks were cut from her head, and the reverence expressed on this occasion for that cherished head, he never belied. It was to him the temple of immortal intellect. He respected his child, however, too much to be an indulgent parent. He called on her for clear judgment, for courage, for honor and fidelity; in short, for such virtues as he knew. In so far as he possessed the keys to the wonders of this universe, he allowed free use of them to her, and by the incentive of a high expectation, he forbade, as far as possible, that she should let the privilege lie idle.

Thus this child was early led to feel herself a child of the spirit. She took her place easily, not only in the world of organized being, but in the world of mind. A dignified sense of self-dependence was given as all her portion, and she found it a sure anchor. Herself securely anchored, her relations with others were established with equal security. She was fortunate in a total absence of those charms which might have drawn to her bewildering flatteries, and in a strong electric nature, which repelled those who did not belong to her, and attracted those who did. With men and women her relations were noble, affectionate without passion, intellectual without coldness. The world was free to her, and she lived freely in it. Outward adversity came, and inward conflict, but that faith and self-respect had early been awakened which must always lead at last, to an outward serenity and an inward peace.

Of Miranda I had always thought as an example, that the restraints upon the sex were insuperable only to those who think them so, or who noisily strive to break them. She had taken a course of her own, and no man stood in her way. Many of her acts had been unusual, but excited no uproar. Few helped, but none checked her, and the many men, who knew her mind and her life, showed to her confidence, as to a brother, gentleness as to a sister. And not only refined, but very coarse men approved and aided one in whom they saw resolution and clearness of design. Her mind was often the leading one, always effective.

When I talked with her upon these matters, and had said very much what I have written, she smilingly replied: 'And yet we must admit that I have been fortunate, and this should not be. My good father's early trust gave the first bias, and the rest followed of course. It is true that I have had less outward aid, in after years, than most women, but that is of little consequence. Religion was early awakened in my soul, a sense that what the soul is capable to ask it must attain, and that, though I might be aided and instructed by others, I must depend on myself as the only constant friend. This self-dependence, which was honored in me, is deprecated as a fault in most women. They are taught to learn their rule from without, not to unfold it from within.

'This is the fault of man, who is still vain, and wishes to be more important to woman than, by right, he should be.'

'Men have not shown this disposition toward you,' I said.

'No! because the position I early was enabled to take was one of self-reliance. And were all women as sure of their wants as I was, the result would be the same. But they are so overloaded with precepts by guardians, who think that nothing is so much to be dreaded for a woman as originality of thought or character, that their minds are impeded by doubts till they lose their chance of fair free proportions. The difficulty is to get them to the point from which they shall naturally develop self-respect, and learn self-help.

'Once I thought that men would help to forward this state of things more than I do now. I saw so many of them wretched in the connections they had formed in weakness and vanity. They seemed so glad to esteem women whenever they could.

"The soft arms of affection," said one of the most discerning spirits, "will not suffice for me, unless on them I see the steel bracelets of strength."

'But early I perceived that men never, in any extreme of

despair, wished to be women. On the contrary they were ever ready to taunt one another at any sign of weakness, with,

"Art thou not like the women, who"—

The passage ends various ways, according to the occasion and rhetoric of the speaker. When they admired any woman they were inclined to speak of her as "above her sex." Silently I observed this, and feared it argued a rooted scepticism, which for ages had been fastening on the heart, and which only an age of miracles could eradicate. Ever I have been treated with great sincerity; and I look upon it as a signal instance of this, that an intimate friend of the other sex said, in a fervent moment, that I "deserved in some star to be a man." He was much surprised when I disclosed my view of my position and hopes, when I declared my faith that the feminine side, the side of love, of beauty, of holiness, was now to have its full chance, and that, if either were better, it was better now to be a woman, for even the slightest achievement of good was furthering an especial work of our time. He smiled incredulous. "She makes the best she can of it," thought he. "Let Jews believe the pride of Jewry, but I am of the better sort, and know better."

'Another used as highest praise, in speaking of a character in literature, the words "a manly woman."'

'So in the noble passage of Ben Jonson:

"I meant the day-star should not brighter ride,
    Nor shed like influence from its lucent seat;
I meant she should be courteous, facile, sweet,
    Free from that solemn vice of greatness, pride;
I meant each softest virtue there should meet,
    Fit in that softer bosom to abide,
Only a learned and a *manly* soul,
    I purposed her, that should with even powers,
The rock, the spindle, and the shears control
    Of destiny, and spin her own free hours." *

'Methinks,' said I, 'you are too fastidious in objecting to this. Jonson in using the word "manly" only meant to heighten the picture of this, the true, the intelligent fate, with one of the deeper colors.' 'And yet,' said she, 'so invariable is the use of this word where a heroic quality is to be described, and I feel so sure that persistence and courage are the most womanly no less than the most manly qualities, that I would exchange these words for others of a larger sense at the risk of marring the fine tissue of the verse. Read, 'a heavenward and instructed soul,' and I should be satisfied. Let it not be said, wherever there is energy or creative genius, "She has a masculine mind." '

This by no means argues a willing want of generosity toward woman. Man is as generous toward her, as he knows how to be.

Wherever she has herself arisen in national or private history, and nobly shone forth in any form of excellence, men have received her, not only willingly, but with triumph. Their encomiums indeed, are always, in some sense, mortifying; they show too much surprise. Can this be you? he cries to the transfigured Cinderella; well I should never have thought it, but I am very glad. We will tell every one that you have 'surpassed your sex.'

In every-day life the feelings of the many are stained with vanity. Each wishes to be lord in a little world, to be superior at least over one; and he does not feel strong enough to retain a life-long ascendancy over a strong nature. Only a Theseus could conquer before he wed the Amazonian Queen.* Hercules wished rather to rest with Dejanira, and received the poisoned robe, as a fit guerdon.* The tale should be interpreted to all those who seek repose with the weak.

But not only is man vain and fond of power, but the same want of development, which thus affects him morally, prevents his intellectually discerning the destiny of woman. The boy wants no woman, but only a girl to play ball with him, and mark his pocket handkerchief.

Thus, in Schiller's Dignity of Woman, beautiful as the poem is, there is no 'grave and perfect man,' but only a great boy to be softened and restrained by the influence of girls. Poets, the elder brothers of their race, have usually seen farther; but what can you expect of every-day men, if Schiller was not more prophetic as to what women must be? Even with Richter,* one foremost thought about a wife was that she would 'cook him something good.' But as this is a delicate subject, and we are in constant danger of being accused of slighting what are called 'the functions,' let me say in behalf of Miranda and myself, that we have high respect for those who cook something good, who create and preserve fair order in houses, and prepare therein the shining raiment for worthy inmates, worthy guests. Only these 'functions' must not be a drudgery, or enforced necessity, but a part of life. Let Ulysses drive the beeves home while Penelope* there piles up the fragrant loaves; they are both well employed if these be done in thought and love, willingly. But Penelope is no more meant for a baker or weaver solely, than Ulysses for a cattle-herd.

The sexes should not only correspond to and appreciate, but prophesy to one another. In individual instances this happens. Two persons love in one another the future good which they aid one another to unfold. This is imperfectly or rarely done in the general life. Man has gone but little way; now he is waiting to see whether woman can keep step with him, but instead of calling out, like a good brother, 'you can do it, if you only think so,' or impersonally; 'any one can do what he tries to do;' he often discourages with school-boy brag: 'Girls can't do that; girls can't play ball.' But let any one defy their taunts, break through and be brave and secure, they rend the air with shouts.

This fluctuation was obvious in a narrative I have lately seen, the story of the life of Countess Emily Plater,* the heroine of the last revolution in Poland. The dignity, the purity, the concentrated resolve, the calm, deep enthusiasm, which yet could, when occasion called, sparkle up a holy, an indignant fire, make of this young maiden the figure I want for my frontispiece. Her portrait is to be seen in the book, a gentle shadow of her soul. Short was the career—like the maid of Orleans, she only did enough to verify her credentials, and then passed from a scene on which she was, probably, a premature apparition.

When the young girl joined the army where the report of her exploits had preceded her, she was received in a manner that marks the usual state of feeling. Some of the officers were disappointed at her quiet manners; that she had not the air and tone of a stage-heroine. They thought she could not have acted heroically unless in buskins; had no idea that such deeds only showed the habit of her mind. Others talked of the delicacy of her sex, advised her to withdraw from perils and dangers, and had no comprehension of the feelings within her breast that made this impossible. The gentle irony of her reply to these self-constituted tutors, (not one of whom showed himself her equal in conduct or reason,) is as good as her indignant reproof at a later period to the general, whose perfidy ruined all.

But though, to the mass of these men, she was an embarrassment and a puzzle, the nobler sort viewed her with a tender enthusiasm worthy of her. 'Her name,' said her biographer, 'is known throughout Europe. I paint her character that she may be as widely loved.'

With pride, he shows her freedom from all personal affections; that, though tender and gentle in an uncommon degree, there was no room for a private love in her consecrated life. She inspired those who knew her with a simple energy of feeling like her own. We have seen, they felt, a woman worthy the name, capable of all sweet affections, capable of stern virtue.

It is a fact worthy of remark, that all these revolutions in favor of liberty have produced female champions that share the same traits, but Emily alone has found a biographer. Only a near friend could have performed for her this task, for the flower was reared in feminine seclusion, and the few and simple traits of her history before her appearance in the field could only have been known to the domestic circle. Her biographer has gathered them up with a brotherly devotion.

No! man is not willingly ungenerous. He wants faith and love, because he is not yet himself an elevated being. He cries, with sneering skepticism, Give us a sign. But if the sign appears, his eyes glisten, and he offers not merely approval, but homage.

The severe nation which taught that the happiness of the race was forfeited through the fault of a woman, and showed its thought of what sort of regard man owed her, by making him accuse her on the first question to his God;* who gave her to the patriarch as a handmaid, and by the Mosaical law, bound her to allegiance like a serf; even they greeted, with solemn rapture, all great and holy women as heroines, prophetesses, judges in Israel; and if they made Eve listen to the serpent, gave Mary as a bride to the Holy Spirit. In other nations it has been the same down to our day. To the woman who could conquer, a triumph was awarded. And not only those whose strength was recommended to the heart by association with goodness and beauty, but those who were bad, if they were steadfast and strong, had their claims allowed. In any age a Semiramis,* an Elizabeth of England, a Catharine of Russia, makes her place good, whether in a large or small circle. How has a little wit, a little genius, been celebrated in a woman! What an intellectual triumph was that of the lonely Aspasia,* and how heartily acknowledged! She, indeed, met a Pericles. But what annalist, the rudest of men, the most plebeian of husbands, will spare from his page one of the few anecdotes of Roman women—Sappho! Eloisa!* The names are of threadbare celebrity. Indeed they were not more suitably met in their own time than the Countess Colonel Plater on her first joining the army. They had much to mourn, and their great impulses did not find due scope. But with time enough, space enough, their kindred appear on the scene. Across the ages, forms lean, trying to touch the hem of their retreating robes. The youth here by my side cannot be weary of the fragments from the life of Sappho. He will not believe they are not addressed to himself, or that he to whom they were addressed could be ungrateful.* A recluse of high powers devotes himself to understand and explain the thought of Eloisa; he asserts her vast superiority in soul and genius to her master; he curses the fate that cast his lot in another age than hers. He could have understood her: he would have been to her a friend, such as Abelard never could. And this one woman he could have loved and reverenced, and she, alas! lay cold in her grave hundreds of years ago. His sorrow is truly pathetic. These responses that come too late to give joy are as tragic as any thing we know, and yet the tears of later ages glitter as they fall on Tasso's prison bars.* And we know how elevating to the captive is the security that somewhere an intelligence must answer to his.

The man habitually most narrow towards women will be flushed, as by the worst assault on Christianity, if you say it has made no improvement in her condition. Indeed, those most opposed to new acts in her favor, are jealous of the reputation of those which have been done.

We will not speak of the enthusiasm excited by actresses, improvvisatrici, female singers, for here mingles the charm of beauty and grace; but female authors, even learned women, if not insufferably ugly and slovenly, from the Italian professor's daughter, who taught behind the curtain, down to Mrs Carter and Madame Dacier,* are sure of an admiring audience, and what is far better, chance to use what they have learned, and to learn more, if they can once get a platform on which to stand.

But how to get this platform, or how to make it of reasonably easy access is the difficulty. Plants of great vigor will almost always struggle into blossom, despite impediments. But there should be encouragement, and a free genial atmosphere for those of more timid sort, fair play for each in its own kind. Some are like the little, delicate flowers which love to hide in the dripping mosses, by the sides of moutain torrents, or in the shade of tall trees. But others require an open field, a rich and loosened soil, or they never show their proper hues.

It may be said that man does not have his fair play either; his energies are repressed and distorted by the interposition of artificial obstacles. Ay, but he himself has put them there; they have grown out of his own imperfections. If there *is* a misfortune in woman's lot, it is in obstacles being interposed by men, which do *not* mark her state; and, if they express her past ignorance, do not her present needs. As every man is of woman born, she has slow but sure means of redress, yet the sooner a general justness of thought makes smooth the path, the better.

Man is of woman born, and her face bends over him in infancy with an expression he can never quite forget. Eminent men have delighted to pay tribute to this image, and it is an hacknied observation, that most men of genius boast some remarkable development in the mother. The rudest tar brushes off a tear with his coat-sleeve at the hallowed name. The other day, I met a decrepit old man of seventy, on a journey, who challenged the stage-company to guess where he was going. They guessed aright, 'To see your mother.' 'Yes,' said he, 'she is ninety-two, but has good eye-sight still, they say. I have not seen her these forty years, and I thought I could not die in peace without.' I should have liked his picture painted as a companion piece to that of a boisterous little boy, whom I saw attempt to declaim at a school exhibition—

> 'O that those lips had language. Life has passed
> With me but roughly since I heard thee last.'*

He got but very little way before sudden tears shamed him from the stage.

Some gleams of the same expression which shone down upon his infancy, angelically pure and benign, visit man again with hopes of pure love, of a holy marriage. Or, if not before, in the eyes of the mother of his child they again are seen, and dim fancies pass before his mind, that woman may not have been born for him alone, but have come from heaven, a commissioned soul, a messenger of truth and love; that she can only make for him a home in which he may lawfully repose, in so far as she is

'True to the kindred points of Heaven and home.'*

In gleams, in dim fancies, this thought visits the mind of common men. It is soon obscured by the mists of sensuality, the dust of routine, and he thinks it was only some meteor, or ignis fatuus* that shone. But, as a Rosicrucian lamp,* it burns unwearied, though condemned to the solitude of tombs; and to its permanent life, as to every truth, each age has in some form borne witness. For the truths, which visit the minds of careless men only in fitful gleams, shine with radiant clearness into those of the poet, the priest, and the artist.

Whatever may have been the domestic manners of the ancients, the idea of woman was nobly manifested in their mythologies and poems, where she appears as Sita in the Ramayana,* a form of tender purity, as the Egyptian Isis,*† of divine wisdom never yet surpassed. In Egypt, too, the Sphinx, walking the earth with lion tread, looked out upon its marvels in the calm, inscrutable beauty of a virgin's face, and the Greek could only add wings to the great emblem. In Greece, Ceres and Proserpine,* significantly termed 'the great goddesses,' were seen seated, side by side. They needed not to rise for any worshipper or any change; they were prepared for all things, as those initiated to their mysteries knew. More obvious is the meaning of these three forms, the Diana, Minerva, and Vesta.* Unlike in the expression of their beauty, but alike in this,—that each was self-sufficing. Other forms were only accessories and illustrations, none the complement to one like these. Another might,

---

† Appendix A. [Fuller's note.]

indeed, be the companion, and the Apollo and Diana set off one another's beauty. Of the Vesta, it is to be observed, that not only deep-eyed, deep-discerning Greece, but ruder Rome, who represents the only form of good man, (the always busy warrior,) that could be indifferent to woman, confided the permanence of its glory to a tutelary goddess, and her wisest legislator spoke of meditation as a nymph.

Perhaps in Rome the neglect of woman was a reaction on the manners of Etruria,* where the priestess Queen, warrior Queen, would seem to have been so usual a character.

An instance of the noble Roman marriage, where the stern and calm nobleness of the nation was common to both, we see in the historic page through the little that is told us of Brutus and Portia.* Shakspeare has seized on the relation in its native lineaments, harmonizing the particular with the universal; and, while it is conjugal love, and no other, making it unlike the same relation, as seen in Cymbeline, or Othello, even as one star differeth from another in glory.

> 'By that great vow
> Which did incorporate and make us one,
> Unfold to me, yourself, your half,
> Why you are heavy.   *   *   *
> Dwell I but in the suburbs
> Of your good pleasure? If it be no more,
> Portia is Brutus' harlot, not his wife.'

Mark the sad majesty of his tone in answer. Who would not have lent a life-long credence to that voice of honor?

> 'You are my true and honorable wife,
> As dear to me as are the ruddy drops
> That visit this sad heart.'

It is the same voice that tells the moral of his life in the last words—

> 'Countrymen,
> My heart doth joy, that yet in all my life,
> I found no man but he was true to me.'

It was not wonderful that it should be so.

Shakspeare, however, was not content to let Portia rest her

plea for confidence on the essential nature of the marriage bond;

> 'I grant I am a woman; but withal,
> A woman that lord Brutus took to wife.
> I grant I am a woman; but withal,
> A woman well reputed—Cato's daughter.*
> Think you I am *no stronger than my sex*,
> Being so fathered and so husbanded?'

And afterwards in the very scene where Brutus is suffering under that 'insupportable and touching loss,' the death of his wife, Cassius pleads—

> 'Have you not love enough to bear with me,
> When that rash humor which my mother gave me
> Makes me forgetful?
> *Brutus.* Yes, Cassius; and henceforth,
> When you are over-earnest with your Brutus,
> He'll think your mother chides and leave you so.'

As indeed it was a frequent belief among the ancients, as with our Indians, that the *body* was inherited from the mother, the *soul* from the father. As in that noble passage of Ovid,* already quoted, where Jupiter, as his divine synod are looking down on the funeral pyre of Hercules, thus triumphs—

> Nic nisi *materna* Vulcanum parte potentem.
> Sentiet. Aeternum est, a me quod traxit, et expers
> At que immune necis, nullaque domabile flamma
> Idque ego defunctum terra cœlestibus oris
> Accipiam, cunctisque meum lætabile factum
> Dis fore confido.

> 'The part alone of gross *maternal* frame
> Fire shall devour, while that from me he drew
> Shall live immortal and its force renew;
> That, when he's dead, I'll raise to realms above;
> Let all the powers the righteous act approve.'

It is indeed a god speaking of his union with an earthly woman, but it expressed the common Roman thought as to marriage, the same which permitted a man to lend his wife to a friend, as if she were a chattel.

'She dwelt but in the suburbs of his good pleasure.'

Yet the same city as I have said leaned on the worship of Vesta, the Preserver, and in later times was devoted to that of Isis. In Sparta,* thought, in this respect as in all others, was expressed in the characters of real life, and the women of Sparta were as much Spartans as the men. The citoyen, citoyenne of France was here actualized. Was not the calm equality they enjoyed as honorable as the devotion of chivalry? They intelligently shared the ideal life of their nation.

Like the men they felt

> 'Honor gone, all's gone,
> Better never have been born.'*

They were the true friends of men. The Spartan, surely, would not think that he received only his body from his mother. The sage, had he lived in that community, could not have thought the souls of 'vain and foppish men will be degraded after death, to the forms of women, and, if they do not there make great efforts to retrieve themselves, will become birds.'

(By the way it is very expressive of the hard intellectuality of the merely *mannish* mind, to speak thus of birds, chosen always by the *feminine* poet as the symbols of his fairest thoughts.)

We are told of the Greek nations in general, that woman occupied there an infinitely lower place than man. It is difficult to believe this when we see such range and dignity of thought on the subject in the mythologies, and find the poets producing such ideals as Cassandra, Iphigenia, Antigone, Macaria,* where Sibylline priestesses* told the oracle of the highest god, and he could not be content to reign with a court of fewer than nine muses. Even victory wore a female form.*

But whatever were the facts of daily life, I cannot complain of the age and nation, which represents its thought by such a symbol as I see before me at this moment. It is a zodiac of the busts of gods and goddesses, arranged in pairs. The circle breathes the music of a heavenly order. Male and female heads are distinct in expression, but equal in beauty, strength and calmness. Each male head is that of a brother and a king— each female of a sister and a queen. Could the thought, thus expressed, be lived out, there would be nothing more to be desired. There would be unison in variety, congeniality in difference.

Coming nearer our own time, we find religion and poetry no less true in their revelations. The rude man, just disengaged from the sod, the Adam, accuses woman to his God, and records her disgrace to their posterity. He is not ashamed to write that he could be drawn from heaven by one beneath him, one made, he says, from but a small part of himself. But in the same nation, educated by time, instructed by a succession of prophets, we find woman in as high a position as she has ever occupied. No figure that has ever arisen to greet our eyes has been received with more fervent reverence than that of the Madonna. Heine* calls her the *Dame du Comptoir* of the Catholic church, and this jeer well expresses a serious truth.

And not only this holy and significant image was worshipped by the pilgrim, and the favorite subject of the artist, but it exercised an immediate influence on the destiny of the sex. The empresses who embraced the cross, converted sons and husbands. Whole calendars of female saints, heroic dames of chivalry, binding the emblem of faith on the heart of the best-beloved, and wasting the bloom of youth in separation and loneliness, for the sake of duties they thought it religion to assume, with innumerable forms of poesy, trace their lineage to this one. Nor, however imperfect may be the action, in our day, of the faith thus expressed, and though we can scarcely think it nearer this ideal, than that of India or Greece was near their ideal, is it in vain that the truth has been recognized, that woman is not only a part of man, bone of his bone, and flesh of his flesh, born that men might not be lonely, but that women are in themselves possessors of and possessed by immortal souls. This truth undoubtedly received a greater outward stability from the belief of the church that the earthly parent of the Saviour of souls was a woman.

The assumption of the Virgin, as painted by sublime artists, Petrarch's Hymn to the Madonna,*† cannot have spoken to the world wholly without result, yet, oftentimes those who had ears heard not.

† Appendix B. [Fuller's note.]

See upon the nations the influence of this powerful example. In Spain look only at the ballads. Woman in these is 'very woman;' she is the betrothed, the bride, the spouse of man, there is on her no hue of the philosopher, the heroine, the savante, but she looks great and noble; why? because she is also, through her deep devotion, the betrothed of heaven. Her upturned eyes have drawn down the light that casts a radiance round her. See only such a ballad as that of 'Lady Teresa's Bridal.'*

Where the Infanta, given to the Moorish bridegroom, calls down the vengeance of Heaven on his unhallowed passion, and thinks it not too much to expiate by a life in the cloister, the involuntary stain upon her princely youth.† It was this constant sense of claims above those of earthly love or happiness that made the Spanish lady who shared this spirit, a guerdon to be won by toils and blood and constant purity, rather than a chattel to be bought for pleasure and service.

Germany did not need to *learn* a high view of woman; it was inborn in that race. Woman was to the Teuton warrior his priestess, his friend, his sister, in truth, a wife. And the Christian statues of noble pairs, as they lie above their graves in stone, expressing the meaning of all the by-gone pilgrimage by hands folded in mutual prayer, yield not a nobler sense of the place and powers of woman, than belonged to the altvater* day. The holy love of Christ which summoned them, also, to choose 'the better part, that which could not be taken from them,' refined and hallowed in this nation a native faith, thus showing that it was not the warlike spirit alone that left the Latins so barbarous in this respect.

But the Germans, taking so kindly to this thought, did it the more justice. The idea of woman in their literature is expressed both to a greater height and depth than elsewhere.

I will give as instances the themes of three ballads.

One is upon a knight who had always the name of the Virgin on his lips. This protected him all his life through, in various and beautiful modes, both from sin and other dangers, and, when he died, a plant sprang from his grave, which so gently

---

† Appendix C. [Fuller's note.]

whispered the Ave Maria that none could pass it by with an unpurified heart.

Another is one of the legends of the famous Drachenfels.* A maiden, one of the earliest converts to Christianity, was carried by the enraged populace to this dread haunt of 'the dragon's fabled brood,' to be their prey. She was left alone, but unafraid, for she knew in whom she trusted. So, when the dragons came rushing towards her, she showed them a crucifix and they crouched reverently at her feet. Next day the people come, and seeing these wonders, are all turned to the faith which exalts the lowly.

The third I have in mind is another of the Rhine legends. A youth is sitting with the maid he loves on the shore of an isle, her fairy kingdom, then perfumed by the blossoming grape vines, which draped its bowers. They are happy; all blossoms with them, and life promises its richest wine. A boat approaches on the tide; it pauses at their feet. It brings, perhaps, some joyous message, fresh dew for their flowers, fresh light on the wave. No! it is the usual check on such great happiness. The father of the Count departs for the crusade; will his son join him, or remain to rule their domain, and wed her he loves? Neither of the affianced pair hesitate a moment. 'I must go with my father.' 'Thou must go with thy father.' It was one thought, one word. 'I will be here again,' he said, 'when these blossoms have turned to purple grapes.' 'I hope so,' she sighed, while the prophetic sense said 'no.'

And there she waited, and the grapes ripened, and were gathered into the vintage, and he came not. Year after year passed thus, and no tidings; yet still she waited.

He, meanwhile, was in a Moslem prison. Long he languished there without hope, till, at last, his patron saint appeared in vision and announced his release, but only on condition of his joining the monastic order for the service of the saint.

And so his release was effected, and a safe voyage home given. And once more he sets sail upon the Rhine. The maiden, still watching beneath the vines, sees at last the object of all this patient love approach. Approach, but not to touch the strand to which she, with outstretched arms, has rushed. He dares not trust himself to land, but in low, heart-broken tones, tells her of heaven's will; and that he, in obedience to his vow, is now on his way to a convent on the river bank, there to pass the rest of his earthly life in the service of the shrine. And then he turns his boat, and floats away from her and hope of any happiness in this world, but urged, as he believes, by the breath of heaven.

The maiden stands appalled, but she dares not murmur, and cannot hesitate long. She also bids them prepare her boat. She follows her lost love to the convent gate, requests an interview with the abbot, and devotes her Elysian isle, where vines had ripened their ruby fruit in vain for her, to the service of the monastery where her love was to serve. Then, passing over to the nunnery opposite, she takes the veil, and meets her betrothed at the altar; and for a life long union, if not the one they had hoped in earlier years.

Is not this sorrowful story of a lofty beauty? Does it not show a sufficiently high view of woman, of marriage? This is commonly the chivalric, still more the German view.

Yet, wherever there was a balance in the mind of man of sentiment, with intellect, such a result was sure. The Greek Xenophon* has not only painted as a sweet picture of the domestic woman, in his Economics, but in the Cyropedia has given, in the picture of Panthea, a view of woman which no German picture can surpass, whether lonely and quiet with veiled lids, the temple of a vestal loveliness, or with eyes flashing, and hair flowing to the free wind, cheering on the hero to fight for his God, his country, or whatever name his duty might bear at the time. This picture I shall copy by and by. Yet Xenophon grew up in the same age with him who makes Iphigenia say to Achilles—*

'Better a thousand women should perish than one man cease to see the light.'

This was the vulgar Greek sentiment. Xenophon, aiming at the ideal man, caught glimpses of the ideal woman also. From the figure of a Cyrus, the Pantheas stand not afar. They do not in thought; they would not in life.

I could swell the catalogue of instances far beyond the reader's patience. But enough have been brought forward to show that, though there has been great disparity betwixt the nations as between individuals in their culture on this point, yet the idea of woman has always cast some rays and often been forcibly represented.

Far less has woman to complain that she has not had her share of power. This, in all ranks of society, except the lowest, has been hers to the extent that vanity would crave, far beyond what wisdom would accept. In the very lowest, where man, pressed by poverty, sees in woman only the partner of toils and cares, and cannot hope, scarcely has an idea of, a comfortable home, he often maltreats her, and is less influenced by her. In all ranks, those who are gentle and uncomplaining, too candid to intrigue, too delicate to encroach, suffer much. They suffer long, and are kind; verily, they have their reward. But wherever man is sufficiently raised above extreme poverty or brutal stupidity, to care for the comforts of the fireside, or the bloom and ornament of life, woman has always power enough, if she choose to exert it, and is usually disposed to do so, in proportion to her ignorance and childish vanity. Unacquainted with the importance of life and its purposes, trained to a selfish coquetry and love of petty power, she does not look beyond the pleasure of making herself felt at the moment, and governments are shaken and commerce broken up to gratify the pique of a female favorite. The English shopkeeper's wife does not vote, but it is for her interest that the politician canvasses by the coarsest flattery. France suffers no woman on her throne, but her proud nobles kiss the dust at the feet of Pompadour and Du Barry;* for such flare in the lighted foreground where a Roland would modestly aid in the closet. Spain, (that same Spain which sang of Ximena* and the Lady Teresa,) shuts up her women in the care of duennas, and allows them no book but the Breviary, but the ruin follows only the more surely from the worthless favorite of a worthless queen.* Relying on mean precautions, men indeed cry peace, peace, where there is no peace.

It is not the transient breath of poetic incense that women want; each can receive that from a lover. It is not life-long sway; it needs but to become a coquette, a shrew, or a good cook, to be sure of that. It is not money, nor notoriety, nor the badges of authority that men have appropriated to themselves. If demands, made in their behalf, lay stress on any of these particulars, those who make them have not searched deeply into the need. It is for that which at once includes these and precludes them; which would not be forbidden power, lest there be temptation to steal and misuse it; which would not have the mind perverted by flattery from a worthiness of esteem. It is for that which is the birthright of every being capable to receive it,—the freedom, the religious, the intelligent freedom of the universe, to use its means; to learn its secret as far as nature has enabled them, with God alone for their guide and their judge.

Ye cannot believe it, men; but the only reason why women ever assume what is more appropriate to you, is because you prevent them from finding out what is fit for themselves. Were they free, were they wise fully to develop the strength and beauty of woman; they would never wish to be men, or manlike. The well-instructed moon flies not from her orbit to seize on the glories of her partner. No; for she knows that one law rules, one heaven contains, one universe replies to them alike. It is with women as with the slave.

> 'Vor dem Sklaven, wenn er die Kette bricht,
> Vor dem freien Menschen erzittert nicht.'*

Tremble not before the free man, but before the slave who has chains to break.

In slavery, acknowledged slavery, women are on a par with men. Each is a work-tool, an article of property, no more! In perfect freedom, such as is painted in Olympus, in Swedenborg's* angelic state, in the heaven where there is no marrying nor giving in marriage,* each is a purifed intelligence, an enfranchised soul,—no less!

> Jene himmlische Gestalten
> Sie fragen nicht nach Mann und Weib,
> Und keine Kleider, keine Falten
> Umgeben den verklarten Leib.*

The child who sang this was a prophetic form, expressive of the longing for a state of perfect freedom, pure love. She could not remain here, but was transplanted to another air. And it may be that the air of this earth will never be so tempered that such can bear it long. But, while they stay, they must bear testimony to the truth they are constituted to demand.

That an era approaches which shall approximate nearer to such a temper than any has yet done, there are many tokens, indeed so many, that only a few of the most prominent can here be enumerated.

The reigns of Elizabeth of England and Isabella of Castile foreboded this era. They expressed the beginning of the new state, while they forwarded its progress. These were strong characters and in harmony with the wants of their time. One showed that this strength did not unfit a woman for the duties of a wife and a mother, the other that it could enable her to live and die alone, a wide energetic life, a courageous death. Elizabeth is certainly no pleasing example. In rising above the weakness, she did not lay aside the weaknesses ascribed to her sex; but her strength must be respected now, as it was in her own time.

Elizabeth and Mary Stuart seem types, moulded by the spirit of the time, and placed upon an elevated platform to show to the coming ages, woman such as the conduct and wishes of man in general is likely to make her, lovely even to allurement, quick in apprehension and weak in judgment, with grace and dignity of sentiment, but no principle; credulous and indiscreet, yet artful; capable of sudden greatness or of crime, but not of a steadfast wisdom, or self-restraining virtue; and woman half-emancipated and jealous of her freedom, such as she has figured before and since in many a combative attitude, mannish, not equally manly, strong and prudent more than great or wise; able to control vanity, and the wish to rule through coquetry and passion, but not to resign these dear deceits, from the very foundation, as unworthy a being capable of truth and nobleness. Elizabeth, taught by adversity, put on her virtues as armor, more than produced them in a natural order from her soul. The time and her position called on her to act the wise sovereign, and she was proud that she could do so, but her tastes and inclinations would have led her to act the weak woman. She was without magnanimity* of any kind.

We may accept as an omen for ourselves, that it was Isabella who furnished Columbus with the means of coming hither. This land must pay back its debt to woman, without whose aid it would not have been brought into alliance with the civilized world.

A graceful and meaning figure is that introduced to us by Mr. Prescott, in the Conquest of Mexico, in the Indian girl Marina, who accompanied Cortes, and was his interpreter in all the various difficulties of his career. She stood at his side, on the walls of the besieged palace, to plead with her enraged country-men. By her name he was known in New Spain, and, after the conquest, her gentle intercession was often of avail to the con-quered. The poem of the Future may be read in some features of the story of 'Malinche.'*

The influence of Elizabeth on literature was real, though, by sympathy with its finer productions, she was no more entitled to give name to an era than Queen Anne.* It was simply that the fact of having a female sovereign on the throne affected the course of a writer's thoughts. In this sense, the presence of a woman on the throne always makes its mark. Life is lived before the eyes of men, by which their imaginations are stimulated as to the possibilities of woman. 'We will die for our King, Maria Theresa,'* cry the wild warriors, clashing their swords, and the sounds vibrate through the poems of that generation. The range of female character in Spenser alone might content us for one period. Britomart and Belphœbe have as much room on the canvass as Florimel; and where this is the case, the haughtiest amazon will not murmur that Una should be felt to be the fairest type.*

Unlike as was the English Queen to a fairy queen, we may yet conceive that it was the image of *a* queen before the poet's mind, that called up this splendid court of women. Shakspeare's range is also great; but he has left out the heroic characters, such as the Macaria of Greece, the Britomart of Spenser. Ford and Massinger* have, in this respect, soared to a higher flight of feeling than he. It was the holy and heroic woman they most loved, and if they could not paint an Imogen, a Desdemona, a Rosalind, yet, in those of a stronger mould, they showed a higher ideal, though with so much less poetic power to em-body it, than we see in Portia or Isabella. The simple truth of Cordelia, indeed, is of this sort. The beauty of Cordelia is neither male nor female; it is the beauty of virtue.*

The ideal of love and marriage rose high in the mind of all the Christian nations who were capable of grave and deep feeling. We may take as examples of its English aspect, the lines,

> 'I could not love thee, dear, so much,
> Loved I not honor more.'*

Or the address of the Commonwealth's man* to his wife, as she looked out from the Tower window to see him for the last time, on his way to the scaffold. He stood up in the cart, waved his hat, and cried, 'To Heaven, my love, to Heaven, and leave you in the storm?'

Such was the love of faith and honor, a love which stopped, like Colonel Hutchinson's,* 'on this side idolatry,' because it was religious. 'The meeting of two such souls' Donne* describes as giving birth to an 'abler soul.'

Lord Herbert* wrote to his love,

> 'Were not our souls immortal made,
> Our equal loves can make them such.'

In the 'Broken Heart' of Ford, Penthea, a character which engages my admiration even more deeply than the famous one of Calanthe,* is made to present to the mind the most beautiful picture of what these relations should be in their purity. Her life cannot sustain the violation of what she so clearly felt.

Shakspeare, too, saw that, in true love as in fire, the utmost ardor is coincident with the utmost purity. It is a true lover that exclaims in the agony of Othello,

> 'If thou art false, O then Heaven mocks itself.'*

The son, framed like Hamlet, to appreciate truth in all the beauty of relations, sinks into deep melancholy, when he finds his natural expectations disappointed. He has no mother. She to whom he gave the name, disgraces from his heart's shrine all the sex.

> 'Frailty, thy name is woman.'

It is because a Hamlet could find cause to say so, that I have put the line, whose stigma has never been removed, at the head of my work. But, as a lover, surely a Hamlet would not have so far mistook, as to have finished with such a conviction. He would have felt the faith of Othello, and that faith could not, in his more dispassionate mind, have been disturbed by calumny.

In Spain, this thought is arrayed in a sublimity, which belongs to the sombre and passionate genius of the nation. Calderon's Justina* resists all the temptation of the Demon, and raises her lover, with her, above the sweet lures of mere temporal happiness. Their marriage is vowed at the stake; their souls are liberated together by the martyr flame into 'a purer state of sensation and existence.'

In Italy, the great poets wove into their lives an ideal love which answered to the highest wants. It included those of the intellect and the affections, for it was a love of spirit for spirit. It was not ascetic, or superhuman, but, interpreting all things, gave their proper beauty to details of the common life, the common day; the poet spoke of his love, not as a flower to place in his bosom, or hold carelessly in his hand, but as a light towards which he must find wings to fly, or 'a stair to heaven.' He delighted to speak of her, not only as the bride of his heart, but the mother of his soul; for he saw that, in cases where the right direction had been taken, the greater delicacy of her frame, and stillness of her life, left her more open to spiritual influx than man is. So he did not look upon her as betwixt him and earth, to serve his temporal needs, but, rather, betwixt him and heaven, to purify his affections and lead him to wisdom through love. He sought, in her, not so much the Eve, as the Madonna.

In these minds the thought, which gleams through all the legends of chivalry, shines in broad intellectual effulgence, not to be misinterpreted, and their thought is reverenced by the world, though it lies so far from the practice of the world as yet, so far, that it seems as though a gulf of death yawned between.

Even with such men, the practice was, often, widely different from the mental faith. I say mental, for if the heart were thoroughly alive with it, the practice could not be dissonant. Lord Herbert's was a marriage of convention, made for him at fifteen; he was not discontented with it, but looked only to the advantages it brought of perpetuating his family on the basis of a great fortune. He paid, in act, what he considered a dutiful attention to the bond; his thoughts travelled elsewhere; and while forming a high ideal of the companionship of minds in marriage, he seems never to have doubted that its realization must be postponed to some other state of being. Dante, almost immediately after the death of Beatrice,* married a lady chosen for him by his friends, and Boccaccio,* in describing the miseries that attended, in this case,

> 'The form of an union where union is none,'

speaks as if these were inevitable to the connection, and the scholar and poet, especially, could expect nothing but misery and obstruction in a domestic partnership with woman.

Centuries have passed since, but civilized Europe is still in a transition state about marriage; not only in practice, but in thought. It is idle to speak with contempt of the nations where polygamy is an institution, or seraglios a custom, when practices far more debasing haunt, well nigh fill, every city and every town. And so far as union of one with one is believed to be the only pure form of marriage, a great majority of societies and individuals are still doubtful whether the earthly bond must be a meeting of souls, or only supposes a contract of convenience and utility. Were woman established in the rights of an immortal being, this could not be. She would not, in some countries, be given away by her father, with scarcely more respect for her feelings than is shown by the Indian chief, who sells his daughter for a horse, and beats her if she runs away from her new home. Nor, in societies where her choice is left free, would she be perverted, by the current of opinion that seizes her, into the belief that she must marry, if it be only to find a protector, and a home of her own.

Neither would man, if he thought the connection of permanent importance, form it so lightly. He would not deem it a trifle, that he was to enter into the closest relations with another soul, which, if not eternal in themselves, must eternally affect his growth.

Neither, did he believe woman capable of friendship,† would he, by rash haste, lose the chance of finding a friend in the person who might, probably, live half a century by his side. Did

---

† See Appendix D, Spinoza's view. [Fuller's note.]

love, to his mind, stretch forth into infinity, he would not miss his chance of its revelations, that he might, the sooner, rest from his weariness by a bright fireside, and secure a sweet and graceful attendant 'devoted to him alone.' Were he a step higher, he would not carelessly enter into a relation where he might not be able to do the duty of a friend, as well as a protector from external ill, to the other party, and have a being in his power pining for sympathy, intelligence and aid, that he could not give.

What deep communion, what real intercourse is implied by the sharing the joys and cares of parentage, when any degree of equality is admitted between the parties! It is true that, in a majority of instances, the man looks upon his wife as an adopted child, and places her to the other children in the relation of nurse or governess, rather than of parent. Her influence with them is sure, but she misses the education which should enlighten that influence, by being thus treated. It is the order of nature that children should complete the education, moral and mental, of parents, by making them think what is needed for the best culture of human beings, and conquer all faults and impulses that interfere with their giving this to these dear objects, who represent the world to them. Father and mother should assist one another to learn what is required for this sublime priesthood of nature. But, for this, a religious recognition of equality is required.

Where this thought of equality begins to diffuse itself, it is shown in four ways.

The household partnership. In our country, the woman looks for a 'smart but kind' husband; the man for a 'capable, sweet-tempered' wife.

The man furnishes the house; the woman regulates it. Their relation is one of mutual esteem, mutual dependence. Their talk is of business, their affection shows itself by practical kindness. They know that life goes more smoothly and cheerfully to each for the other's aid; they are grateful and content. The wife praises her husband as a 'good provider;' the husband, in return, compliments her as a 'capital house-keeper.' This relation is good, as far as it goes.

Next comes a closer tie, which takes the two forms, either of mutual idolatry, or of intellectual companionship. The first, we suppose, is to no one a pleasing subject of contemplation. The parties weaken and narrow one another; they lock the gate against all the glories of the universe, that they may live in a cell together. To themselves they seem the only wise, to all others steeped in infatuation; the gods smile as they look forward to the crisis of cure; to men, the woman seems an unlovely syren; to women, the man an effeminate boy.

The other form, of intellectual companionship, has become more and more frequent. Men engaged in public life, literary men, and artists, have often found in their wives companions and confidants in thought no less than in feeling. And as the intellectual development of woman has spread wider and risen higher, they have, not unfrequently, shared the same employment. As in the case of Roland and his wife,* who were friends in the household and in the nation's councils, read, regulated home affairs, or prepared public documents together, indifferently.

It is very pleasant, in letters begun by Roland, and finished by his wife, to see the harmony of mind, and the difference of nature; one thought, but various ways of treating it.

This is one of the best instances of a marriage of friendship. It was only friendship, whose basis was esteem; probably neither party knew love, except by name.

Roland was a good man, worthy to esteem, and be esteemed; his wife as deserving of admiration, as able to do without it. Madame Roland is the fairest specimen we have yet of her class, as clear to discern her aim, as valiant to pursue it, as Spenser's Britomart; austerely set apart from all that did not belong to her, whether as woman or as mind. She is an antetype of a class to which the coming time will afford a field, the Spartan matron, brought by the culture of the age of Books to intellectual consciousness and expansion.

Self-sufficingness, strength, and clear-sightedness were, in her, combined with a power of deep and calm affection. She, too, would have given a son or husband the device for his shield, 'Return with it or upon it;' and this, not because she loved little, but much. The page of her life is one of unsullied dignity.

Her appeal to posterity is one against the injustice of those who committed such crimes in the name of Liberty. She makes it in behalf of herself and her husband. I would put beside it, on the shelf, a little volume, containing a similar appeal from the verdict of contemporaries to that of mankind, made by Godwin in behalf of his wife, the celebrated, the, by most men, detested, Mary Wolstonecraft.* In his view, it was an appeal from the injustice of those who did such wrong in the name of virtue.

Were this little book interesting for no other cause, it would be so for the generous affection evinced under the peculiar circumstances. This man had courage to love and honor this woman in the face of the world's sentence, and of all that was repulsive in her own past history. He believed he saw of what soul she was, and that the impulses she had struggled to act out were noble, though the opinions to which they had led might not be thoroughly weighed. He loved her, and he defended her for the meaning and tendency of her inner life. It was a good fact.

Mary Wolstonecraft, like Madame Dudevant, (commonly known as George Sand,)* in our day, was a woman whose existence better proved the need of some new interpretation of woman's rights, than any thing she wrote. Such beings as these, rich in genius, of most tender sympathies, capable of high virtue and a chastened harmony, ought not to find themselves, by birth, in a place so narrow, that, in breaking bonds, they become outlaws. Were there as much room in the world for such, as in Spenser's poem for Britomart, they would not run their heads so wildly against the walls, but prize their shelter rather. They find their way, at last, to light and air, but the world will not take off the brand it has set upon them. The champion of the Rights of Woman found, in Godwin, one who would plead that cause like a brother. He who delineated with such purity of traits the form of woman in the Marguerite, of whom the weak St Leon* could never learn to be worthy, a pearl indeed whose price was above rubies, was not false in life to the faith by which he had hallowed his romance. He acted as he wrote, like a brother. This form of appeal rarely fails to touch the basest man. 'Are you acting towards other women in the way you would have men act towards your sister?' George Sand smokes,

wears male attire, wishes to be addressed as 'Mon frère;'—
perhaps, if she found those who were as brothers, indeed, she
would not care whether she were brother or sister.[†]

[†] Since writing the above, I have read with great satisfaction, the following
sonnets addressed to George Sand by a woman who has precisely the qualities
that the author of Simon and Indiana* lacks. It is such a woman, so unblemished
in character, so high in aim, and pure in soul, that should address this other, as
noble in nature, but clouded by error, and struggling with circumstances. It is
such women that will do justice. They are not afraid to look for virtue and reply
to aspiration, among those who have *not* 'dwelt in decencies forever.' It is a source
of pride and happiness to read this address from the heart of Elizabeth Barrett.*

TO GEORGE SAND.

A DESIRE.

Thou large-brained woman and large-hearted man,
   Self-called George Sand! whose soul, amid the lions
   Of thy tumultuous senses moans defiance,
And answers roar for roar, as spirits can:
I would some mild miraculous thunder ran
   Above the applauded circus, in appliance
   Of thine own nobler nature's strength and science,
   Drawing two pinions, white as wings of swan,
From the strong shoulders, to amaze the place
   With holier light! that thou to woman's claim,
And man's might join, beside, the angel's grace
   Of a pure genius sanctified from blame;
Till child and maiden pressed to thine embrace,
   To kiss upon thy lips a stainless fame.

TO THE SAME.

A RECOGNITION.

True genius, but true woman! dost deny
   Thy woman's nature with a manly scorn,
And break away the gauds and armlets worn
   By weaker women in captivity?
Ah, vain denial! that revolted cry
   Is sobbed in by a woman's voice forlorn:—
Thy woman's hair, my sister, all unshorn,
   Floats back dishevelled strength in agony,
Disproving thy man's name, and while before
   The world thou burnest a poet-fire,
We see thy woman-heart beat evermore
   Through the large flame. Beat purer, heart, and higher,
Till God unsex thee on the spirit-shore;
   To which alone unsexing, purely aspire.

We rejoice to see that she, who expresses such a painful contempt for men in most of her works, as shows she must have known great wrong from them, depicting in 'La Roche Mauprat,'* a man raised by the workings of love, from the depths of savage sensualism, to a moral and intellectual life. It was love for a pure object, for a steadfast woman, one of those who, the Italian said, could make the stair to heaven.

This author, beginning like the many in assault upon bad institutions, and external ills, yet deepening the experience through comparative freedom, sees at last, that the only efficient remedy must come from individual character. These bad institutions, indeed, it may always be replied, prevent individuals from forming good character, therefore we must remove them. Agreed, yet keep steadily the higher aim in view. Could you clear away all the bad forms of society, it is vain, unless the individual begin to be ready for better. There must be a parallel movement in these two branches of life. And all the rules left by Moses availed less to further the best life than the living example of one Messiah.

Still, still the mind of the age struggles confusedly with these problems, better discerning as yet the ill it can no longer bear, than the good by which it may supersede it. But women, like Sand, will speak now and cannot be silenced; their characters and their eloquence alike foretell an era when such as they shall easier learn to lead true lives. But though such forebode, not such shall be the parents of it.† Those who would reform the world must show that they do not speak in the heat of wild impulse, their lives must be unstained by passionate error; they must be severe lawgivers to themselves. They must be religious students of the divine purpose with regard to man, if they would not confound the fancies of a day with the requisitions of eternal good. Their liberty must be the liberty of law and knowledge. But, as to the transgressions against custom which

This last sonnet seems to have been written after seeing the picture of Sand, which represents her in a man's dress, but with long loose hair, and an eye whose mournful fire is impressive even in the caricatures. [Fuller's note.]

† Appendix E. [Fuller's note.]

have caused such outcry against those of noble intention, it may be observed, that the resolve of Eloisa to be only the mistress of Abelard, was that of one who saw in practice around her, the contract of marriage made the seal of degradation. Shelley* feared not to be fettered, unless so to be was to be false. Wherever abuses are seen, the timid will suffer; the bold will protest. But society has a right to outlaw them till she has revised her law; and this she must be taught to do, by one who speaks with authority, not in anger or haste.

If Godwin's choice of the calumniated authoress of the 'Rights of Woman,'* for his honored wife, be a sign of a new era, no less so is an article to which I have alluded some pages back, published five or six years ago in one of the English Reviews, where the writer, in doing full justice to Eloisa, shows his bitter regret that she lives not now to love him, who might have known better how to prize her love than did the egotistical Abelard.

These marriages, these characters, with all their imperfections, express an onward tendency. They speak of aspiration of soul, of energy of mind, seeking clearness and freedom. Of a like promise are the tracts lately published by Goodwyn Barmby,* (the European Pariah, as he calls himself,) and his wife Catharine. Whatever we may think of their measures, we see in them wedlock; the two minds are wed by the only contract that can permanently avail, of a common faith and a common purpose.

We might mention instances, nearer home, of minds, partners in work and in life, sharing together, on equal terms, public and private interests, and which wear not, on any side, the aspect of offence shown by those last-named: persons who steer straight onward, yet, in our comparatively free life, have not been obliged to run their heads against any wall. But the principles which guide them might, under petrified and oppressive institutions, have made them warlike, paradoxical, and in some sense, Pariahs. The phenomena are different, the law is the same, in all these cases. Men and women have been obliged to build up their house anew from the very foundation. If they found stone ready in the quarry, they took it peaceably, otherwise they alarmed the country by pulling down old towers to get materials.

These are all instances of marriage as intellectual companionship. The parties meet mind to mind, and a mutual trust is produced, which can buckler them against a million. They work together for a common purpose, and, in all these instances, with the same implement, the pen. The pen and the writing-desk furnish forth as naturally the retirement of woman as of man.

A pleasing expression, in this kind, is afforded by the union in the names of the Howitts. William and Mary Howitt* we heard named together for years, supposing them to be brother and sister; the equality of labors and reputation, even so, was auspicious; more so, now we find them man and wife. In his late work on Germany, Howitt mentions his wife, with pride, as one among the constellation of distinguished English-women, and in a graceful simple manner.

Our pleasure, indeed, in this picture, is marred by the vulgar apparition which has of late displaced the image, which we had from her writings cherished of a pure and gentle Quaker poetess. The surprise was painful as that of the little sentimentalist in the tale of 'L'Amie Inconnue' when she found her correspondent, the poetess, the 'adored Araminta,' scolding her servants in Welsh, and eating toasted cheese and garlic. Still, we cannot forget what we have thought of the partnership in literature and affection between the Howitts, the congenial pursuits and productions, the pedestrian tours where the married pair showed that marriage, on a wide enough basis, does not destroy the 'inexhaustible' entertainment which lovers found in one another's company.

In naming these instances, I do not mean to imply that community of employment is essential to union of husband and wife, more than to the union of friends. Harmony exists in difference, no less than in likeness, if only the same key-note govern both parts. Woman the poem, man the poet! Woman the heart, man the head! Such divisions are only important when they are never to be transcended. If nature is never bound down, nor the voice of inspiration stifled, that is enough. We are pleased that women should write and speak, if they feel the need of it, from having something to tell; but silence for ages would be no misfortune, if that silence be from divine command, and not from man's tradition.

While Goetz Von Berlichingen* rides to battle, his wife is busy in the kitchen; but difference of occupation does not prevent that community of inward life, that perfect esteem, with which he says—

> 'Whom God loves, to him gives he such a wife.'

Manzoni thus dedicates his 'Adelchi.'*

'To his beloved and venerated wife, Enrichetta Luigia Blondel, who, with conjugal affection and maternal wisdom, has preserved a virgin mind, the author dedicates this 'Adelchi,' grieving that he could not, by a more splendid and more durable monument, honor the dear name, and the memory of so many virtues.'

The relation could not be fairer, or more equal, if she, too, had written poems. Yet the position of the parties might have been the reverse as well; the woman might have sung the deeds, given voice to the life of the man, and beauty would have been the result, as we see, in pictures of Arcadia, the nymph singing to the shepherds, or the shepherd, with his pipe, alluring the nymphs; either makes a good picture. The sounding lyre requires, not muscular strength, but energy of soul to animate the hand which would control it. Nature seems to delight in varying the arrangements, as if to show that she will be fettered by no rule, and we must admit the same varieties that she admits.

The fourth and highest grade of marriage union, is the religious, which may be expressed as pilgrimage towards a common shrine. This includes the others; home sympathies and household wisdom, for these pilgrims must know how to assist each other along the dusty way; intellectual communion, for how sad it would be on such a journey to have a companion to whom you could not communicate thoughts and aspirations as they sprang to life; who would have no feeling for the prospects that open, more and more glorious as we advance; who would never see the flowers that may be gathered by the most industrious traveller. It must include all these. Such a fellow-pilgrim Count Zinzendorf* seems to have found in his Countess, of whom he thus writes:

'Twenty-five years' experience has shown me that just the help-mate whom I have, is the only one that could suit my vocation. Who else could have so carried through my family affairs? Who lived so spotlessly before the world? Who so wisely aided me in my rejection of a dry morality? Who so clearly set aside the Pharisaism which, as years passed, threatened to creep in among us? Who so deeply discerned as to the spirits of delusion, which sought to bewilder us? Who would have governed my whole economy so wisely, richly, and hospitably, when circumstances commanded? Who have taken indifferently the part of servant or mistress, without, on the one side, affecting an especial spirituality; on the other, being sullied by any wordly pride? Who, in a community where all ranks are eager to be on a level, would, from wise and real causes, have known how to maintain inward and outward distinctions? Who, without a murmur, have seen her husband encounter such dangers by land and sea? Who undertaken with him, and *sustained* such astonishing pilgrimages? Who, amid such difficulties, always held up her head and supported me? Who found such vast sums of money, and acquitted them on her own credit? And, finally, who, of all human beings, could so well understand and interpret to others my inner and outer being as this one, of such nobleness in her way of thinking, such great intellectual capacity, and free from the theological perplexities that enveloped me!'

Let any one peruse, with all their power, the lineaments of this portrait, and see if the husband had not reason, with this air of solemn rapture and conviction, to challenge comparison? We are reminded of the majestic cadence of the line whose feet step in the just proportions of Humanity,

'Daughter of God and Man, accomplished Eve!'*

An observer* adds this testimony:

'We may, in many marriages, regard it as the best arrangement, if the man has so much advantage over his wife, that she can, without much thought of her own, be, by him, led and directed as by a father. But it was not so with the Count and his consort. She was not made to be a copy; she was an original; and, while she loved and honored him, she thought for herself, on all subjects, with so much intelligence, that he could and did look on her as sister and friend also.'

Compare with this refined specimen of a religiously civilized life, the following imperfect sketch of a North American Indian, and we shall see that the same causes will always produce the same results. The Flying Pigeon (Ratchewaine) was the wife of a barbarous chief, who had six others, but she was his only true wife, because the only one of a strong and pure character, and, having this, inspired a veneration, as like as the mind of the man permitted, to that inspired by the Countess Zinzendorf. She died when her son was only four years old, yet left on his mind a feeling of reverent love worthy the thought of Christian chivalry. Grown to manhood, he shed tears on seeing her portrait.

THE FLYING PIGEON

'Ratchewaine was chaste, mild, gentle in her disposition, kind, generous, and devoted to her husband. A harsh word was never known to proceed from her mouth; nor was she ever known to be in a passion. Mahaskah used to say of her, after her death, that her hand was shut, when those, who did not want, came into her presence; but when the really poor came in, it was like a strainer full of holes, letting all she held in it pass through. In the exercise of generous feeling she was uniform. It was not indebted for its exercise to whim, or caprice, or partiality. No matter of what nation the applicant for her bounty was, or whether at war or peace with her nation; if he were hungry, she fed him; if naked, she clothed him; and if houseless, she gave him shelter. The continued exercise of this generous feeling kept her poor. And she has been known to give away her last blanket—all the honey that was in the lodge, the last bladder of bear's oil, and the last piece of dried meat.

'She was scrupulously exact in the observance of all the religious rites which her faith imposed upon her. Her conscience is represented to have been extremely tender. She often feared that her acts were displeasing to the Great Spirit, when she would blacken her face, and retire to some lone place, and fast and pray.'

To these traits should be added, but for want of room, anecdotes which show the quick decision and vivacity of her mind. Her face was in harmony with this combination. Her brow is as ideal and the eyes and lids as devout and modest as the Italian pictures of the Madonna, while the lower part of the face has the simplicity and childish strength of the Indian race. Her picture presents the finest specimen of Indian beauty we have ever seen.

Such a woman is the sister and friend of all beings, as the worthy man is their brother and helper.

With like pleasure we survey the pairs wedded on the eve of missionary effort. They, indeed, are fellow pilgrims on a well-made road, and whether or no they accomplish all they hope for the sad Hindoo, or the nearer savage, we feel that, in the burning waste, their love is like to be a healing dew, in the forlorn jungle, a tent of solace to one another. They meet, as children of one Father, to read together one book of instruction.

We must insert in this connection the most beautiful picture presented by ancient literature of wedded love under this noble form.

It is from the romance in which Xenophon,* the chivalrous Greek, presents his ideal of what human nature should be.

The generals of Cyrus had taken captive a princess, a woman of unequalled beauty, and hastened to present her to the prince as the part of the spoil he would think most worthy of his acceptance.

Cyrus visits the lady, and is filled with immediate admiration by the modesty and majesty with which she receives him. He finds her name is Panthea, and that she is the wife of Abradatus, a young king whom she entirely loves. He protects her as a sister, in his camp, till he can restore her to her husband.

After the first transports of joy at this re-union, the heart of Panthea is bent on showing her love and gratitude to her magnanimous and delicate protector. And as she has nothing so precious to give as the aid of Abradatus, that is what she most wishes to offer. Her husband is of one soul with her in this, as in all things.

The description of her grief and self-destruction, after the death which ensued upon this devotion, I have seen quoted, but never that of their parting when she sends him forth to battle. I shall copy both. If they have been read by any of my readers, they may be so again with profit in this connexion, for never were the heroism of a true woman, and the purity of love, in a true marriage, painted in colors more delicate or more lively.

'The chariot of Abradatus, that had four perches and eight horses, was completely adorned for him; and when he was going to put on his linen corslet, which was a sort of armor used by those of his country, Panthea brought him a golden helmet, and arm-pieces, broad bracelets for his wrists, a purple habit that reached down to his feet, and hung in folds at the bottom, and a crest dyed of a violet color. These things she had made unknown to her husband, and by taking the measure of his armor. He wondered when he saw them, and inquired thus of Panthea: "And have you made me these arms, woman, by destroying your own ornaments?" "No, by Jove," said Panthea, "not what is the most valuable of them; for it is you, if you appear to others to be what I think you, that will be my greatest ornament." And, saying that, she put on him the armor, and, though she endeavored to conceal it, the tears poured down her cheeks. When Abradatus, who was before a man of fine appearance, was set out in those arms, he appeared the most beautiful and noble of all, especially, being likewise so by nature. Then, taking the reins from the driver, he was just preparing to mount the chariot, when Panthea, after she had desired all that were there to retire, thus said:

"O Abradatus! if ever there was a woman who had a greater regard to her husband than to her own soul, I believe you know that I am such an one; what need I therefore speak of things in particular? for I reckon that my actions have convinced you more than any words I can now use. And yet, though I stand thus affected towards you, as you know I do, I swear by this friendship of mine and yours, that I certainly would rather choose to be put under ground jointly with you, approving yourself a brave man, than to live with you in disgrace and shame; so much do I think you and myself worthy of the noblest things. Then I think that we both lie under great obligations to Cyrus, that, when I was a captive, and chosen out for himself, he thought fit to treat me neither as a slave, nor, indeed, as a woman of mean account, but he took and kept me for you, as if I were his brother's wife. Besides, when Araspes, who was my guard, went away from him, I promised him, that, if he would allow me to send for you, you would come to him, and approve yourself a much better and more faithful friend than Araspes."

'Thus she spoke; and Abradatus being struck with admiration at her discourse, laying his hand gently on her head, and lifting up his eyes to heaven, made this prayer: "Do thou, O greatest Jove! grant me to appear a husband worthy of Panthea, and a friend worthy of Cyrus, who has done us so much honor!"

'Having said this, he mounted the chariot by the door of the driver's seat; and, after he had got up, when the driver shut the door, Panthea, who had now no other way to salute him, kissed the seat of the chariot. The chariot then moved, and she, unknown to him, followed, till Abradatus turning about, and seeing her, said: "Take courage, Panthea! Fare you happily and well, and now go your ways." On this her women and servants carried her to her conveyance, and, laying her down, concealed her by throwing the covering of a tent over her. The people, though Abradatus and his chariot made a noble spectacle, were not able to look at him till Panthea was gone.'

After the battle—

'Cyrus calling to some of his servants, "Tell me," said he, "has any one seen Abradatus? for I admire that he now does not appear." One replied, "My sovereign, it is because he is not living, but died in the battle as he broke in with his chariot on the Egyptians. All the rest, except his particular companions, they say, turned off when they saw the Egyptians' compact body. His wife is now said to have taken up his dead body, to have placed it in the carriage that she herself was conveyed in, and to have brought it hither to some place on the river Pactolus, and her servants are digging a grave on a certain elevation. They say that his wife, after setting him out with all the ornaments she has, is sitting on the ground with his head on her knees." Cyrus, hearing this, gave himself a blow on the thigh, mounted his horse at a leap, and taking with him a thousand horse, rode away to this scene of affliction; but gave orders to Gadatas and Gobryas to take with them all the rich ornaments proper for a friend and an excellent man deceased, and to follow after him; and whoever had herds of cattle with him, he ordered them to take both oxen, and horses, and sheep in good number, and to bring them away to the place where, by inquiry, they should find him to be, that he might sacrifice these to Abradatus.

'As soon as he saw the woman sitting on the ground, and the dead body there lying, he shed tears at the afflicting sight, and said: "Alas! thou brave and faithful soul, hast thou left us, and art thou gone?" At the same time he took him by the right hand, and the hand of the deceased came away, for it had been cut off, with a sword, by the Egyptians. He, at the sight of this, became yet much more concerned than before. The woman shrieked out in a lamentable manner, and, taking the hand from Cyrus, kissed it, fitted it to its proper place again, as well as she could, and said, "The rest, Cyrus, is in the same condition, but what need you see it? And I know that I was not one of the least concerned in these his sufferings, and, perhaps, you were not less so, for I, fool that I was! frequently exhorted him to behave in such a manner as to appear a friend to you, worthy of notice; and I know he never thought of what he himself should suffer, but of what he should do to please you. He is dead, therefore," said she, "without reproach, and I, who urged him on, sit here alive." Cyrus, shedding tears for some time in silence, then spoke—"He has died, woman, the noblest death; for he has died victorious! do you adorn him with these things that I furnish you with." (Gobryas and Gadatas were then come up and had brought rich ornaments in great abundance with them.) "Then," said he, "be assured that he shall not want respect and honor in all other things: but, over and above, multitudes shall concur in raising him a monument that shall be worthy of us, and all the sacrifices shall be made him that are proper to be made in honor of a brave man. You shall not be left destitute, but, for the sake of your modesty and every other virtue, I will pay you all other honors, as well as place those about you who will conduct you wherever you please. Do you but make it known to me where it is that you desire to be conveyed to." And Panthea replied, "Be confident, Cyrus," said she, "I will not conceal from you to whom it is that I desire to go."

'He, having said this, went away with great pity for her that she should have lost such a husband, and for the man that he should have left such a wife behind him, never to see her more. Panthea then gave orders for her servants to retire, "Till such time," said she, "as I shall have lamented my husband, as I please." Her nurse she bid to stay, and gave orders that, when she was dead, she would wrap her and her husband up in one mantle together. The nurse, after having repeatedly begged her not to do this, and meeting with no success, but observing her to grow angry, sat herself down, breaking out into tears. She, being before-hand provided with a sword, killed herself, and, laying her head down on her husband's breast, she died. The nurse set up a lamentable cry, and covered them both as Panthea had directed.

'Cyrus, as soon as he was informed of what the woman had done, being struck with it, went to help her if he could. The servants, three in number, seeing what had been done, drew their swords and killed themselves, as they stood at the place where she had ordered them. And the monument is now said to have been raised by continuing the mount on to the servants; and on a pillar above, they say, the names of the man and woman were written in Syriac letters.

'Below were three pillars, and they were inscribed thus, "Of the servants." Cyrus, when he came to this melancholy scene, was struck with admiration of the woman, and, having lamented over her, went away. He took care, as was proper, that all the funeral rites should be paid them in the noblest manner, and the monument, they say, was raised up to a very great size.'

These be the ancients, who, so many assert had no idea of the dignity of woman, or of marriage. Such love Xenophon could paint as subsisting between those who after death 'would see one another never more.' Thousands of years have passed since, and with the reception of the cross, the nations assume the belief that those who part thus, may meet again and forever, if spiritually fitted to one another, as Abradatus and Panthea were, and yet do we see such marriages among them? If at all, how often?

I must quote two more short passages from Xenophon, for he is a writer who pleases me well.

Cyrus receiving the Armenians whom he had conquered.

'Tigranes,' said he, 'at what rate would you purchase the regaining of your wife?' Now Tigranes happened to be *but lately married*, and had a very great love for his wife,' (that clause perhaps sounds *modern*.)

'Cyrus,' said he, 'I would ransom her at the expense of my life.'

'Take then your own to yourself,' said he. * * *

When they came home, one talked of Cyrus' wisdom, another of his patience and resolution, another of his mildness. One spoke of his beauty and the smallness of his person, and, on that, Tigranes asked his wife, 'And do you, Armenian dame, think Cyrus handsome?' 'Truly,' said she, 'I did not look at him.' 'At whom, then, did you look?' said Tigranes. 'At him who said that, to save me from servitude, he would ransom me at the expense of his own life.'

From the Banquet.*—

Socrates, who observed her with pleasure, said, 'This young girl has confirmed me in the opinion I have had, for a long time, that the female sex are nothing inferior to ours, excepting only in strength of body, or, perhaps, in steadiness of judgment.'

In the Economics,* the manner in which the husband gives counsel to his young wife, presents the model of politeness and refinement. Xenophon is thoroughly the gentleman, gentle in breeding and in soul. All the men he describes are so, while the shades of manner are distinctly marked. There is the serene dignity of Socrates, with gleams of playfulness thrown across its cool religious shades, the princely mildness of Cyrus, and the more domestic elegance of the husband in the Economics.

There is no way that men sin more against refinement, as well as discretion, than in their conduct towards their wives. Let them look at the men of Xenophon. Such would know how to give counsel, for they would know how to receive it. They would feel that the most intimate relations claimed most, not least, of refined courtesy. They would not suppose that confidence justified carelessness, nor the reality of affection want of delicacy in the expression of it.

Such men would be too wise to hide their affairs from the wife and then expect her to act as if she knew them. They would know that if she is expected to face calamity with courage, she must be instructed and trusted in prosperity, or, if they had failed in wise confidence such as the husband shows in the Economics, they would be ashamed of anger or querulous surprise at the results that naturally follow.

Such men would not be exposed to the bad influence of bad wives, for all wives, bad or good, loved or unloved, inevitably influence their husbands, from the power their position not merely gives, but necessitates, of coloring evidence and infusing feelings in hours when the patient, shall I call him? is off his guard. Those who understand the wife's mind, and think it worthwhile to respect her springs of action, know better where they are. But to the bad or thoughtless man who lives carelessly and irreverently so near another mind, the wrong he does daily back upon himself recoils. A Cyrus, an Abradatus knows where he stands.

But to return to the thread of my subject.

Another sign of the times is furnished by the triumphs of female authorship. These have been great and constantly increasing. Women have taken possession of so many provinces for which men had pronounced them unfit, that though these still declare there are some inaccessible to them, it is difficult to say just *where* they must stop.

The shining names of famous women have cast light upon the path of the sex, and many obstructions have been removed. When a Montague* could learn better than her brother, and use her lore afterward to such purpose, as an observer, it seemed amiss to hinder woman from preparing themselves to see, or from seeing all they could, when prepared. Since Somerville* has achieved so much, will any young girl be prevented from seeking a knowledge of the physical sciences, if she wishes it? De Stael's name* was not so clear of offence; she could not forget the woman in the thought; while she was instructing you as a mind, she wished to be admired as a woman; sentimental tears often dimmed the eagle glance. Her intellect too, with all its splendor, trained in a drawing-room, fed on flattery, was tainted and flawed; yet its beams make the obscurest school-house in New-England warmer and lighter to the little rugged girls, who are gathered together on its wooden bench. They may never through life hear her name, but she is not the less their benefactress.

The influence has been such, that the aim certainly is, now, in arranging school instruction for girls, to give them as fair a field as boys. As yet, indeed, these arrangements are made with little judgment or reflection; just as the tutors of Lady Jane Grey,* and other distinguished women of her time, taught them Latin and Greek, because they knew nothing else themselves, so now the improvement in the education of girls is to be made by giving them young men as teachers, who only teach what has been taught themselves at college, while methods and topics need revision for these new subjects, which could better be made by those who had experienced the same wants. Women are, often, at the head of these institutions, but they have, as yet, seldom been thinking women, capable to organize a new whole for the wants of the time, and choose persons to officiate in the departments. And when some portion of instruction is got of a good sort from the school, the far greater proportion which is infused from the general atmosphere of society contradicts its purport. Yet books and a little elementary instruction are not furnished, in vain. Women are better aware how great and rich the universe is, not so easily blinded by narrowness or partial views of a home circle. 'Her mother did so before her,' is no longer a sufficient excuse. Indeed, it was never received as an excuse to mitigate the severity of censure, but was adduced as a reason, rather, why there should be no effort made for reformation.

Whether much or little has been done or will be done, whether women will add to the talent of narration, the power of systematizing, whether they will carve marble, as well as draw and paint, is not important. But that it should be acknowledged that they have intellect which needs developing, that they should not be considered complete, if beings of affection and habit alone, is important.

Yet even this acknowledgement, rather conquered by woman than proffered by man, has been sullied by the usual selfishness. So much is said of women being better educated, that they may become better companions and mothers *for men*. They should be fit for such companionship, and we have mentioned, with satisfaction, instances where it has been established. Earth knows no fairer, holier relation than that of a mother. It is one which, rightly understood, must both promote and require the highest attainments. But a being of infinite scope must not be treated with an exclusive view to any one relation. Give the soul free course, let the organization, both of body and mind, be freely developed, and the being will be fit for any and every relation to which it may be called. The intellect, no more than the sense of hearing, is to be cultivated merely that she may be a more valuable companion to man, but because the Power who gave a power, by its mere existence, signifies that it must be brought out towards perfection.

In this regard of self-dependence, and a greater simplicity and fulness of being, we must hail as a preliminary the increase of the class contemptuously designated as old maids.

We cannot wonder at the aversion with which old bachelors and old maids have been regarded. Marriage is the natural means of forming a sphere, of taking root on the earth; it requires more strength to do this without such an opening; very many have failed, and their imperfections have been in every one's way. They have been more partial, more harsh, more officious and impertinent than those compelled by severer friction to render themselves endurable. Those, who have a more full experience of the instincts, have a distrust, as to whether they can be thoroughly human and humane, such as is hinted in the saying, 'Old maids' and bachelors' children are well cared for,' which derides at once their ignorance and their presumption.

Yet the business of society has become so complex, that it could now scarcely be carried on without the presence of these despised auxiliaries; and detachments from the army of aunts and uncles are wanted to stop gaps in every hedge. They rove about, mental and moral Ishmaelites,* pitching their tents amid the fixed and ornamented homes of men.

In a striking variety of forms, genius of late, both at home and abroad, has paid its tribute to the character of the Aunt, and the Uncle, recognizing in these personages the spiritual parents, who had supplied defects in the treatment of the busy or careless actual parents.*

They also gain a wider, if not so deep experience. Those who are not intimately and permanently linked with others, are thrown upon themselves, and, if they do not there find peace and incessant life, there is none to flatter them that they are not very poor and very mean.

A position which so constantly admonishes, may be of inestimable benefit. The person may gain, undistracted by other relationships, a closer communion with the one. Such a use is made of it by saints and sibyls. Or she may be one of the lay sisters of charity, a Canoness, bound by an inward vow! Or the useful drudge of all men, the Martha,* much sought, little prized! Or the intellectual interpreter of the varied life she sees; the Urania* of a half-formed world's twilight.

Or she may combine all these. Not 'needing to care that she may please a husband,' a frail and limited being, her thoughts may turn to the centre, and she may, by steadfast contemplation entering into the secret of truth and love, use it for the use of all men, instead of a chosen few, and interpret through it all the forms of life. It is possible, perhaps, to be at once a priestly servant, and a loving muse.

Saints and geniuses have often chosen a lonely position in the faith that if, undisturbed by the pressure of near ties, they would give themselves up to the inspiring spirit, it would enable them to understand and reproduce life better than actual experience could.

How many old maids take this high stand, we cannot say: it is an unhappy fact, that too many who have come before the eye are gossips rather, and not always good-natured gossips. But if these abuse, and none make the best of their vocation, yet it has not failed to produce some good results. It has been seen by others, if not by themselves, that beings, likely to be left alone, need to be fortified and furnished within themselves, and education and thought have tended more and more to regard these beings as related to absolute Being, as well as to other men. It has been seen that, as the breaking of no bond ought to destroy a man, so ought the missing of none to hinder him from growing. And thus a circumstance of the time, which springs rather from its luxury than its purity, has helped to place women on the true platform.

Perhaps the next generation, looking deeper into this matter, will find that contempt is put upon old maids, or old women at all, merely because they do not use the elixir which would keep them always young. Under its influence a gem brightens yearly which is only seen to more advantage through the fissures

Time makes in the casket. No one thinks of Michael Angelo's Persican Sibyl, or St Theresa, or Tasso's Leonora, or the Greek Electra, as an old maid, more than of Michael Angelo or Canova* as old bachelors, though all had reached the period in life's course appointed to take that degree.

See a common woman at forty; scarcely has she the remains of beauty, of any soft poetic grace which gave her attraction as woman, which kindled the hearts of those who looked on her to sparkling thoughts, or diffused round her a roseate air of gentle love. See her, who was, indeed, a lovely girl, in the coarse full-blown dahlia flower of what is commonly called matron-beauty, fat, fair, and forty, showily dressed, and with manners as broad and full as her frill or satin cloak. People observe, 'how well she is preserved;' 'she is a fine woman still,' they say. This woman, whether as a duchess in diamonds, or one of our city dames in mosaics, charms the poet's heart no more, and would look much out of place kneeling before the Madonna. She 'does well the honors of her house,' 'leads society,' is, in short, always spoken and thought of upholstery-wise.

Or see that care-worn face, from which every soft line is blotted, those faded eyes from which lonely tears have driven the flashes of fancy, the mild white beam of a tender enthusiasm. This woman is not so ornamental to a tea party; yet she would please better, in picture. Yet surely she, no more than the other, looks as a human being should at the end of forty years. Forty years! have they bound those brows with no garland? shed in the lamp no drop of ambrosial oil?

Not so looked the Iphigenia in Aulis.* Her forty years had seen her in anguish, in sacrifice, in utter loneliness. But those pains were borne for her father and her country; the sacrifice she had made pure for herself and those around her. Wandering alone at night in the vestal solitude of her imprisoning grove, she has looked up through its 'living summits' to the stars, which shed down into her aspect their own lofty melody. At forty she would not misbecome the marble.

Not so looks the Persica. She is withered, she is faded; the drapery that enfolds her has, in its dignity an angularity, too, that tells of age, of sorrow, of a stern composure to the *must*.

But her eye, that torch of the soul, is untamed, and in the intensity of her reading, we see a soul invincibly young in faith and hope. Her age is her charm, for it is the night of the Past that gives this beacon fire leave to shine. Wither more and more, black Chrysalid!* Thou dost but give the winged beauty time to mature its splendors.

Not so looked Vittoria Colonna,* after her life of a great hope, and of true conjugal fidelity. She had been, not merely a bride, but a wife, and each hour had helped to plume the noble bird. A coronet of pearls will not shame her brow; it is white and ample, a worthy altar for love and thought.

Even among the North American Indians, a race of men as completely engaged in mere instinctive life as almost any in the world, and where each chief, keeping many wives as useful servants, of course looks with no kind eye on celibacy in woman, it was excused in the following instance mentioned by Mrs Jameson.* A woman dreamt in youth that she was betrothed to the Sun. She built her a wigwam apart, filled it with emblems of her alliance, and means of an independent life. There she passed her days, sustained by her own exertions, and true to her supposed engagement.

In any tribe, we believe, a woman, who lived as if she was betrothed to the Sun, would be tolerated, and the rays which made her youth blossom sweetly, would crown her with a halo in age.

There is, on this subject, a nobler view than heretofore, if not the noblest, and improvement here must coincide with that in the view taken of marriage.

We must have units before we can have union, says one of the ripe thinkers of the times.

If larger intellectual resources begin to be deemed needful to woman, still more is a spiritual dignity in her, or even the mere assumption of it, looked upon with respect. Joanna Southcott* and Mother Anne Lee* are sure of a band of disciples; Ecstatica, Dolorosa,* of enraptured believers who will visit them in their lowly huts, and wait for days to revere them in their trances. The foreign noble traverses land and sea to hear a few words from the lips of the lowly peasant girl, whom he believes especially visited by the Most High. Very beautiful, in this way, was the influence of the invalid of St Petersburg, as described by De Maistre.*

Mysticism, which may be defined as the brooding soul of the world, cannot fail of its oracular promise as to woman. 'The mothers'—'The mother of all things,' are expressions of thought which lead the mind towards this side of universal growth. Whenever a mystical whisper was heard, from Behmen down to St Simon,* sprang up the thought, that, if it be true, as the legend says, that humanity withers through a fault committed by and a curse laid upon woman, through her pure child, or influence, shall the new Adam, the redemption, arise. Innocence is to be replaced by virtue, dependence by a willing submission, in the heart of the Virgin Mother of the new race.

The spiritual tendency is towards the elevation of woman, but the intellectual by itself is not so. Plato sometimes seems penetrated by that high idea of love, which considers man and woman as the two-fold expression of one thought. This the angel of Swedenborg, the angel of the coming age, cannot surpass, but only explain more fully. But then again Plato, the man of intellect, treats woman in the Republic as property,* and, in the Timæus, says that man, if he misuse the privileges of one life, shall be degraded into the form of woman, and then, if he do not redeem himself, into that of a bird. This, as I said above, expresses most happily how antipoetical is this state of mind. For the poet, contemplating the world of things, selects various birds as the symbols of his most gracious and ethereal thoughts, just as he calls upon his genius, as muse, rather than as God. But the intellect, cold, is ever more masculine than feminine; warmed by emotion, it rushes towards mother earth, and puts on the forms of beauty.

The electrical, the magnetic element in woman has not been fairly brought out at any period. Every thing might be expected from it; she has far more of it than man. This is commonly expressed by saying that her intuitions are more rapid and more correct. You will often see men of high intellect absolutely stupid in regard to the atmospheric changes, the fine invisible links which connect the forms of life around them, while common women, if pure and modest, so that a vulgar self do not overshadow the mental eye, will seize and delineate these with unerring discrimination.

Women who combine this organization with creative genius, are very commonly unhappy at present. They see too much to act in conformity with those around them, and their quick impulses seem folly to those who do not discern the motives. This is an usual effect of the apparition of genius, whether in man or woman, but is more frequent with regard to the latter, because a harmony, an obvious order and self-restraining decorum, is most expected from her.

Then women of genius, even more than men, are likely to be enslaved by an impassioned sensibility. The world repels them more rudely, and they are of weaker bodily frame.

Those, who seem overladen with electricity, frighten those around them. 'When she merely enters the room, I am what the French call *hérissé*,'* said a man of petty feelings and worldly character of such a woman, whose depth of eye and powerful motion announced the conductor of the mysterious fluid.

Woe to such a woman who finds herself linked to such a man in bonds too close. It is the cruellest of errors. He will detest her with all the bitterness of wounded self-love. He will take the whole prejudice of manhood upon himself, and to the utmost of his power imprison and torture her by its imperious rigors.

Yet, allow room enough, and the electric fluid will be found to invigorate and embellish, not destroy life. Such women are the great actresses, the songsters. Such traits we read in a late searching, though too French analysis of the character of Mademoiselle Rachel,* by a modern La Rochefoucauld.* The Greeks thus represent the muses; they have not the golden serenity of Apollo; they are *over*-flowed with thought; there is something tragic in their air. Such are the Sibyls of Guercino,* the eye is over-full of expression, dilated and lustrous; it seems to have drawn the whole being into it.

Sickness is the frequent result of this over-charged existence. To this region, however misunderstood, or interpreted with presumptuous carelessness, belong the phenomena of magnetism, or mesmerism, as it is now often called, where the trance of the Ecstatica* purports to be produced by the agency of one human being on another, instead of, as in her case, direct from the spirit.

The worldling has his sneer at this as at the services of religion. 'The churches can always be filled with women.' 'Show me a man in one of your magnetic states, and I will believe.'

Women are, indeed, the easy victims both of priestcraft and self-delusion, but this would not be, if the intellect was developed in proportion to the other powers. They would, then, have a regulator, and be more in equipoise, yet must retain the same nervous susceptibility, while their physical structure is such as it is.

It is with just that hope, that we welcome every thing that tends to strengthen the fibre and develop the nature on more sides. When the intellect and affections are in harmony; when intellectual consciousness is calm and deep; inspiration will not be confounded with fancy.

> Then, 'she who advances
>   With rapturous, lyrical glances,
>   Singing the song of the earth, singing
>   Its hymn to the Gods,'*

will not be pitied, as a madwoman, nor shrunk from as unnatural.

The Greeks, who saw every thing in forms, which we are trying to ascertain as law, and classify as cause, embodied all this in the form of Cassandra. Cassandra was only unfortunate in receiving her gift too soon. The remarks, however, that the world still makes in such cases, are well expressed by the Greek dramatist.

In the Trojan Dames,* there are fine touches of nature with regard to Cassandra. Hecuba shows that mixture of shame and reverence that prosaic kindred always do towards the inspired child, the poet, the elected sufferer for the race.

When the herald announces that Cassandra is chosen to be the mistress of Agamemnon, Hecuba answers, with indignation, betraying the pride and faith she involuntarily felt in this daughter.

Hec. 'The maiden of Phoebus, to whom the golden haired
       Gave as a privilege a virgin life!

Tal. Love of the inspired maiden hath pierced him.
Hec. Then cast away, my child, the sacred keys, and from thy person
  The consecrated garlands which thou wearest.'

Yet, when a moment after, Cassandra appears, singing, wildly, her inspired song, Hecuba calls her, 'My *frantic* child.'

Yet how graceful she is in her tragic *raptus*,* the chorus shows.

  Chor. 'How sweetly at thy house's ills thou smil'st,
    Chanting what, haply, thou wilt not show true.'

If Hecuba dares not trust her highest instinct about her daughter, still less can the vulgar mind of the herald Talthybius, a man not without feeling, but with no princely, no poetic blood, abide the wild prophetic mood which insults all his prejudices.

  Tal. 'The venerable, and that accounted wise,
    Is nothing better than that of no repute,
    For the greatest king of all the Greeks,
    The dear son of Atreus, is possessed with the love
    Of this madwoman. I, indeed, am poor,
    Yet, I would not receive her to my bed.'

The royal Agamemnon could see the beauty of Cassandra, HE was not afraid of her prophetic gifts.

The best topic for a chapter on this subject in the present day, would be the history of the Seeress of Prevorst,* the best observed subject of magnetism in our present times, and who, like her ancestresses of Delphos, was roused to ecstacy or phrenzy by the touch of the laurel.

I observe in her case, and in one known to me here, that, what might have been a gradual and gentle disclosure of remarkable powers, was broken and jarred into disease by an unsuitable marriage. Both these persons were unfortunate in not understanding what was involved in this relation, but acted ignorantly as their friends desired. They thought that this was the inevitable destiny of woman. But when engaged in the false position, it was impossible for them to endure its dissonances, as those of less delicate perceptions can, and the fine flow of life was checked and sullied. They grew sick, but, even so, learnt and disclosed more than those in health are wont to do.

In such cases, worldlings sneer, but reverent men learn wondrous news, either from the person observed, or by thoughts caused in themselves by the observation. Fenelon learns from Guyon,* Kerner, from his Seeress, what we fain would know. But to appreciate such disclosures one must be a child, and here the phrase, 'women and children' may, perhaps, be interpreted aright, that only little children shall enter into the kingdom of heaven.

All these motions of the time, tides that betoken a waxing moon, overflow upon our land. The world, at large, is readier to let woman learn and manifest the capacities of her nature than it ever was before, and here is a less encumbered field and freer air than any where else. And it ought to be so; we ought to pay for Isabella's jewels.*

The names of nations are feminine—religion, virtue, and victory are feminine. To those who have a superstition, as to outward reigns, it is not without significance that the name of the queen of our mother-land should at this crisis be Victoria— Victoria the First. Perhaps to us it may be given to disclose the era thus outwardly presaged.

Another Isabella* too at this time ascends the throne. Might she open a new world to her sex! But, probably, these poor little women are, least of any, educated to serve as examples or inspirers for the rest. The Spanish queen is younger; we know of her that she sprained her foot the other day, dancing in her private apartments; of Victoria, that she reads aloud, in a distinct voice and agreeable manner, her addresses to parliament on certain solemn days, and, yearly, that she presents to the nation some new prop of royalty. These ladies have, very likely, been trained more completely to the puppet life than any other. The queens, who have been queens indeed, were trained by adverse circumstances to know the world around them and their own powers.

It is moving, while amusing. to read of the Scottish peasant measuring the print left by the queen's foot as she walks, and priding himself on its beauty. It is so natural to wish to find what is fair and precious in high places, so astonishing to find the Bourbon a glutton, or the Guelph* a dullard or gossip.

In our own country, women are, in many respects, better situated than men. Good books are allowed, with more time to read them. They are not so early forced into the bustle of life, nor so weighed down by demands for outward success. The perpetual changes, incident to our society, make the blood circulate freely through the body politic, and, if not favorable at present to the grace and bloom of life, they are so to activity, resource, and would be to reflection, but for a low materialist tendency, from which the women are generally exempt in themselves, though its existence, among the men, has a tendency to repress their impulses and make them doubt their instincts, thus, often, paralyzing their action during the best years.

But they have time to think, and no traditions chain them, and few conventionalities compared with what must be met in other nations. There is no reason why they should not discover that the secrets of nature are open, the revelations of the spirit waiting for whoever will seek them. When the mind is once awakened to this consciousness, it will not be restrained by the habits of the past, but fly to seek the seeds of a heavenly future.

Their employments are more favorable to meditation than those of men.

Woman is not addressed religiously here, more than elsewhere. She is told she should be worthy to be the mother of a Washington, or the companion of some good man. But in many, many instances, she has already learnt that all bribes have the same flaw; that truth and good are to be sought solely for their own sakes. And, already, an ideal sweetness floats over many forms, shines in many eyes.

Already deep questions are put by young girls on the great theme: What shall I do to enter upon the eternal life?

Men are very courteous to them. They praise them often, check them seldom. There is chivalry in the feeling towards 'the ladies,' which gives them the best seats in the stagecoach, frequent admission, not only to lectures of all sorts, but to courts of justice, halls of legislature, reform conventions. The newspaper editor 'would be better pleased that the Lady's Book* should be filled up exclusively by ladies. It would then, indeed, be a true gem, worthy to be presented by young men to the mistresses of their affections.' Can gallantry go further?

In this country is venerated, wherever seen, the character which Goethe spoke of an Ideal, which he saw actualized in his friend and patroness, the Grand Duchess Amelia. 'The excellent woman is she, who, if the husband dies, can be a father to the children.' And this, if read aright, tells a great deal.

Women who speak in public, if they have a moral power, such as has been felt from Angelina Grimke* and Abby Kelley;* that is, if they speak for conscience' sake, to serve a cause which they hold sacred, invariably subdue the prejudices of their hearers, and excite an interest proportionate to the aversion with which it had been the purpose to regard them.

A passage in a private letter so happily illustrates this, that it must be inserted here.

Abby Kelley in the Town-House of——.

'The scene was not unheroic—to see that woman, true to humanity and her own nature, a centre of rude eyes and tongues, even gentlemen feeling licensed to make part of a species of mob around a female out of her sphere. As she took her seat in the desk amid the great noise, and in the throng, full, like a wave, of something to ensue, I saw her humanity in a gentleness and unpretension, tenderly open to the sphere around her, and, had she not been supported by the power of the will of genuineness and principle, she would have failed. It led her to prayer, which, in woman especially, is childlike; sensibility and will going to the side of God and looking up to him; and humanity was poured out in aspiration.

'She acted like a gentle hero, with her mild decision and womanly calmness. All heroism is mild and quiet and gentle, for it is life and possession, and combativeness and firmness show a want of actualness. She is as earnest, fresh, and simple as when she first entered the crusade. I think she did much good, more than the men in her place could do, for woman feels more as being and reproducing, this brings the subject more into home relations. Men speak through, and mostly from intellect, and this addresses itself in others, which creates and is combative.'

Not easily shall we find elsewhere, or before this time, any written observations on the same subject, so delicate and profound.

The late Dr Channing,* whose enlarged and tender and religious nature, shared every onward impulse of his time, though his thoughts followed his wishes with a deliberative caution, which belonged to his habits and temperament, was greatly interested in these expectations for women. His own treatment of them was absolutely and thoroughly religious. He regarded them as souls, each of which had a destiny of its own, incalculable to other minds, and whose leading it must follow, guided by the light of a private conscience. He had sentiment, delicacy, kindness, taste; but they were all pervaded and ruled by this one thought, that all beings had souls, and must vindicate their own inheritance. Thus all beings were treated by him with an equal, and sweet, though solemn, courtesy. The young and unknown, the woman and the child, all felt themselves regarded with an infinite expectation, from which there was no reaction to vulgar prejudice. He demanded of all he met, to use his favorite phrase, 'great truths.'

His memory, every way dear and reverend, is, by many, especially cherished for this intercourse of unbroken respect.

At one time, when the progress of Harriet Martineau* through this country, Angelina Grimke's appearance in public, and the visit of Mrs Jameson had turned his thoughts to this subject, he expressed high hopes as to what the coming era would bring to woman. He had been much pleased with the dignified courage of Mrs Jameson in taking up the defence of her sex, in a way from which women usually shrink, because, if they express themselves on such subjects with sufficient force and clearness to do any good, they are exposed to assaults whose vulgarity makes them painful. In intercourse with such a woman, he had shared her indignation at the base injustice, in many respects, and in many regions, done to the sex; and been led to think of it far more than ever before. He seemed to think that he might some time write upon the subject. That his aid is withdrawn from the cause is a subject of great regret, for, on this question as on others, he would have known how to sum up the evidence and take, in the noblest spirit, middle ground. He always furnished a platform on which opposing parties could stand, and look at one another under the influence of his mildness and enlightened candor.

Two younger thinkers, men both, have uttered noble prophecies, auspicious for woman. Kinmont,* all whose thoughts tended towards the establishment of the reign of love and peace, thought that the inevitable means of this would be an increased predominance given to the idea of woman. Had he lived longer, to see the growth of the peace party, the reforms in life and medical practice which seek to substitute water for wine and drugs, pulse for animal food, he would have been confirmed in his view of the way in which the desired changes are to be effected.

In this connection, I must mention Shelley, who, like all men of genius, shared the feminine development, and, unlike many, knew it. His life was one of the first pulse-beats in the present reform-growth. He, too, abhorred blood and heat, and, by his system and his song, tended to reinstate a plant-like gentleness in the development of energy. In harmony with this, his ideas of marriage were lofty, and, of course, no less so of woman, her nature, and destiny.

For woman, if, by a sympathy as to outward condition she is led to aid the enfranchisement of the slave, must be no less so, by inward tendency, to favor measures which promise to bring the world more thoroughly and deeply into harmony with her nature. When the lamb takes place of the lion as the emblem of nations, both women and men will be as children of one spirit, perpetual learners of the word and doers thereof, not hearers only.

A writer in the New-York Pathfinder, in two articles headed 'Femality,'* has uttered a still more pregnant word than any we have named. He views woman truly from the soul, and not from society, and the depth and leading of his thoughts are proportionably remarkable. He views the feminine nature as a harmonizer of the vehement elements, and this has often been hinted elsewhere; but what he expresses most forcibly is the lyrical, the inspiring, and inspired apprehensiveness of her being.

This view being identical with what I have before attempted to indicate, as to her superior susceptibility to magnetic or electric influence, I will now try to express myself more fully.

There are two aspects of woman's nature, represented by the ancients as Muse and Minerva. It is the former to which the writer in the Pathfinder looks. It is the latter which Wordsworth has in mind, when he says—

> 'With a placid brow,
> Which woman ne'er should forfeit, keep thy vow.'*

The especial genius of woman I believe to be electrical in movement, intuitive in function, spiritual in tendency. She excels not so easily in classification, or re-creation, as in an instinctive seizure of causes, and a simple breathing out of what she receives that has the singleness of life, rather than the selecting and energizing of art.

More native is it to her to be the living model of the artist than to set apart from herself any one form in objective reality; more native to inspire and receive the poem, than to create it. In so far as soul is in her completely developed, all soul is the same; but as far as it is modified in her as woman, it flows, it breathes, it sings, rather than deposits soil, or finishes work, and that which is especially feminine flushes, in blossom, the face of earth, and pervades, like air and water, all this seeming solid globe, daily renewing and purifying its life. Such may be the especially feminine element, spoken of as Femality. But it is no more the order of nature that it should be incarnated pure in any form, than that the masculine energy should exist un-mingled with it in any form.

Male and female represent the two sides of the great radical dualism. But, in fact, they are perpetually passing into one another. Fluid hardens to solid, solid rushes to fluid. There is no wholly masculine man, no purely feminine woman.

History jeers at the attempts of physiologists to bind great original laws by the forms which flow from them. They make a rule; they say from observation, what can and cannot be. In vain! Nature provides exceptions to every rule. She sends women to battle, and sets Hercules spinning;* she enables women to bear immense burdens, cold, and frost; she enables the man, who feels maternal love, to nourish his infant like a mother. Of late she plays still gayer pranks. Not only she deprives organizations, but organs, of a necessary end. She enables people to read with the top of the head, and see with the pit of the stomach. Presently she will make a female Newton, and a male Syren.

Man partakes of the feminine in the Apollo, woman of the masculine as Minerva.

What I mean by the Muse is the unimpeded clearness of the intuitive powers which a perfectly truthful adherence to every admonition of the higher instincts would bring to a finely organized human being. It may appear as prophecy or as poesy. It enabled Cassandra to foresee the results of actions passing round her; the Seeress to behold the true character of the person through the mask of his customary life. (Sometimes she saw a feminine form behind the man, sometimes the reverse.) It enabled the daughter of Linnæus* to see the soul of the flower exhaling from the flower.† It gave a man, but a poet man, the power of which he thus speaks: 'Often in my contemplation of nature, radiant intimations, and as it were sheaves of light appear before me as to the facts of cosmogony in which my mind has, perhaps, taken especial part.' He wisely adds, 'but it is necessary with earnestness to verify the knowledge we gain by these flashes of light.'* And none should forget this. Sight must be verified by life before it can deserve the honors of piety and genius. Yet sight comes first, and of this sight of the world of causes, this approximation to the region of primitive motions, women I hold to be especially capable. Even without equal freedom with the other sex, they have already shown themselves so, and should these faculties have free play, I believe they will open new, deeper and purer sources of joyous inspiration than have as yet refreshed the earth.

Let us be wise and not impede the soul. Let her work as she will. Let us have one creative energy, one incessant revelation. Let it take what form it will, and let us not bind it by the past to man or woman, black or white. Jove sprang from Rhea, Pallas from Jove.* So let it be.

If it has been the tendency of these remarks to call woman rather to the Minerva side,—if I, unlike the more generous writer, have spoken from society no less than the soul,—let it be pardoned! It is love that has caused this, love for many incarcerated souls, that might be freed, could the idea of religious self-dependence be established in them, could the weakening habit of dependence on others be broken up.

---

† The daughter of Linnaeus states, that while looking steadfastly at the red lily, she saw its spirit hovering above it, as a red flame. It is true, this, like many fair spirit-stories, may be explained away as an optical illusion, but its poetic beauty and meaning would, even then, make it valuable, as an illustration of the spiritual fact. [Fuller's note.]

Proclus* teaches that every life has, in its sphere, a totality or wholeness of the animating powers of the other spheres; having only, as its own characteristic, a predominance of some one power. Thus Jupiter comprises, within himself, the other twelve powers, which stand thus: The first triad is *demiurgic or fabricative*, i.e., Jupiter, Neptune, Vulcan; the second, *defensive*, Vesta, Minerva, Mars; the third, *vivific*, Ceres, Juno, Diana; and the fourth, Mercury, Venus, Apollo, *elevating and harmonic*. In the sphere of Jupiter, energy is predominant—with Venus, beauty; but each comprehends and apprehends all the others.

When the same community of life and consciousness of mind begins among men, humanity will have, positively and finally, subjugated its brute elements and Titanic* childhood; criticism will have perished; arbitrary limits and ignorant censure be impossible; all will have entered upon the liberty of law, and the harmony of common growth.

Then Apollo will sing to his lyre what Vulcan forges on the anvil, and the Muse weave anew the tapestries of Minerva.

It is, therefore, only in the present crisis that the preference is given to Minerva. The power of continence must establish the legitimacy of freedom, the power of self-poise the perfection of motion.

Every relation, every gradation of nature is incalculably precious, but only to the soul which is poised upon itself, and to whom no loss, no change, can bring dull discord, for it is in harmony with the central soul.

If any individual live too much in relations, so that he becomes a stranger to the resources of his own nature, he falls, after a while, into a distraction, or imbecility, from which he can only be cured by a time of isolation, which gives the renovating fountains time to rise up. With a society it is the same. Many minds, deprived of the traditionary or instinctive means of passing a cheerful existence, must find help in self-impulse, or perish. It is therefore that, while any elevation, in the view of union, is to be hailed with joy, we shall not decline celibacy as the great fact of the time. It is one from which no vow, no arrangement, can at present save a thinking mind. For now the rowers are pausing on their oars; they wait a change before they can pull together. All tends to illustrate the thought of a wise contemporary. Union is only possible to those who are units. To be fit for relations in time, souls, whether of man or woman, must be able to do without them in the spirit.

It is therefore that I would have woman lay aside all thought, such as she habitually cherishes, of being taught and led by men. I would have her, like the Indian girl, dedicate herself to the Sun, the Sun of Truth, and go nowhere if his beams did not make clear the path. I would have her free from compromise, from complaisance, from helplessness, because I would have her good enough and strong enough to love one and all beings, from the fulness, not the poverty of being.

Men, as at present instructed, will not help this work, because they also are under the slavery of habit. I have seen with delight their poetic impulses. A sister is the fairest ideal, and how nobly Wordsworth, and even Byron, have written of a sister.*

There is no sweeter sight than to see a father with his little daughter. Very vulgar men become refined to the eye when leading a little girl by the hand. At that moment the right relation between the sexes seems established, and you feel as if the man would aid in the noblest purpose, if you ask him in behalf of his little daughter. Once two fine figures stood before me, thus. The father of very intellectual aspect, his falcon eye softened by affection as he looked down on his fair child, she the image of himself, only more graceful and brilliant in expression. I was reminded of Southey's Kehama;* when lo, the dream was rudely broken. They were talking of education, and he said.

'I shall not have Maria brought too forward. If she knows too much, she will never find a husband; superior women hardly ever can.'

'Surely,' said his wife, with a blush, 'you wish Maria to be as good and wise as she can, whether it will help her to marriage or not.'

'No,' he persisted, 'I want her to have a sphere and a home, and some one to protect her when I am gone.'

It was a trifling incident, but made a deep impression. I felt that the holiest relations fail to instruct the unprepared and perverted mind. If this man, indeed, could have looked at it on the other side, he was the last that would have been willing to have been taken himself for the home and protection he could give, but would have been much more likely to repeat the tale of Alcibiades with his phials.*

But men do *not* look at both sides, and women must leave off asking them and being influenced by them, but retire within themselves, and explore the groundwork of life till they find their peculiar secret. Then, when they come forth again, renovated and baptized, they will know how to turn all dross to gold, and will be rich and free though they live in a hut, tranquil, if in a crowd. Then their sweet singing shall not be from passionate impulse, but the lyrical over-flow of a divine rapture, and a new music shall be evolved from this many-chorded world.

Grant her, then, for a while, the armor and the javelin. Let her put from her the press of other minds and meditate in virgin loneliness. The same idea shall re-appear in due time as Muse, or Ceres, the all-kindly patient Earth-Spirit.

Among the throng of symptoms which denote the present tendency to a crisis in the life of woman, which resembles the change from girlhood with its beautiful instincts, but unharmonized thoughts, its blind pupilage and restless seeking, to self-possessed, wise, and graceful womanhood, I have attempted to select a few.

One of prominent interest is the unison of three male minds, upon the subject, which, for width of culture, power of self-concentration and dignity of aim, take rank as the prophets of the coming age, while their histories and labors are rooted in the past.

Swedenborg came, he tells us, to interpret the past revelation and unfold a new. He announces the new church that is to prepare the way for the New Jerusalem, a city built of precious stones, hardened and purified by secret processes in the veins of earth through the ages.

Swedenborg approximated to that harmony between the scientific and poetic lives of mind, which we hope from the perfected man. The links that bind together the realms of nature, the mysteries that accompany her births and growths, were unusually plain to him. He seems a man to whom insight was given at a period when the mental frame was sufficiently matured to retain and express its gifts.

His views of woman are, in the main, satisfactory. In some details, we may object to them as, in all his system, there are still remains of what is arbitrary and seemingly groundless; fancies that show the marks of old habits, and a nature as yet not thoroughly leavened with the spiritual leaven. At least so it seems to me now. I speak reverently, for I find such reason to venerate Swedenborg, from an imperfect knowledge of his mind, that I feel one more perfect might explain to me much that does not now secure my sympathy.

His idea of woman is sufficiently large and noble to interpose no obstacle to her progress. His idea of marriage is consequently sufficient. Man and woman share an angelic ministry, the union is from one to one, permanent and pure.

As the New Church extends its ranks, the needs of woman must be more considered.

Quakerism also establishes woman on a sufficient equality with man.* But though the original thought of Quakerism is pure, its scope is too narrow, and its influence, having established a certain amount of good and made clear some truth, must, by degrees, be merged in one of wider range.† The mind of Swedenborg appeals to the various nature of man and allows room for æsthetic culture and the free expression of·energy.

As apostle of the new order, of the social fabric that is to rise from love, and supersede the old that was based on strife, Charles Fourier* comes next, expressing, in an outward order, many facts of which Swedenborg saw the secret springs. The mind of Fourier, though grand and clear, was, in some respects, superficial. He was a stranger to the highest experiences. His eye was fixed on the outward more than the inward needs of man. Yet he, too, was a seer of the divine order, in its musical expression, if not in its poetic soul. He has filled one depart-

---

† In worship at stated periods, in daily expression, whether by word or deed, the Quakers have placed woman on the same platform with man. Can anyone assert that they have reason to repent this? [Fuller's note.]

ment of instruction for the new era, and the harmony in action, and freedom for individual growth he hopes shall exist; and if the methods he proposes should not prove the true ones, yet his fair propositions shall give many hints, and make room for the inspiration needed for such.

He, too, places woman on an entire equality with man, and wishes to give to one as to the other that independence which must result from intellectual and practical development.

Those who will consult him for no other reason, might do so to see how the energies of woman may be made available in the pecuniary way. The object of Fourier was to give her the needed means of self help, that she might dignify and unfold her life for her own happiness, and that of society. The many, now, who see their daughters liable to destitution, or vice to escape from it, may be interested to examine the means, if they have not yet soul enough to appreciate the ends he proposes.

On the opposite side of the advancing army, leads the great apostle of individual culture, Goethe. Swedenborg makes organization and union the necessary results of solitary thought. Fourier, whose nature was, above all, constructive, looked to them too exclusively. Better institutions, he thought, will make better men. Goethe expressed, in every way, the other side. If one man could present better forms, the rest could not use them till ripe for them.

Fourier says, As the institutions, so the men! All follies are excusable and natural under bad institutions.

Goethe thinks, As the man, so the institutions! There is no excuse for ignorance and folly. A man can grow in any place, if he will.

Ay! but Goethe, bad institutions are prison walls and impure air that make him stupid, so that he does not will.

And thou, Fourier, do not expect to change mankind at once, or even 'in three generations' by arrangement of groups and series, or flourish of trumpets for attractive industry. If these attempts are made by unready men, they will fail.

Yet we prize the theory of Fourier no less than the profound suggestion of Goethe. Both are educating the age to a clearer consciousness of what man needs, what man can be, and better life must ensue.

Goethe, proceeding on his own track, elevating the human being in the most imperfect states of society, by continual efforts at self-culture, takes as good care of women as of men. His mother, the bold, gay Frau Aja, with such playful freedom of nature; the wise and gentle maiden, known in his youth, over whose sickly solitude 'the Holy Ghost brooded as a dove;' his sister, the intellectual woman *par excellence*: the Duchess Amelia; Lili,* who combined the character of the woman of the world with the lyrical sweetness of the shepherdess, on whose chaste and noble breast flowers and gems were equally at home; all these had supplied abundant suggestions to his mind, as to the wants and the possible excellencies of woman. And, from his poetic soul, grew up forms new and more admirable than life has yet produced, for whom his clear eye marked out paths in the future.

In Faust, we see the redeeming power, which, at present, upholds woman, while waiting for a better day, in Margaret.* The lovely little girl, pure in instinct, ignorant in mind, is misled and profaned by man abusing her confidence.† To the Mater *Dolorosa*＊ she appeals for aid. It is given to the soul, if not against outward sorrow; and the maiden, enlightened by her sufferings, refusing to receive temporal salvation by the aid of an evil power, obtains the eternal in its stead.

In the second part, the intellectual man, after all his manifold strivings, owes to the interposition of her whom he had betrayed *his* salvation. She intercedes, this time herself a glorified spirit, with the Mater *Gloriosa*.＊

Leonora,* too, is woman, as we see her now, pure, thoughtful, refined by much acquaintance with grief.

Iphigenia* he speaks of in his journals as his 'daughter,' and she is the daughter† whom a man will wish, even if he has chosen his wife from very mean motives. She is the virgin, steadfast soul, to whom falsehood is more dreadful than any other death.

---

† As Faust says, her only fault was a 'Kindly delusion,'—'ein guter wahn.' [Fuller's note.]

† Goethe was as false to his ideas in practice, as Lord Herbert. And his punishment was the just and usual one of connections formed beneath the standard of right, from the impulses of the baser self. Iphigenia was the worthy

But it is to Wilhelm Meister's Apprenticeship and Wandering Years* that I would especially refer, as these volumes contain the sum of the Sage's observations during a long life, as to what man should do, under present circumstances, to obtain mastery over outward, through an initiation into inward life, and severe discipline of faculty.

As Wilhelm advances in the upward path he becomes acquainted with better forms of woman by knowing how to seek, and how to prize them when found. For the weak and immature man will, often, admire a superior woman, but he will not be able to abide by a feeling, which is too severe a tax on his habitual existence. But, with Wilhelm, the gradation is natural and expresses ascent in the scale of being. At first he finds charm in Mariana and Philina, very common forms of feminine character, not without redeeming traits, no less than charms, but without wisdom or purity. Soon he is attended by Mignon, the finest expression ever yet given to what I have called the lyrical element in woman. She is a child, but too full-grown for this man; he loves, but cannot follow her; yet is the association not without an enduring influence. Poesy has been domesticated in his life, and, though he strives to bind down her heavenward impulse, as art or apothegm, these are only the tents, beneath which he may sojourn for a while, but which may be easily struck, and carried on limitless wanderings.

Advancing into the region of thought, he encounters a wise philanthropy in Natalia, (instructed, let us observe, by an *uncle*,) practical judgment and the outward economy of life in Theresa, pure devotion in the Fair Saint.

Farther and last he comes to the house of Macaria, the soul of a star, *i.e.* a pure and perfected intelligence embodied in feminine form, and the centre of a world whose members revolve harmoniously round her. She instructs him in the

daughter of his mind, but the son, the child of his degrading connection* in actual life, corresponded with that connection. This son, on whom Goethe vainly lavished so much thought and care, was like his mother, and like Goethe's attachment for his mother. 'This young man,' says a late well informed writer, (M. Henri Blaze,*) 'Wieland, with good reason, was called the son of the servant, *der Sohn der Magd*. He inherited from his father only his name and his *physique*.' [Fuller's note.]

archives of a rich human history, and introduces him to the contemplation of the heavens.

From the hours passed by the side of Mariana to these with Macaria, is a wide distance for human feet to traverse. Nor has Wilhelm travelled so far, seen and suffered so much in vain. He now begins to study how he may aid the next generation; he sees objects in harmonious arrangement, and from his observations deduces precepts by which to guide his course as a teacher and a master, 'help-full, comfort-full.'

In all these expressions of woman, the aim of Goethe is satisfactory to me. He aims at a pure self-subsistence, and free development of any powers with which they may be gifted by nature as much for them as for men. They are units, addressed as souls. Accordingly the meeting between man and woman, as represented by him, is equal and noble, and, if he does not depict marriage, he makes it possible.

In the Macaria, bound with the heavenly bodies in fixed revolutions, the centre of all relations, herself unrelated, he expresses the Minerva side of feminine nature. It was not by chance that Goethe gave her this name. Macaria, the daughter of Hercules, who offered herself as a victim for the good of her country, was canonized by the Greeks, and worshipped as the Goddess of true Felicity. Goethe has embodied this Felicity as the Serenity that arises from Wisdom, a Wisdom, such as the Jewish wise man venerated, alike instructed in the designs of heaven, and the methods necessary to carry them into effect upon earth.

Mignon is the electrical, inspired, lyrical nature. And wherever it appears we echo in our aspirations that of the child,

> 'So let me seem until I be:—
> Take not the *white robe* away.'
>
> * * *
>
> 'Though I lived without care and toil,
> Yet felt I sharp pain enough,
> Make me again forever young.'*

All these women, though we see them in relations, we can think of as unrelated. They all are very individual, yet seem, nowhere, restrained. They satisfy for the present, yet arouse an infinite expectation.

The economist Theresa, the benevolent Natalia, the fair Saint, have chosen a path, but their thoughts are not narrowed to it. The functions of life to them are not ends, but suggestions.

Thus, to them, all things are important, because none is necessary. Their different characters have fair play, and each is beautiful in its minute indications, for nothing is enforced or conventional, but every thing, however slight, grows from the essential life of the being.

Mignon and Theresa wear male attire when they like, and it is graceful for them to do so, while Macaria is confined to her arm-chair behind the green curtain, and the Fair Saint could not bear a speck of dust on her robe.

All things are in their places in this little world, because all is natural and free, just as 'there is room for everything out of doors.' Yet all is rounded in by natural harmony, which will always arise where Truth and Love are sought in the light of Freedom.

Goethe's book bodes an era of freedom like its own of 'extraordinary generous seeking,' and new revelations. New individualities shall be developed in the actual world, which shall advance upon it as gently as the figures come out upon his canvas.*

I have indicated on this point the coincidence between his hopes and those of Fourier, though his are directed by an infinitely higher and deeper knowledge of human nature. But, for our present purpose, it is sufficient to show how surely these different paths have conducted to the same end two earnest thinkers. In some other place I wish to point out similar coincidences between Goethe's model school and the plans of Fourier, which may cast light upon the page of prophecy.

Many women have observed that the time drew nigh for a better care of the sex, and have thrown out hints that may be useful. Among these may be mentioned—

Miss Edgeworth,* who, although restrained by the habits of her age and country, and belonging more to the eighteenth than the nineteenth century, has done excellently as far as she goes. She had a horror of sentimentalism, and the love of notoriety, and saw how likely women, in the early stages of culture, were to aim at these. Therefore she bent her efforts to recommending domestic life. But the methods she recommends are such as will fit a character for any position to which it may be called. She taught a contempt of falsehood, no less in its most graceful, than in its meanest apparitions; the cultivation of a clear, independent judgment, and adherence to its dictates; habits of various and liberal study and employment, and a capacity for friendship. Her standard of character is the same for both sexes. Truth, honor, enlightened benevolence, and aspiration after knowledge. Of poetry, she knows nothing, and her religion consists in honor and loyalty to obligations once assumed, in short, in 'the great idea of duty which holds us upright.' Her whole tendency is practical.

Mrs Jameson* is a sentimentalist, and, therefore, suits us ill in some respects, but she is full of talent, has a just and refined perception of the beautiful, and a genuine courage when she finds it necessary. She does not appear to have thought out, thoroughly, the subject on which we are engaged, and her opinions, expressed as opinions, are sometimes inconsistent with one another. But from the refined perception of character, admirable suggestions are given in her 'Women of Shakspeare,' and 'Loves of the Poets.'

But that for which I most respect her is the decision with which she speaks on a subject which refined women are usually afraid to approach, for fear of the insult and scurrile jest they may encounter; but on which she neither can nor will restrain the indignation of a full heart. I refer to the degradation of a large portion of women into the sold and polluted slaves of men, and the daring with which the legislator and man of the world lifts his head beneath the heavens, and says 'this must be; it cannot be helped; it is a necessary accompaniment of *civilization*.'

So speaks the *citizen*. Man born of woman, the father of daughters, declares that he will and must buy the comforts and commercial advantages of his London, Vienna, Paris, New-York, by conniving at the moral death, the damnation, so far as the action of society can insure it, of thousands of women for each splendid metropolis.

O men! I speak not to you. It is true that your wickedness (for you must not deny that, at least, nine thousand out of the ten fall through the vanity you have systematically flattered, or the promises you have treacherously broken;) yes, it is true that your wickedness is its own punishment. Your forms degraded and your eyes clouded by secret sin; natural harmony broken and fineness of perception destroyed in your mental and bodily organization; God and love shut out from your hearts by the foul visitants you have permitted there; incapable of pure marriage; incapable of pure parentage; incapable of worship; oh wretched men, your sin is its own punishment! You have lost the world in losing yourselves. Who ruins another has admitted the worm to the root of his own tree, and the fuller ye fill the cup of evil, the deeper must be your own bitter draught. But I speak not to you—you need to teach and warn one another. And more than one voice rises in earnestness. And all that *women* say to the heart that has once chosen the evil path, is considered prudery, or ignorance, or perhaps, a feebleness of nature which exempts from similar temptations.

But to you, women, American women, a few words may not be addressed in vain. One here and there may listen.

You know how it was in the Oriental clime. One man, if wealth permitted, had several wives and many hand-maidens. The chastity and equality of genuine marriage, with 'the thousand decencies that flow,' from its communion, the precious virtues that gradually may be matured, within its enclosure, were unknown.

But this man did not wrong according to his light. What he did, he might publish to God and Man; it was not a wicked secret that hid in vile lurking-places and dens, like the banquets of beasts of prey. Those women were not lost, not polluted in their own eyes, nor those of others. If they were not in a state of knowledge and virtue, they were at least in one of comparative innocence.

You know how it was with the natives of this continent. A chief had many wives whom he maintained and who did his household work; those women were but servants, still they enjoyed the respect of others and their own. They lived together in peace. They knew that a sin against what was in their nation esteemed virtue, would be as strictly punished in man as in woman.

Now pass to the countries where marriage is between one and one. I will not speak of the Pagan nations, but come to those which own the Christian rule. We all know what that enjoins; there is a standard to appeal to.

See now, not the mass of the people, for we all know that it is a proverb and a bitter jest to speak of the 'down-trodden million.' We know that, down to our own time, a principle never had so fair a chance to pervade the mass of the people, but that we must solicit its illustration from select examples.

Take the Paladin, take the Poet.* Did *they* believe purity more impossible to man than to woman? Did they wish woman to believe that man was less amenable to higher motives, that pure aspirations would not guard him against bad passions, that honorable employments and temperate habits would not keep him free from slavery to the body. O no! Love was to them a part of heaven, and they could not even wish to receive its happiness, unless assured of being worthy of it. Its highest happiness to them was, that it made them wish to be worthy. They courted probation. They wished not the title of knight, till the banner had been upheld in the heats of battle, amid the rout of cowards.

I ask of you, young girls—I do not mean *you*, whose heart is that of an old coxcomb, though your locks have not yet lost their sunny tinge. Not of you whose whole character is tainted with vanity, inherited or taught, who have early learnt the love of coquettish excitement, and whose eyes rove restlessly in search of a 'conquest' or a 'beau.' You who are ashamed *not* to be seen by others the mark of the most contemptuous flattery or injurious desire. To such I do not speak. But to thee, maiden, who, if not so fair, art yet of that unpolluted nature which Milton saw when he dreamed of Comus and the Paradise. Thou, child of an unprofaned wedlock, brought up amid the teachings of the woods and fields, kept fancy-free by useful employment and a free flight into the heaven of thought, loving to please only those whom thou wouldst not be ashamed to love; I ask of thee, whose cheek has not forgotten its blush nor thy heart its lark-like hopes, if he whom thou mayst hope the Father will send thee, as the companion of life's toils and joys, is not to thy thought pure? Is not manliness to thy thought purity, *not* lawlessness? Can his lips speak falsely? Can he do, in secret, what he could not avow to the mother that bore him? O say, dost thou not look for a heart free, open as thine own, all whose thoughts may be avowed, incapable of wronging the innocent, or still farther degrading the fallen. A man, in short, in whom brute nature is entirely subject to the impulses of his better self.

Yes! it was thus that thou didst hope, for I have many, many times seen the image of a future life, of a destined spouse, painted on the tablets of a virgin heart.

It might be that she was not true to these hopes. She was taken into what is called 'the world,' froth and scum as it mostly is on the social cauldron. There, she saw fair woman carried in the waltz close to the heart of a being who appeared to her a Satyr. Being warned by a male friend that he was in fact of that class, and not fit for such familiar nearness to a chaste being, the advised replied that 'women should know nothing about such things.' She saw one fairer given in wedlock to a man of the same class. 'Papa and mamma said that "all men were faulty, at some time in their lives; they had a great many temptations. Frederick would be so happy at home; he would not want to do wrong."' She turned to the married women; they, oh tenfold horror! laughed at her supposing 'men were like women.' Sometimes, I say, she was not true and either sadly accommodated herself to 'woman's lot,' or acquired a taste for satyr-society, like some of the Nymphs, and all the Bacchanals* of old. But to these who could not and would not accept a mess of pottage, or a Circe* cup, in lieu of their birthright, and to these others who have yet their choice to make, I say, Courage! I have some words of cheer for you. A man, himself of unbroken purity, reported to me the words of a foreign artist, that 'the world would never be better till men subjected themselves to the same laws they had imposed on women;' that artist, he added, was true to the thought. The same was true of Canova, the same of Beethoven. 'Like each other demi-god, they kept themselves free from stain,' and Michael Angelo, looking over here from the loneliness of his century, might meet some eyes that need not shun his glance.

In private life, I am assured by men who are not so sustained and occupied by the worship of pure beauty, that a similar consecration is possible, is practiced. That many men feel that no temptation can be too strong for the will of man, if he invokes the aid of the Spirit instead of seeking extenuation from the brute alliances of his nature. In short, what the child fancies is really true, though almost the whole world declares it a lie. Man is a child of God; and if he seek His guidance to keep the heart with diligence, it will be so given that all the issues of life may be pure. Life will then be a temple.

> The temple round
> Spread green the pleasant ground;
>   The fair colonnade
> Be of pure marble pillars made;
> Strong to sustain the roof,
>   Time and tempest proof,
> Yet, amidst which, the lightest breeze
>   Can play as it please;
>   The audience hall
>   Be free to all
>   Who revere
> The Power worshipped here,
>   Sole guide of youth
>   Unswerving Truth:
>   In the inmost shrine
>   Stands the image divine,
>   Only seen
> By those whose deeds have worthy been—
>   Priestlike clean.
> Those, who initiated are,
>   Declare,
>   As the hours
> Usher in varying hopes and powers;
>   It changes its face,
>   It changes its age,
>   Now a young beaming Grace,
>   Now Nestorian Sage:*
>   But, to the pure in heart,
>   This shape of primal art
>   In age is fair,
>   In youth seems wise,

> Beyond compare,
> Above surprise;
> What it teaches native seems
> Its new lore our ancient dreams;
> Incense rises from the ground,
> Music flows around;
> Firm rest the feet below, clear gaze the
> eyes above,
> When Truth to point the way through Life
> assumes the wand of Love;
> But, if she cast aside the robe of green,
> Winter's silver sheen,
> White, pure as light,
> Makes gentle shroud as worthy weed as bridal robe had been.[†]

We are now in a transition state, and but few steps have yet been taken. From polygamy, Europe passed to the marriage *de convenance*.* This was scarcely an improvement. An attempt was then made to substitute genuine marriage, (the mutual choice of souls inducing a permanent union,) as yet baffled on every side by the haste, the ignorance, or the impurity of man.

Where man assumes a high principle to which he is not yet ripened; it will happen, for a long time, that the few will be nobler than before; the many worse. Thus now. In the country of Sidney* and Milton, the metropolis is a den of wickedness, and a stye of sensuality; in the country of Lady Russell,* the custom of English Peeresses, of selling their daughters to the highest bidder, is made the theme and jest of fashionable novels by unthinking children who would stare at the idea of sending them to a Turkish slave dealer, though the circumstances of the bargain are there less degrading, as the will and thoughts of the person sold are not so degraded by it, and it is not done in defiance of an acknowledged law of right in the land and the age.

[†] (*As described by the historian.*)
The temple of Juno is like what the character of woman should be.
Columns! graceful decorums, attractive yet sheltering.
Porch! noble inviting aspect of the life.
Kaos! receives the worshippers. See here the statue of the Divinity.
Ophistodomos! Sanctuary where the most precious possessions were kept safe from the hand of the spoiler and the eye of the world. [Fuller's note.]

I must here add that I do not believe there ever was put upon record more depravation of man, and more despicable frivolity of thought and aim in woman, than in the novels which purport to give the picture of English fashionable life, which are read with such favor in our drawing rooms, and give the tone to the manners of some circles. Compared with the hard-hearted cold folly there described, crime is hopeful, for it, at least, shows some power remaining in the mental constitution.

To return: Attention has been awakened among men to the stains of celibacy, and the profanations of marriage. They begin to write about it and lecture about it. It is the tendency now to endeavor to help the erring by showing them the physical law. This is wise and excellent; but forget not the better half. Cold bathing and exercise will not suffice to keep a life pure, without an inward baptism and noble and exhilarating employment for the thoughts and the passions. Early marriages are desirable, but if, (and the world is now so out of joint that there are a hundred thousand chances to one against it,) a man does not early, or at all, find the person to whom he can be united in the marriage of souls, will you give him in the marriage *de convenance*, or if not married, can you find no way for him to lead a virtuous and happy life? Think of it well, ye who think yourselves better than pagans, for many of *them* knew this sure way.[†]

To you, women of America, it is more especially my business to address myself on this subject, and my advice may be classed under three heads:

Clear your souls from the taint of vanity.

Do not rejoice in conquests, either that your power to allure

---

[†] The Persian sacred books, the Desatir, describe the great and holy prince Ky Khosrou, as being 'an angel, and the son of an angel,' one to whom the Supreme says, 'Thou art not absent from before me for one twinkling of an eye. I am never out of thy heart. And I am contained in nothing but in thy heart, and in a heart like thy heart. And I am nearer unto thee than thou art to thyself.' This Prince had in his Golden Seraglio three ladies of surpassing beauty, and all four, in this royal monastery, passed their lives, and left the world, as virgins.

The Persian people had no scepticism when the history of such a mind was narrated. They were Catholics. [Fuller's note.]

may be seen by other women, or for the pleasure of rousing passionate feelings that gratify your love of excitement.

It must happen, no doubt, that frank and generous women will excite love they do not reciprocate, but, in nine cases out of ten, the woman has, half consciously, done much to excite. In this case she shall not be held guiltless, either as to the unhappiness or injury to the lover. Pure love, inspired by a worthy object, must ennoble and bless, whether mutual or not; but that which is excited by coquettish attraction of any grade of refinement, must cause bitterness and doubt, as to the reality of human goodness, so soon as the flush of passion is over. And that you may avoid all taste for these false pleasures

'Steep the soul
In one pure love, and it will last thee long.'*

The love of truth, the love of excellence, which, whether you clothe them in the person of a special object or not, will have power to save you from following Duessa, and lead you in the green glades where Una's feet have trod.*

It was on this one subject that a venerable champion of good, the last representative of the spirit which sanctified the revolution and gave our country such a sunlight of hope in the eyes of the nations, the same who lately in Boston offered anew to the young men the pledge taken by the young men of his day, offered, also, his counsel, on being addressed by the principal of a girl's school, thus:

REPLY OF MR ADAMS*

Mr Adams was so deeply affected by the address of Miss Foster, as to be for some time inaudible. When heard, he spoke as follows:

'This is the first instance in which a lady has thus addressed me personally; and I trust that all the ladies present will be able sufficiently to enter into my feelings to know, that I am more affected by this honor, than by any other I could have received.

'You have been pleased, Madam, to allude to the character of my father,* and the history of my family, and their services to the country. It is indeed true, that from the existence of the Republic as an independent nation, my father and myself have been in the public service of the country, almost without interruption. I came into the world, as a person having personal responsibilities, with the Declaration of Independence, which constituted us a nation. I was a child at that time, and had then perhaps the greatest of blessings that can be bestowed on man—a mother* who was anxious and capable to form her children to what they ought to be. From that mother I derived whatever instruction—religious especially, and moral—has pervaded a long life; I will not say perfectly, and as it ought to be; but I will say, because it is justice only to the memory of her whom I revere, that if, in the course of my life, there has been any imperfection, or deviation from what she taught me, the fault is mine, and not hers.

'With such a mother, and such other relations with the sex, of sister, wife, and daughter, it has been the perpetual instruction of my life to love and revere the female sex. And in order to carry that sentiment of love and reverence to its highest degree of perfection, I know of nothing that exists in human society better adapted to produce that result, than institutions of the character that I have now the honor to address.

'I have been taught, as I have said, through the course of my life, to love and to revere the female sex; but I have been taught, also—and that lesson has perhaps impressed itself on my mind even more strongly, it may be, than the other—I have been taught not to flatter them. It is not unusual in the intercourse of man with the other sex—and especially for young men—to think, that the way to win the hearts of ladies is by flattery.—To love and to revere the sex, is what I think the duty of man; but *not to flatter them*; and this I would say to the young ladies here; and if they, and others present, will allow me, with all the authority which nearly four score years may have with those who have not yet attained one score—I would say to them what I have no doubt they say to themselves, and are taught here, not to take the flattery of men as proof of perfection.

'I am now, however, I fear, assuming too much of a character that does not exactly belong to me. I therefore conclude, by assuring you, Madam, that your reception of me has affected me, as you perceive, more than I can express in words; and that I shall offer my best prayers, till my latest hour, to the Creator of us all, that this institution especially, and all others of a similar kind, designed to form the female mind to wisdom and virtue, may prosper to the end of time.'

It will be interesting to add here the character of Mr Adams's mother, as drawn by her husband, the first John Adams, in a family letter† written just before his death.

'I have reserved for the last the life of Lady Russell. This I have not yet read, because I read it more than forty years ago. On this hangs a tale which you ought to know and communicate it to your children. I bought the life and letters of Lady Russell, in the year 1775, and sent it to your grandmother, with an express intent and desire, that she should consider it a mirror in which to contemplate herself; for, at that time, I thought it extremely probable, from the daring and dangerous career I was determined to run, that she would one day find herself in the situation of Lady Russell, her husband without a head.* This lady was more beautiful than Lady Russell, had a brighter genius, more information, a more refined taste, and, at least, her equal in the virtues of the heart; equal fortitude and firmness of character, equal resignation to the will of Heaven, equal in all the virtues and graces of the christian life. Like Lady Russell, she never, by word or look, discouraged me from running all hazards for the salvation of my country's liberties; she was willing to share with me, and that her children should share with us both, in all the dangerous consequences we had to hazard.'

Will a woman who loves flattery or an aimless excitement, who wastes the flower of her mind on transitory sentiments, ever be loved with a love like that, when fifty years trial have entitled to the privileges of 'the golden marriage?'

Such was the love of the iron-handed warrior for her, not his hand-maid, but his help-meet:

'Whom God loves, to him gives he such a wife.'

I find the whole of what I want in this relation, in the two epithets by which Milton makes Adam address *his* wife.

† Journal and Correspondence of Miss Adams, vol. i, p. 246. [Fuller's note.]*

In the intercourse of every day he begins:

'Daughter of God and man, *accomplished* Eve.'†

In a moment of stronger feeling,

'Daughter of God and man, IMMORTAL Eve.'*

What majesty in the cadence of the line; what dignity, what reverence in the attitude, both of giver and receiver!

The woman who permits, in her life, the alloy of vanity; the woman who lives upon flattery, coarse or fine, shall never be thus addressed. She is *not* immortal as far as her will is concerned, and every woman who dose so creates miasma, whose spread is indefinite. The hand, which casts into the waters of life a stone of offence, knows not how far the circles thus caused, may spread their agitations.

A little while since, I was at one of the most fashionable places of public resort. I saw there many women, dressed without regard to the season or the demands of the place, in apery, or, as it looked, in mockery of European fashions. I saw their eyes restlessly courting attention. I saw the way in which it was paid, the style of devotion, almost an open sneer, which it pleased those ladies to receive from men whose expression marked their own low position in the moral and intellectual world. Those women went to their pillows with their heads full of folly, their hearts of jealousy, or gratified vanity: those men, with the low opinion they already entertained of woman confirmed. These were American *ladies*; i.e., they were of that class who have wealth and leisure to make full use of the day, and confer benefits on others. They were of that class whom the possession of external advantages makes of pernicious example to many, if these advantages be misused.

Soon after, I met a circle of women, stamped by society as among the most degraded of their sex. 'How,' it was asked of them, 'did you come here?' for, by the society that I saw in the former place, they were shut up in a prison. The causes were not difficult to trace: love of dress, love of flattery, love of excitement. They had not dresses like the other ladies, so they

† See Appendix H. [Fuller's note.]

stole them; they could not pay for flattery by distinctions, and the dower of a worldly marriage, so they paid by the profanation of their persons. In excitement, more and more madly sought from day to day, they drowned the voice of conscience.

Now I ask you, my sisters, if the women at the fashionable house be not answerable for those women being in the prison?

As to position in the world of souls, we may suppose the women of the prison stood fairest, both because they had misused less light, and because loneliness and sorrow had brought some of them to feel the need of better life, nearer truth and good. This was no merit in them, being an effect of circumstance, but it was hopeful. But you, my friends, (and some of you I have already met,) consecrate yourselves without waiting for reproof, in free love and unbroken energy, to win and to diffuse a better life. Offer beauty, talents, riches, on the altar; thus shall ye keep spotless your own hearts, and be visibly or invisibly the angels to others.

I would urge upon those women who have not yet considered this subject, to do so. Do not forget the unfortunates who dare not cross your guarded way. If it do not suit you to act with those who have organized measures of reform, then hold not yourself excused from acting in private. Seek out these degraded women, give them tender sympathy, counsel, employment. Take the place of mothers, such as might have saved them originally.

If you can do little for those already under the ban of the world, and the best considered efforts have often failed, from a want of strength in those unhappy ones to bear up against the sting of shame and the prejudices of the world, which makes them seek oblivion again in their old excitements, you will at least leave a sense of love and justice in their hearts that will prevent their becoming utterly embittered and corrupt. And you may learn the means of prevention for those yet uninjured. There will be found in a diffusion of mental culture, simple tastes, best taught by your example, a genuine self-respect, and above all, what the influence of man tends to hide from woman, the love and fear of a divine, in preference to a human tribunal.

But suppose you save many who would have lost their bodily innocence (for as to mental, the loss of that is incalculably more general,) through mere vanity and folly; there still remain many, the prey and spoil of the brute passions of man. For the stories frequent in our newspapers outshame antiquity, and vie with the horrors of war.

As to this, it must be considered that, as the vanity and proneness to seduction of the imprisoned women represented a general degradation in their sex; so do these acts a still more general and worse in the male. Where so many are weak it is natural there should be many lost, where legislators admit that ten thousand prostitutes are a fair proportion to one city, and husbands tell their wives that it is folly to expect chastity from men, it is inevitable that there should be many monsters of vice.

I must in this place mention, with respect and gratitude, the conduct of Mrs Child in the case of Amelia Norman.* The action and speech of this lady was of straight-forward nobleness, undeterred by custom or cavil from duty towards an injured sister. She showed the case and the arguments the counsel against the prisoner had the assurance to use in their true light to the public. She put the case on the only ground of religion and equity. She was successful in arresting the attention of many who had before shrugged their shoulders, and let sin pass as necessarily a part of the company of men. They begin to ask whether virtue is not possible, perhaps necessary, to man as well as to woman. They begin to fear that the perdition of a woman must involve that of a man. This is a crisis. The results of this case will be important.

In this connection I must mention Eugene Sue,* the French novelist, several of whose works have been lately transplanted among us, as having the true spirit of reform as to women. Like every other French writer, he is still tainted with the transmissions of the old regime. Still falsehood may be permitted for the sake of advancing truth, evil as the way to good. Even George Sand, who would trample on every graceful decorum, and every human law for the sake of a sincere life, does not see that she violates it by making her heroines able to tell falsehoods in a good cause. These French writers need ever to be confronted by the clear perception of the English and German mind, that the only good man, consequently the only good reformer, is he

'Who bases good on good alone, and owes
To virtue every triumph that he knows.'*

Still, Sue has the heart of a reformer, and especially towards women, he sees what they need, and what causes are injuring them. From the histories of Fleur de Marie and La Louve, from the lovely and independent character of Rigolette, from the distortion given to Matilda's* mind, by the present views of marriage, and from the truly noble and immortal character of the 'hump-backed Sempstress' in the 'Wandering Jew,' may be gathered much that shall elucidate doubt and direct inquiry on this subject. In reform, as in philosophy, the French are the interpreters to the civilized world. Their own attainments are not great, but they make clear the past, and break down barriers to the future.

Observe that the good man of Sue is pure as Sir Charles Grandison.*

Apropos to Sir Charles, women are accustomed to be told by men that the reform is to come *from them*. 'You,' say the men, 'must frown upon vice, you must decline the attentions of the corrupt, you must not submit to the will of your husband when it seems to you unworthy, but give the laws in marriage, and redeem it from its present sensual and mental pollutions.'

This seems to us hard. Men have, indeed, been, for more than a hundred years, rating women for countenancing vice. But at the same time, they have carefully hid from them its nature, so that the preference often shown by women for bad men, arises rather from a confused idea that they are bold and adventurous, acquainted with regions which women are forbidden to explore, and the curiosity that ensues, than a corrupt heart in the woman. As to marriage it has been inculcated on women for centuries, that men have not only stronger passions than they, but of a sort that it would be shameful for them to share or even understand. That, therefore, they must 'confide in their husbands,' i.e., submit implicitly to their will. That the least appearance of coldness or withdrawal, from whatever cause, in the wife is wicked, because liable to turn her husband's thoughts to illicit indulgence; for a man is so constituted that he must indulge his passions or die!

Accordingly a great part of women look upon men as a kind of wild beasts, but 'suppose they are all alike;' the unmarried are assured by the married that, 'if they knew men as they do,' i.e., by being married to them, 'they would not expect continence or self-government from them.'

I might accumulate illustrations on this theme, drawn from acquaintance with the histories of women, which would startle and grieve all thinking men, but I forbear. Let Sir Charles Grandison preach to his own sex, or if none there be, who feels himself able to speak with authority from a life unspotted in will or deed, let those who are convinced of the practicability and need of a pure life, as the foreign artist was, advise the others, and warn them by their own example, if need be.

The following passage from a female writer on female affairs, expresses a prevalent way of thinking on this subject.

'It may be that a young woman, exempt from all motives of vanity, determines to take for a husband a man who does not inspire her with a very decided inclination. Imperious circumstances, the evident interest of her family, or the danger of a suffering celibacy, may explain such a resolution. If, however, she were to endeavor to surmount a personal repugnance, we should look upon this as *injudicious*. Such a rebellion of nature marks the limit that the influence of parents, or the self-sacrifice of the young girl, should never pass. *We shall be told that this repugnance is an affair of the imagination*; it may be so; but imagination is a power which it is temerity to brave; and its antipathy is more difficult to conquer than its preference.'[†]

Among ourselves, the exhibition of such a repugnance from a woman who had been given in marriage 'by advice of friends,' was treated by an eminent physician as sufficient proof of insanity. If he had said sufficient cause for it, he would have been nearer right.

It has been suggested by men who were pained by seeing bad men admitted, freely, to the society of modest women, thereby encouraged to vice by impunity, and corrupting the atmosphere of homes; that there should be a senate of the matrons in each

---

[†] Madame Necker de Saussure. [Fuller's note.]

city and town, who should decide what candidates were fit for admission to their houses and the society of their daughters.[†]

Such a plan might have excellent results, but it argues a moral dignity and decision, which does not yet exist, and needs to be induced by knowledge and reflection. It has been the tone to keep women ignorant on these subjects, or when they were not, to command that they should seem so. 'It is indelicate,' says the father or husband, 'to inquire into the private character of such an one. It is sufficient that I do not think him unfit to visit you.' And so, this man, who would not tolerate these pages in his house, 'unfit for family reading,' because they speak plainly, introduces there a man whose shame is written on his brow, as well as the open secret of the whole town, and, presently, if *respectable* still, and rich enough, gives him his daughter to wife. The mother affects ignorance, 'supposing he is no worse than most men.' The daughter *is* ignorant; something in the mind of the new spouse seems strange to her, but she supposes it is 'woman's lot' not to be perfectly happy in her affections; she has always heard, 'men could not understand women,' so she weeps alone, or takes to dress and the duties of the house. The husband, of course, makes no avowal, and dreams of no redemption.

'In the heart of every young woman,' says the female writer, above quoted, addressing herself to the husband, 'depend upon it, there is a fund of exalted ideas; she conceals, represses, without succeeding in smothering them. *So long as these ideas in your wife are directed to* YOU, *they are, no doubt, innocent*, but take care that they be not accompanied with *too much* pain. In other respects, also, spare her delicacy. Let all the antecedent parts of your life, if there are such, which would give her pain, be concealed from her; *her happiness and her respect for you would suffer from this misplaced confidence*. Allow her to retain that flower of purity, *which should distinguish her in your eyes from every other woman*.' We should think so, truly, under this canon. Such a man must esteem purity an exotic that could only be

---

[†] See Goethe's Tasso. 'A synod of good women should decide,'—if the golden age is to be restored. [Fuller's note.]

preserved by the greatest care. Of the degree of mental intimacy possible, in such a marriage, let everyone judge for himself!

On this subject, let every woman, who has once begun to think, examine herself, see whether she does not suppose virtue possible and necessary to man, and whether she would not desire for her son a virtue which aimed at a fitness for a divine life, and involved, if not asceticism, that degree of power over the lower self, which shall 'not exterminate the passions, but keep them chained at the feet of reason.' The passions, like fire, are a bad master; but confine them to the hearth and the altar, and they give life to the social economy, and make each sacrifice meet for heaven.

When many women have thought upon this subject, some will be fit for the Senate, and one such Senate in operation would affect the morals of the civilized world.

At present I look to the young. As preparatory to the Senate, I should like to see a society of novices, such as the world has never yet seen, bound by no oath, wearing no badge. In place of an oath they should have a religious faith in the capacity of man for virtue; instead of a badge, should wear in the heart a firm resolve not to stop short of the destiny promised him as a son of God. Their service should be action and conservatism, not of old habits, but of a better nature, enlightened by hopes that daily grow brighter.

If sin was to remain in the world, it should not be by their connivance at its stay, or one moment's concession to its claims.

They should succor the oppressed, and pay to the upright the reverence due in hero-worship by seeking to emulate them. They would not denounce the willingly bad, but they could not be with them, for the two classes could not breathe the same atmosphere.

They would heed no detention from the time-serving, the worldly and the timid.

They could love no pleasures that were not innocent and capable of good fruit.

I saw, in a foreign paper, the title now given to a party abroad, 'Los Exaltados.' Such would be the title now given these children by the world: Los Exaltados, Las Exaltadas;* but the world would not sneer always, for from them would issue a virtue by which it would, at last, be exalted too.

I have in my eye a youth and a maiden whom I look to as the nucleus of such a class. They are both in early youth, both as yet uncontaminated, both aspiring without rashness, both thoughtful, both capable of deep affection, both of strong nature and sweet feelings, both capable of large mental development. They reside in different regions of earth, but their place in the soul is the same. To them I look, as, perhaps, the harbingers and leaders of a new era, for never yet have I known minds so truly virgin, without narrowness or ignorance.

When men call upon women to redeem them, they mean such maidens. But such are not easily formed under the present influences of society. As there are more such young men to help give a different tone, there will be more such maidens.

The English novelist, D'Israeli,* has, in his novel of the 'Young Duke,' made a man of the most depraved stock be redeemed by a woman who despises him when he has only the brilliant mask of fortune and beauty to cover the poverty of his heart and brain, but knows how to encourage him when he enters on a better course. But this woman was educated by a father who valued character in women.

Still there will come now and then, one who will, as I hope of my young Exaltada, be example and instruction to the rest. It was not the opinion of woman current among Jewish men that formed the character of the mother of Jesus.

Since the sliding and backsliding men of the world, no less than the mystics, declare that, as through woman man was lost, so through woman must man be redeemed, the time must be at hand. When she knows herself indeed as 'accomplished,' still more as 'immortal Eve,' this may be.

As an immortal, she may also know and inspire immortal love, a happiness not to be dreamed of under the circumstances advised in the last quotation. Where love is based on conceal-ment, it must, of course, disappear when the soul enters the scene of clear vision!

And, without this hope, how worthless every plan, every bond, every power!

'The giants,' said the Scandinavian Saga, 'had induced Loke, (the spirit that hovers between good and ill,) to steal for them Iduna, (Goddess of Immortality,) and her apples of pure gold. He lured her out, by promising to show, on a marvellous tree he had discovered, apples beautiful as her own, if she would only take them with her for a comparison. Thus, having lured her beyond the heavenly domain, she was seized and carried away captive by the powers of misrule.'

As now the gods could not find their friend Iduna, they were confused with grief; indeed they began visibly to grow old and gray. Discords arose, and love grew cold. Indeed, Odur, spouse of the goddess of love and beauty, wandered away and returned no more. At last, however, the gods, discovering the treachery of Loke, obliged him to win back Iduna from the prison in which she sat mourning. He changed himself into a falcon, and brought her back as a swallow, fiercely pursued by the Giant King, in the form of an eagle. So she strives to return among us, light and small as a swallow. We must welcome her form as the speck on the sky that assures the glad blue of Summer. Yet one swallow does not make a summer. Let us solicit them in flights and flocks!

Returning from the future to the present, let us see what forms Iduna takes, as she moves along the declivity of centuries to the valley where the lily flower may concentrate all its fragrance.

It would seem as if this time were not very near to one fresh from books, such as I have of late been—no: *not* reading, but sighing over. A crowd of books having been sent me since my friends knew me to be engaged in this way, on Woman's 'Sphere,' Woman's 'Mission,' and Woman's 'Destiny,' I believe that almost all that is extant of formal precept has come under my eye. Among these I read with refreshment, a little one called 'The Whole Duty of Woman,'* 'indited by a noble lady at the request of a noble lord,' and which has this much of nobleness, that the view it takes is a religious one. It aims to fit woman for heaven, the main bent of most of the others is to fit her to please, or, at least, not to disturb a husband.

Among these I select as a favorable specimen, the book I have already quoted, 'The Study† of the Life of Woman, by Madame Necker de Saussure,* of Geneva, translated from the

† This title seems to be incorrectly translated from the French. I have not seen the original. [Fuller's note.]

French.' This book was published at Philadelphia, and has been read with much favor here. Madame Necker is the cousin of Madame de Staël, and has taken from her works the motto prefixed to this.

'Cette vie n'a quelque prix que si elle sert à' l'éducation morale de notre cœur.'*

Mme Necker is, by nature, capable of entire consistency in the application of this motto, and, therefore, the qualifications she makes, in the instructions given to her own sex, show forcibly the weight which still paralyzes and distorts the energies of that sex.

The book is rich in passages marked by feeling and good suggestions, but taken in the whole the impression it leaves is this:

Woman is, and *shall remain* inferior to man and subject to his will, and, in endeavoring to aid her, we must anxiously avoid any thing that can be misconstrued into expression of the contrary opinion, else the men will be alarmed, and combine to defeat our efforts.

The present is a good time for these efforts, for men are less occupied about women than formerly. Let us, then, seize upon the occasion, and do what we can to make our lot tolerable. But we must sedulously avoid encroaching on the territory of man. If we study natural history, our observations may be made useful, by some male naturalist; if we draw well, we may make our services acceptable to the artists. But our names must not be known, and, to bring these labors to any result, we must take some man for our head, and be his hands.

The lot of woman is sad. She is constituted to expect and need a happiness that cannot exist on earth. She must stifle such aspirations within her secret heart, and fit herself, as well as she can, for a life of resignations and consolations.

She will be very lonely while living with her husband. She must not expect to open her heart to him fully, or that, after marriage, he will be capable of the refined service of love. The man is not born for the woman, only the woman for the man. 'Men cannot understand the hearts of women.' The life of woman must be outwardly a well-intentioned, cheerful dis- simulation of her real life.

Naturally, the feelings of the mother, at the birth of a female child, resemble those of the Paraguay woman, described by Southey as lamenting in such heart-breaking tones that her mother did not kill her the hour she was born. 'Her mother, who knew what the life of a woman must be;'—or those women seen at the north by Sir A. Mackenzie,* who performed this pious duty towards female infants whenever they had an opportunity.

'After the first delight, the young mother experiences feelings a little different, according as the birth of a son or a daughter has been announced.

'Is it a son? A sort of glory swells at this thought the heart of the mother; she seems to feel that she is entitled to gratitude. She has given a citizen, a defender to her country. To her husband an heir of his name, to herself a protector. And yet the contrast of all these fine titles with this being, so humble, soon strikes her. At the aspect of this frail treasure, opposite feelings agitate her heart; she seems to recognize in him *a nature superior to her own*, but subjected to a low condition, and she honors a future greatness in the object of extreme compassion. Somewhat of that respect and adoration for a feeble child, of which some fine pictures offer the expression in the features of the happy Mary, seem reproduced with the young mother who has given birth to a son.

'Is it a daughter? There is usually a slight degree of regret; so deeply rooted is the idea of the superiority of man in happiness and dignity, and yet, as she looks upon this child, she is more and more *softened* towards it—a deep sympathy—a sentiment of identity with this delicate being takes possession of her; an extreme pity for so much weakness, a more pressing need of prayer stirs her heart. Whatever sorrows she may have felt, she dreads for her daughter; but she will guide her to become much wiser, much better than herself. And then the gayety, the frivolity of the young woman have their turn. This little creature is a flower to cultivate, a doll to decorate.'

Similar sadness at the birth of a daughter I have heard mothers express not unfrequently.

As to this living so entirely for men, I should think when it was proposed to women they would feel, at least, some spark of the old spirit of races allied to our own. If he is to be my bridegroom *and lord*, cries Brunhilda,*† he must first be able to pass through fire and water. I will serve at the banquet, says the Valkyrie, but only him who, in the trial of deadly combat, has shown himself a hero.

If women are to be bond-maids, let it be to men superior to women in fortitude, in aspiration, in moral power, in refined sense of beauty! You who give yourselves 'to be supported,' or because 'one must love something,' are they who make the lot of the sex such that mothers are sad when daughters are born.

It marks the state of feeling on this subject that it was mentioned, as a bitter censure on a woman who had influence over those younger than herself. 'She makes those girls want to see heroes!'

'And will that hurt them?'

'Certainly; how *can* you ask? They will find none, and so they will never be married.'

'*Get* married' is the usual phrase, and the one that correctly indicates the thought, but the speakers, on this occasion, were persons too outwardly refined to use it. They were ashamed of the word, but not of the thing. Madame Necker, however, sees good possible in celibacy.

Indeed, I know not how the subject could be better illustrated, than by separating the wheat from the chaff in Madame Necker's book; place them in two heaps and then summon the reader to choose; giving him first a near-sighted glass to examine the two; it might be a christian, an astronomical, or an artistic glass, any kind of good glass to obviate acquired defects in the eye. I would lay any wager on the result.

But time permits not here a prolonged analysis. I have given the clues for fault-finding.

As a specimen of the good take the following passage, on the phenomena of what I have spoken of, as the lyrical or electric element in woman.

'Women have been seen to show themselves poets in the most pathetic pantomimic scenes, where all the passions were depicted full of beauty; and these poets used a language un-

---

† See the Nibelungen Lays. [Fuller's note.]

known to themselves, and the performance once over, their inspiration was a forgotten dream. Without doubt there is an interior development to beings so gifted, but their sole mode of communication with us is their talent. They are, in all besides, the inhabitants of another planet.'

Similar observations have been made by those who have seen the women at Irish wakes, or the funeral ceremonies of modern Greece or Brittany, at times when excitement gave the impulse to genius; but, apparently, without a thought that these rare powers belonged to no other planet, but were a high development of the growth of this, and might by wise and reverent treatment, be made to inform and embellish the scenes of every day. But, when woman has her fair chance, they will do so, and the poem of the hour will vie with that of the ages. I come now with satisfaction to my own country, and to a writer, a female writer, whom I have selected as the clearest, wisest, and kindliest, who has as yet, used pen here on these subjects. This is Miss Sedgwick.*

Miss Sedgwick, though she inclines to the private path, and wishes that, by the cultivation of character, might should vindicate right, sets limits nowhere, and her objects and inducements are pure. They are the free and careful cultivation of the powers that have been given, with an aim at moral and intellectual perfection. Her speech is moderate and sane, but never palsied by fear or sceptical caution.

Herself a fine example of the independent and beneficent existence that intellect and character can give to woman, no less than man, if she know how to seek and prize it; also that the intellect need not absorb or weaken, but rather will refine and invigorate the affections, the teachings of her practical good sense come with great force, and cannot fail to avail much. Every way her writings please me both as to the means and the ends. I am pleased at the stress she lays on observance of the physical laws, because the true reason is given. Only in a strong and clean body can the soul do its message fitly.

She shows the meaning of the respect paid to personal neatness both in the indispensable form of cleanliness, and of that love of order and arrangement, that must issue from a true harmony of feeling.

The praises of cold water seem to me an excellent sign in the age. They denote a tendency to the true life. We are now to have, as a remedy for ills, not orvietan, or opium, or any quack medicine, but plenty of air and water, with due attention to warmth and freedom in dress, and simplicity of diet.

Every day we observe signs that the natural feelings on these subjects are about to be reinstated, and the body to claim care as the abode and organ of the soul, not as the tool of servile labor, or the object of voluptuous indulgence.

A poor woman who had passed through the lowest grades of ignominy, seemed to think she had never been wholly lost, 'for,' said she, 'I would always have good underclothes;' and, indeed, who could doubt that this denoted the remains of private self-respect in the mind?

A woman of excellent sense said, 'it might seem childish, but to her one of the most favorable signs of the times, was that the ladies had been persuaded to give up corsets.'

Yes! let us give up all artificial means of distortion. Let life be healthy, pure, all of a piece. Miss Sedgwick, in teaching that domestics must have the means of bathing as much as their mistresses, and time, too, to bathe, has symbolized one of the most important of human rights.

Another interesting sign of the time is the influence exercised by two women, Miss Martineau and Miss Barrett,* from their sick rooms. The lamp of life which, if it had been fed only by the affections, depended on precarious human relations, would scarce have been able to maintain a feeble glare in the lonely prison, now shines far and wide over the nations, cheering fellow sufferers and hallowing the joy of the healthful.

These persons need not health or youth, or the charms of personal presence, to make their thoughts available. A few more such, and old woman† shall not be the synonym for imbecility, nor old maid a term of contempt, nor woman be spoken of as a reed shaken in the wind.

It is time, indeed, that men and women both should cease to grow old in any other way than as the tree does, full of grace and honor. The hair of the artist turns white, but his eye shines

† An apposite passage is quoted in Appendix F. [Fuller's note.]

clearer than ever, and we feel that age brings him maturity, not decay. So would it be with all were the springs of immortal refreshment but unsealed within the soul, then like these women they would see, from the lonely chamber window, the glories of the universe; or, shut in darkness, be visited by angels.

I now touch on my own place and day, and, as I write, events are occurring that threaten the fair fabric approached by so long an avenue. Week before last the Gentile was requested to aid the Jew to return to Palestine, for the Millennium, the reign of the Son of Mary, was near. Just now, at high and solemn mass, thanks were returned to the Virgin for having delivered O'Connell* from unjust imprisonment, in requital of his having consecrated to her the league formed in behalf of Liberty on Tara's Hill. But, last week brought news which threatens that a cause identical with the enfranchisement of Jews, Irish, women, ay, and of Americans in general, too, is in danger, for the choice of the people threatens to rivet the chains of slavery and the leprosy of sin permanently on this nation, through the annexation of Texas!*

Ah! if this should take place, who will dare again to feel the throb of heavenly hope, as to the destiny of this country? The noble thought that gave unity to all our knowledge, harmony to all our designs;—the thought that the progress of history had brought on the era, the tissue of prophecies pointed out the spot, where humanity was, at last, to have a fair chance to know itself, and all men be born free and equal for the eagle's flight, flutters as if about to leave the breast, which, deprived of it, will have no more a nation, no more a home on earth.

Women of my country!—Exaltadas! if such there be,— Women of English, old English nobleness, who understand the courage of Boadicea, the sacrifice of Godiva, the power of Queen Emma to tread the red hot iron unharmed. Women who share the nature of Mrs Hutchinson,* Lady Russell, and the mothers of our own revolution: have you nothing to do with this? You see the men, how they are willing to sell shamelessly, the happiness of countless generations of fellow-creatures, the honor of their country, and their immortal souls, for a money market and political power. Do you not feel within you that which can reprove them, which can check, which can convince them? You would not speak in vain; whether each in her own home, or banded in unison.

Tell these men that you will not accept the glittering baubles, spacious dwellings, and plentiful service, they mean to offer you through these means. Tell them that the heart of women demands nobleness and honor in man, and that, if they have not purity, have not mercy, they are no longer fathers, lovers, husbands, sons of yours.

This cause is your own,* for as I have before said, there is a reason why the foes of African slavery seek more freedom for women;* but put it not upon that ground, but on the ground of right.

If you have a power, it is a moral power. The films of interest are not so close around you as around the men. If you will but think, you cannot fail to wish to save the country from this disgrace. Let not slip the occasion, but do something to lift off the curse incurred by Eve.

You have heard the women engaged in the abolition movement accused of boldness, because they lifted the voice in public, and lifted the latch of the stranger. But were these acts, whether performed judiciously or no, *so* bold as to dare before God and man to partake the fruits of such offence as this?

You hear much of the modesty of your sex. Preserve it by filling the mind with noble desires that shall ward off the corruptions of vanity and idleness. A profligate woman, who left her accustomed haunts and took service in a New-York boarding-house, said 'she had never heard talk so vile at the Five Points,* as from the ladies at the boarding-house.' And why? Because they were idle; because, having nothing worthy to engage them, they dwelt, with unnatural curiosity, on the ill they dared not go to see.

It will not so much injure your modesty to have your name, by the unthinking, coupled with idle blame, as to have upon your soul the weight of not trying to save a whole race of women from the scorn that is put upon *their* modesty.

Think of this well! I entreat, I conjure you, before it is too late. It is my belief that something effectual might be done by women, if they would only consider the subject, and enter upon it in the true spirit, a spirit gentle, but firm, and which feared the offence of none, save One who is of purer eyes than to behold iniquity.

And now I have designated in outline, if not in fulness, the stream which is ever flowing from the heights of my thought.

In the earlier tract,* I was told, I did not make my meaning sufficiently clear. In this I have consequently tried to illustrate it in various ways, and may have been guilty of much repetition. Yet, as I am anxious to leave no room for doubt, I shall venture to retrace, once more, the scope of my design in points, as was done in old-fashioned sermons.*

Man is a being of two-fold relations, to nature beneath, and intelligences above him. The earth is his school, if not his birth-place: God his object: life and thought, his means of interpreting nature, and aspiring to God.

Only a fraction of this purpose is accomplished in the life of any one man. Its entire accomplishment is to be hoped only from the sum of the lives of men, or man considered as a whole.

As this whole has one soul and one body, any injury or obstruction to a part, or to the meanest member, affects the whole. Man can never be perfectly happy or virtuous, till all men are so.

To address man wisely, you must not forget that his life is partly animal, subject to the same laws with nature.

But you cannot address him wisely unless you consider him still more as soul, and appreciate the conditions and destiny of soul.

The growth of man is two-fold, masculine and feminine.

As far as these two methods can be distinguished they are so as

Energy and Harmony.

Power and Beauty.

Intellect and Love.

Or by some such rude classification, for we have not language primitive and pure enough to express such ideas with precision.

These two sides are supposed to be expressed in man and woman, that is, as the more and less, for the faculties have not been given pure to either, but only in preponderance. There are also exceptions in great number, such as men of far more beauty than power, and the reverse. But as a general rule, it seems to have been the intention to give a preponderance on the one side, that is called masculine, and on the other, one that is called feminine.

There cannot be a doubt that, if these two developments were in perfect harmony, they would correspond to and fulfil one another, like hemispheres, or the tenor and bass in music.

But there is no perfect harmony in human nature; and the two parts answer one another only now and then, or, if there be a persistent consonance, it can only be traced, at long intervals, instead of discoursing an obvious melody.

What is the cause of this?

Man, in the order of time, was developed first; as energy comes before harmony; power before beauty.

Woman was therefore under his care as an elder. He might have been her guardian and teacher.

But as human nature goes not straight forward, but by excessive action and then reaction in an undulated course, he misunderstood and abused his advantages, and became her temporal master instead of her spiritual sire.

On himself came the punishment. He educated woman more as a servant than a daughter, and found himself a king without a queen.*

The children of this unequal union showed unequal natures, and, more and more, men seemed sons of the handmaid, rather than princes.

At last there were so many Ishmaelites that the rest grew frightened and indignant. They laid the blame on Hagar, and drove her forth into the wilderness.

But there were none the fewer Ishmaelites for that.

At last men became a little wiser, and saw that the infant Moses was, in every case, saved by the pure instincts of woman's breast. For, as too much adversity is better for the moral nature than too much prosperity, woman, in this respect, dwindled less than man, though in other respects, still a child in leading strings.

So man did her more and more justice, and grew more and more kind.

But yet, his habits and his will corrupted by the past, he did not clearly see that woman was half himself, that her interests were identical with his, and that, by the law of their common being, he could never reach his true proportions while she remained in any wise shorn of hers.

And so it has gone on to our day; both ideas developing, but more slowly than they would under a clearer recognition of truth and justice, which would have permitted the sexes their due influence on one another, and mutual improvement from more dignified relations.

Wherever there was pure love, the natural influences were, for the time, restored.

Wherever the poet or artist gave free course to his genius, he saw the truth, and expressed it in worthy forms, for these men especially share and need the feminine principle. The divine birds need to be brooded into life and song by mothers.

Wherever religion (I mean the thirst for truth and good, not the love of sect and dogma,) had its course, the original design was apprehended in its simplicity, and the dove presaged sweetly from Dodona's oak.*

I have aimed to show that no age was left entirely without a witness of the equality of the sexes in function, duty and hope.

Also that, when there was unwillingness or ignorance, which prevented this being acted upon, women had not the less power for their want of light and noble freedom. But it was power which hurt alike them and those against whom they made use of the arms of the servile; cunning, blandishment, and unreasonable emotion.

That now the time has come when a clearer vision and better action are possible. When man and woman may regard one another as brother and sister, the pillars of one porch, the priests of one worship.

I have believed and intimated that this hope would receive an ampler fruition, than ever before, in our own land.

And it will do so if this land carry out the principles from which sprang our national life.

I believe that, at present, women are the best helpers of one another.

Let them think; let them act; till they know what they need.

We only ask of men to remove arbitrary barriers. Some would

like to do more. But I believe it needs for woman to show herself in her native dignity, to teach them how to aid her; their minds are so encumbered by tradition.

When Lord Edward Fitzgerald* travelled with the Indians, his manly heart obliged him at once, to take the packs from the squaws and carry them. But we do not read that the red men followed his example, though they are ready enough to carry the pack of the white woman, because she seems to them a superior being.

Let woman appear in the mild majesty of Ceres, and rudest churls will be willing to learn from her.

You ask, what use will she make of liberty, when she has so long been sustained and restrained?

I answer; in the first place, this will not be suddenly given. I read yesterday a debate of this year on the subject of enlarging women's rights over property. It was a leaf from the class-book that is preparing for the needed instruction. The men learned visibly as they spoke. The champions of woman saw the fallacy of arguments, on the opposite side, and were startled by their own convictions. With their wives at home, and the readers of the paper, it was the same. And so the stream flows on; thought urging action, and action leading to the evolution of still better thought.

But, were this freedom to come suddenly, I have no fear of the consequences. Individuals might commit excesses, but there is not only in the sex a reverence for decorums and limits inherited and enhanced from generation to generation, which many years of other life could not efface, but a native love, in woman as woman, of proportion, of 'the simple art of not too much,' a Greek moderation, which would create immediately a restraining party, the natural legislators and instructors of the rest, and would gradually establish such rules as are needed to guard, without impeding, life.

The Graces would lead the choral dance, and teach the rest to regulate their steps to the measure of beauty.

But if you ask me what offices they may fill; I reply—any. I do not care what case you put; let them be sea-captains, if you will.* I do not doubt there are women well fitted for such an office, and, if so, I should be glad to see them in it, as to welcome the maid of Saragossa, or the maid of Missolonghi, or the Suliote heroine,* or Emily Plater.

I think women need, especially at this juncture, a much greater range of occupation than they have, to rouse their latent powers. A party of travellers lately visited a lonely hut on a mountain. There they found an old woman that told them she and her husband had lived there forty years. 'Why,' they said, 'did you choose so barren a spot?' She 'did not know; *it was the man's notion.*'

And, during forty years, she had been content to act, without knowing why, upon 'the man's notion.' I would not have it so.

In families that I know, some little girls like to saw wood, others to use carpenters' tools. Where these tastes are indulged, cheerfulness and good humor are promoted. Where they are forbidden, because 'such things are not proper for girls,' they grow sullen and mischievous.

Fourier had observed these wants of women, as no one can fail to do who watches the desires of little girls, or knows the ennui that haunts grown women, except where they make to themselves a serene little world by art of some kind. He, therefore, in proposing a great variety of employments, in manufactures or the care of plants and animals, allows for one third of woman, as likely to have a taste for masculine pursuits, one third of men for feminine.

Who does not observe the immediate glow and serenity that is diffused over the life of women, before restless or fretful, by engaging in gardening, building, or the lowest department of art. Here is something that is not routine, something that draws forth life toward the infinite.

I have no doubt, however, that a large proportion of women would give themselves to the same employments as now, because there are circumstances that must lead them. Mothers will delight to make the nest soft and warm. Nature would take care of that; no need to clip the wings of any bird that wants to soar and sing, or finds in itself the strength of pinion for a migratory flight unusual to its kind. The difference would be that *all* need not be constrained to employments, for which *some* are unfit.

I have urged upon the sex self-subsistence in its two forms of self-reliance and self-impulse, because I believe them to be the needed means of the present juncture.

I have urged on woman independence of man, not that I do not think the sexes mutually needed by one another, but because in woman this fact has led to an excessive devotion, which has cooled love, degraded marriage, and prevented either sex from being what it should be to itself or the other.

I wish woman to live, *first* for God's sake. Then she will not make an imperfect man her god, and thus sink to idolatry. Then she will not take what is not fit for her from a sense of weakness and poverty. Then, if she finds what she needs in man embodied, she will know how to love, and be worthy of being loved.

By being more a soul, she will not be less woman, for nature is perfected through spirit.

Now there is no woman, only an overgrown child.

That her hand may be given with dignity, she must be able to stand alone. I wish to see men and women capable of such relations as are depicted by Landor in his Pericles and Aspasia, where grace is the natural garb of strength, and the affections are calm, because deep. The softness is that of a firm tissue, as when

> 'The gods approve
> The depth, but not the tumult of the soul,
> A fervent, not ungovernable love.'*

A profound thinker* has said, 'no married woman can represent the female world, for she belongs to her husband. The idea of woman must be represented by a virgin.'

But that is the very fault of marriage, and of the present relation between the sexes, that the woman does belong to the man, instead of forming a whole with him. Were it otherwise, there would be no such limitation to the thought.

Woman, self-centred, would never be absorbed by any relation; it would be only an experience to her as to man. It is a vulgar error that love, *a* love to woman is her whole existence; she also is born for Truth and Love in their universal energy. Would she but assume her inheritance, Mary would not be the only virgin mother. Not Manzoni alone would celebrate in his wife the virgin mind with the maternal wisdom and conjugal affections. The soul is ever young, ever virgin.

And will not she soon appear? The woman who shall vindicate their birthright for all women; who shall teach them what to claim, and how to use what they obtain? Shall not her name be for her era Victoria, for her country and life Virginia? Yet predictions are rash; she herself must teach us to give her the fitting name.

An idea not unknown to ancient times has of late been revived, that, in the metamorphoses of life, the soul assumes the form, first of man, then of woman, and takes the chances, and reaps the benefits of either lot. Why then, say some, lay such emphasis on the rights or needs of woman? What she wins not, as woman, will come to her as man.

That makes no difference. It is not woman, but the law of right, the law of growth, that speaks in us, and demands the perfection of each being in its kind, apple as apple, woman as woman. Without adopting your theory I know that I, a daughter, live through the life of man; but what concerns me now is, that my life be a beautiful, powerful, in a word, a complete life in its kind. Had I but one more moment to live, I must wish the same.

Suppose, at the end of your cycle, your great world-year, all will be completed, whether I exert myself or not (and the supposition is *false*,) but suppose it true, am I to be indifferent about it? Not so! I must beat my own pulse true in the heart of the world; for *that* is virtue, excellence, health.

Thou, Lord of Day! didst leave us to-night so calmly glorious, not dismayed that cold winter is coming, not postponing thy beneficence to the fruitful summer! Thou didst smile on thy day's work when it was done, and adorn thy down-going as thy up-rising, for thou art loyal, and it is thy nature to give life, if thou canst, and shine at all events!

I stand in the sunny noon of life.* Objects no longer glitter in the dews of morning, neither are yet softened by the shadows of evening. Every spot is seen, every chasm revealed. Climbing the dusty hill, some fair effigies that once stood for symbols of human destiny have been broken; those I still have with me, show defects in this broad light. Yet enough is left, even by experience, to point distinctly to the glories of that destiny; faint, but not to be mistaken streaks of the future day. I can say with the bard,

'Though many have suffered shipwreck, still beat noble hearts.'*

Always the soul says to us all: Cherish your best hopes as a faith, and abide by them in action. Such shall be the effectual fervent means to their fulfilment,

> For the Power to whom we bow
> Has given its pledge that, if not now,
> They of pure and stedfast mind,
> By faith exalted, truth refined,
> *Shall* hear all music loud and clear,
> Whose first notes they ventured here.
> Then fear not thou to wind the horn,
> Though elf and gnome thy courage scorn;
> Ask for the Castle's King and Queen;
> Though rabble rout may rush between,
> Beat thee senseless to the ground,
> In the dark beset thee round;
> Persist to ask and it will come,
> Seek not for rest in humbler home;
> So shalt thou see what few have seen,
> The palace home of King and Queen.*

15th November, 1844.

APPENDIX

A.

Apparition of the goddess Isis to her votary, from Apuleius.*

'Scarcely had I closed my eyes, when behold (I saw in a dream) a divine form emerging from the middle of the sea, and raising a countenance venerable, even to the gods themselves. Afterwards, the whole of the most splendid image seemed to stand before me, having gradually shaken off the sea. I will endeavor to explain to you its admirable form, if the poverty of human language will but afford me the power of an appropriate narration; or if the divinity itself, of the most luminous form, will supply me with a liberal abundance of fluent diction. In the first place, then, her most copious and long hairs, being gradually intorted, and promiscuously scattered on her divine neck, were softly defluous. A multiform crown, consisting of various flowers, bound the sublime summit of her head. And in the middle of the crown, just on her forehead, there was a smooth orb resembling a mirror, or rather a white refulgent light, which indicated that she was the moon. Vipers rising up after the manner of furrows, environed the crown on the right hand and on the left, and Cerealian ears of corn were also extended from above. Her garment was of many colors, and woven from the finest flax, and was at one time lucid with a white splendor, at another yellow from the flower of crocus, and at another flaming with a rosy redness. But that which most excessively dazzled my sight, was a very black robe, fulgid with a dark splendor, and which, spreading round and passing under her right side, and ascending to her left shoulder, there rose protuberant, like the centre of a shield, the dependent part of her robe falling in many folds, and having small knots of fringe, gracefully flowing in its extremities. Glittering stars were dispersed through the embroidered border of the robe, and through the whole of its surface, and the full moon, shining in the middle of the stars, breathed forth flaming fires. A crown, wholly consisting of flowers and fruits of every kind, adhered with indivisible connexion to the border of the conspicuous robe, in all its undulating motions.

'What she carried in her hands also consisted of things of a very different nature. Her right hand bore a brazen rattle, through the narrow lamina of which, bent like a belt, certain rods passing, produced a sharp triple sound through the vibrating motion of her arm. An oblong vessel, in the shape of a boat, depended from her left hand, on the handle of which, in that part which was conspicuous, an asp raised its erect head and largely swelling neck. And shoes, woven from the leaves of the victorious palm tree, covered her immortal feet. Such, and so great a goddess, breathing the fragrant odour of the shores of Arabia the happy, deigned thus to address me.'

The foreign English of the translator, Thomas Taylor,* gives the description the air of being, itself, a part of the Mysteries. But its majestic beauty requires no formal initiation to be enjoyed.

B.

I give this, in the original, as it does not bear translation. Those who read Italian will judge whether it is not a perfect description of a perfect woman.

LODI E PREGHIERE A MARIA.*

Vergine bella che di sol vestita,
Coronata di stelle, al sommo Sole
    Piacesti si, che'n te sua luce ascose;
Amor mi spinge a dir di te parole:
    Ma non so 'ncominciar senza tu' aita,
E di Colui che amando in te si pose.
Invoco lei che ben sempre rispose,
Chi la chiamò con fede.
    Vergine, s'a mercede
Miseria extrema dell' smane cose
    Giammai ti volse, al mio prego t'inchina:
Soccorri alla mia guerra;
    Bench' i' sia terra, e tu del ciel Regina.

Vergine saggia, e del bel numero una
Delle beate vergini prudenti;
    Anzi la prima, e con più chiara lampa;
O saldo scudo dell' afflitte gente
    Contra colpi di Morte e di Fortuna,
Sotto' l qual si trionfa, non pur scampa:
    O refrigerio alcieco ardor ch' avvampa
Qui fra mortali sciocchi,
    Vergine, que' begli occhi
Che vider tristi la spietata stampa
    Ne' dolci membri del tuo caro figlio,
Volgi al mio dnbbio stato;
    Che sconsigliato a te vien per consiglio.

Vergine pura, d'ogni parte intera,
Del tuo parto gentil figliuola e madre;
    Che allumi questa vita, e l'altra adorni;
Per te il tuo Figlio e quel del sommo Padre,
    O finestra del ciel lucente altera,
Venne a salvarne in su gli estremi giorni,
    E fra tutt' i terreni altri soggiorni
Sola tu fusti eletta,
    Vergine benedetta;
Che 'l pianto d' Eva in allegrezza torni';
    Fammi; che puoi; della sua grazia degno,
Senza fine o beata,
    Già coronata nel superno regno.

Vergine santa d'ogni grazia piena;
Che per vera e altissima umiltate
    Salisti al ciel, onde miei preghi ascolti;
Tu partoristi il fonte di pietate,
    E di giustizia il Sol, che rasserena
Il secol pien d'errori oscuri e folti:
    Tre dolci e eari nomi ha' in te raccolti,
Madre, Figliuola, e Sposa;
    Vergine gloriosa,
Donna del Re che nostri lacci ha sciolti,
    E fatto 'l mondo libero e felice;
Nelle cui sante piaghe
    Prego ch'appaghe il cor, vera beatrice.
    Vergine sola al mondo senza esempio,
Che 'l ciel di tue bellezze innamorasti,
    Cui nè prima fu simil, nè seconda;

Santi pensieri, atti pietosi e casti
   Al vero Dio sacrato, e vivo tempio
Fecero in tua virginita feconda.
   Per te può la mia vita esser gioconda,
S' a' tuoi preghi, o MARIA
   Vergine dolce, e pia,
Ove 'l fallo abbondò, la grazia abbonda.
   Con le ginocchia della mente inchine
Prego che sia mia scorta;
   E la mia torta via drizzi a buon fine.

Vergine chiara, e stabile in eterno,
Di questo tempestoso mare stella;
   D'ogni fedel nocchier fidata guida;
Pon mente in che terribile procella
   I mi ritrovo sol senza governo,
Ed ho gia' da vicin l'ultime strida:
   Ma pur' in te l'anima mia si fida;
Peccatrice; i' nol nego,
   Vergine: ma te prego
Che 'l tuo nemico del mia mal non rida:
   Ricorditi che fece il peccar nostro
Prender Dio, per scamparne,
   Umana carne al tuo virginal christro.

Vergine, quante lagrime ho già sparte,
Quante lusinghe, e quanti preghi indarno,
   Pur per mia pena, e per mio grave danno!
Da poi ch' i nacqui in su la riva d' Arno;
   Cercando or questa ed or quell altra parte,
Non è stata mia vita altro ch' affanno.
   Mortal bellezza, atti, e parole m' hanno
Tutta ingombrata l' alma.
   Vergine sacra, ed alma,
Non tardar; ch' i' non forse all' ultim 'ann,
   I di miei piu correnti che saetta,
Fra miserie e peccati
   Sonsen andati, e sol Morte n'aspetta.

Vergine, tale è terra, e posto ha in doglia
Lo mio cor; che vivendo in pianto il tenne;
   E di mille miei mali un non sapea;
E per saperlo, pur quel che n'avvenne,
   Fora avvenuto: ch' ogni altra sua voglia

Era a me morte, ed a lei fama rea
    Or tu, donna del ciel, tu nostra Dea,
Se dir lice, e conviensi;
    Vergine d'alti sensi,
Tu vedi il tutto; e quel che non potea
    Far altri, è nulla a e la tua gran virtute;
Pon fine al mio dolore;
    Ch'a te onore ed a me fia salute.

Vergine, in cui ho tutta mia speranza
Che possi e vogli al gran bisogno aitarme;
    Non mi lasciare in su l'estremo passo.
Non guardar me, ma chi degnò crearme;
    No'l mio valor, ma l'alta sua sembianza;
Che in me ti mova a curar d'uorm si basso.
    Medusa, e l'error mio io han fatto un sasso
D'umor vano stillante;
    Vergine, tu di sante
Lagrime, e pie adempi 'l mio cor lasso;
    Ch' almen l'ultimo pianto sia divoto,
        Senza terrestro limo;
Come fu'l primo non d'insania voto.

Vergine umana, e nemica d'orgoglio,
Del comune principio amor t'induca;
    Miserere d' un cor contrito umile;
Che se poca mortal terra caduca
    Amar con si mirabil fede soglio;
Che devro far di te cosa gentile?
    Se dal mio stato assai misero, e vile
Per le tue man resurgo,
    Vergine; è' sacro, e purgo
Al tuo nome e pens ieri e'ngegno, e stile;
    La lingua, e'l cor, le lagrime, e i sospiri,
Scorgimi al miglior guado;
    E prendi in gràdo i cangiati desiri.

Il di s'appressa, e non pote esser lunge;
    Si corre il tempo, e vola,
Vergine uuica, e sola;
    E'l cor' or conscienza, or morte punge.
Raccommandami al tuo Figliuol, verace
    Uomo, e verace Dio;
Ch accolga I mio spirto ultimo in pace.

As the Scandinavian represented Frigga* the Earth, or World mother, knowing all things, yet never herself revealing them, though ready to be called to counsel by the gods. It represents her in action, decked with jewels and gorgeously attended. But, says the Mythos, when she ascended the throne of Odin, her consort (Haaven) she left with mortals, her friend, the Goddess of Sympathy, to protect them in her absence.

Since, Sympathy goes about to do good. Especially she devotes herself to the most valiant and the most oppressed. She consoled the Gods in some degree even for the death of their darling Baldur.* Among the heavenly powers she has no consort.

C.

'THE WEDDING OF THE LADY THERESA.'

FROM LOCKHART'S SPANISH BALLADS.*

' 'Twas when the fifth Alphonso in Leon held his sway,
   King Abdalla of Toledo an embassy did send;
He asked his sister for a wife, and in an evil day
   Alphonso sent her, for he feared Abdalla to offend;
He feared to move his anger, for many times before
He had received in danger much succor from the Moor.

Sad heart had fair Theresa, when she their paction knew;
   With streaming tears she heard them tell she 'mong the Moors
      must go;
That she, a Christian damsel, a Christian firm and true,
   Must wed a Moorish husband, it well might cause her wo;
But all her tears and all her prayers they are of small avail;
   At length she for her fate prepares, a victim sad and pale.

The king hath sent his sister to fair Toledo town,
   Where then the Moor Abdalla his royal state did keep;
When she drew near, the Moslem from his golden throne came
      down,
   And courteously received her, and bade her cease to weep;
With loving words he pressed her to come his bower within;
With kisses he caressed her, but still she feared the sin.

"Sir King, Sir King, I pray thee,"—'twas thus Theresa spake,
   "I pray thee, have compassion, and do to me no wrong;

For sleep with thee I may not, unless the vows I break,
   Whereby I to the holy church of Christ my Lord belong;
For thou hast sworn to serve Mahoun, and if this thing should be,
The curse of God it must bring down upon thy realm and thee.

"The angel of Christ Jesu, to whom my heavenly Lord
   Hath given my soul in keeping, is ever by my side;
If thou dost me dishonor, he will unsheath his sword,
   And smite thy body fiercely, at the crying of thy bride;
Invisible he standeth; his sword like fiery flame,
Will penetrate thy bosom, the hour that sees my shame."

The Moslem heard her with a smile; the earnest words she said,
   He took for bashful maiden's wile, and drew her to his bower:
In vain Theresa prayed and strove,—she pressed Abdalla's bed,
   Perforce received his kiss of love, and lost her maiden flower.
A woful woman there she lay, a loving lord beside,
And earnestly to God did pray, her succor to provide.

The angel of Christ Jesu her sore complaint did hear,
   And plucked his heavenly weapon from out his sheath unseen,
He waved the brand in his right hand, and to the King came near,
   And drew the point o'er limb and joint, beside the weeping
      Queen:
A mortal weakness from the stroke upon the King did fall;
He could not stand when daylight broke, but on his knees must
   crawl.

Abdalla shuddered inly, when he this sickness felt,
   And called upon his barons, his pillow to come nigh;
"Rise up," he said "my liegemen," as round his bed they knelt,
   "And take this Christian lady, else certainly I die;
Let gold be in your girdles, and precious stones beside,
   And swiftly ride to Leon, and render up my bride."

When they were come to Leon, Theresa would not go
   Into her brother's dwelling, where her maiden years were spent;
But o'er her downcast visage a white veil she did throw,
   And to the ancient nunnery of Las Huelgas went.
There, long, from worldly eyes retired, a holy life she led;
There she, an aged saint, expired; there sleeps she with the dead.'

D.

The following extract from Spinoza* is worthy of attention, as
expressing the view which a man of the largest intellectual scope

may take of woman, if that part of his life to which her influence appeals, has been left unawakened.

He was a man of the largest intellect, of unsurpassed reasoning powers, yet he makes a statement false to history, for we well know how often men and women have ruled together without difficulty, and one in which very few men even at the present day, I mean men who are thinkers, like him, would acquiesce.

I have put in contrast with it three expressions of the latest literature.

1st. From the poems of W. E. Channing,* a poem called 'Reverence,' equally remarkable for the deep wisdom of its thought and the beauty of its utterance, and containing as fine a description of one class of women as exists in literature.

In contrast with this picture of woman, the happy Goddess of Beauty, the wife, the friend, 'the summer queen,' I add one by the author of 'Festus,'* of a woman of the muse, the sibyl kind, which seems painted from living experience.

And thirdly, I subjoin Eugene Sue's description of a wicked, but able woman of the practical sort, and appeal to all readers whether a species that admits of three such varieties is so easily to be classed away, or kept within prescribed limits, as Spinoza, and those who think like him, believe.

SPINOZA. TRACTATUS POLITICI, DE DEMOCRATIA, CAPUT XI.

'Perhaps some one will here ask, whether the supremacy of man over woman is attributable to nature or custom? For if it be human institutions alone to which this fact is owing, there is no reason why we should exclude women from a share in government. Experience, however, most plainly teaches that it is woman's weakness which places her under the authority of man. Since it has nowhere happened that men and women ruled together; but wherever men and women are found the world over, there we see the men ruling and the women ruled, and in this order of things men and women live together in peace and harmony. The Amazons, it is true, are reputed formerly to have held the reins of government, but they drove men from their dominions; the male of their offspring they invariably destroyed, permitting their daughters alone to live. Now if women were by nature upon an equality with men, if they equalled men in fortitude, in genius (qualities which give to men might, and consequently, right) it surely would be the case, that among the numerous and diverse nations of the earth, some would be found where both sexes ruled conjointly, and others where the men were ruled by the women, and so educated as to be mentally inferior: since this state of things nowhere exists, it is perfectly fair to infer that the rights of women are not equal to those of men; but that women must be subordinate, and therefore cannot have an equal, far less a superior place in the government. If, too, we consider the passions of men—how the love men feel towards women is seldom any thing but lust and impulse, and much less a reverence for qualities of soul than an admiration of physical beauty, observing, too, how men are afflicted when their sweethearts favor other wooers, and other things of the same character,—we shall see at a glance that it would be, in the highest degree, detrimental to peace and harmony, for men and women to possess an equal share in government.'

'REVERENCE.'

'As an ancestral heritage revere
All learning, and all thought. The painter's fame
Is thine, whate'er thy lot, who honorest grace.
And need enough in this low time, when they,
Who seek to captivate the fleeting notes
Of heaven's sweet beauty, must despair almost,
So heavy and obdurate show the hearts
Of their companions. Honor kindly then
Those who bear up in their so generous arms
The beautiful ideas of matchless forms;
For were these not portrayed, our human fate,—
Which is to be all high, majestical,
To grow to goodness with each coming age,
Till virtue leap and sing for joy to see
So noble, virtuous men,—would brief decay;
And the green, festering slime, oblivious, haunt
About our common fate. Oh honor them!

But what to all true eyes has chiefest charm,
And what to every breast where beats a heart
Framed to one beautiful emotion,—to
One sweet and natural feeling, lends a grace
To all the tedious walks of common life,
This is fair woman,—woman, whose applause
Each poet sings—woman the beautiful.
Not that her fairest brow, or gentlest form
Charm us to tears; not that the smoothest cheek,
Where ever rosy tints have made their home,
So rivet us on her; but that she is
The subtle, delicate grace,—the inward grace,
For words too excellent; the noble, true,
The majesty of earth; the summer queen:
In whose conceptions nothing but what's great
Has any right. And, O! her love for him,
Who does but his small part in honoring her;
Discharging a sweet office, sweeter none,
Mother and child, friend, counsel and repose;—
Nought matches with her, nought has leave with her
To highest human praise. Farewell to him
Who reverences not with an excess
Of faith the beauteous sex; all barren he
Shall live a living death of mockery.

Ah! had but words the power, what could we say
Of woman! We, rude men, of violent phrase,
Harsh action, even in repose inwardly harsh;
Whose lives walk blustering on high stilts, removed
From all the purely gracious influence
Of mother earth. To single from the host
Of angel forms one only, and to her
Devote our deepest heart and deepest mind
Seems almost contradiction. Unto her
We owe our greatest blessings, hours of cheer,
Gay smiles, and sudden tears, and more than these
A sure perpetual love. Regard her as
She walks along the vast still earth; and see!
Before her flies a laughing troop of joys,
And by her side treads old experience,
With never-failing voice admonitory;
The gentle, though infallible, kind advice,
The watchful care, the fine regardfulness,

Whatever mates with what we hope to find,
All consummate in her—the summer queen.

To call past ages better than what now
Man is enacting on life's crowded stage,
Cannot improve our worth; and for the world
Blue is the sky as ever, and the stars
Kindle their crystal flames at soft-fallen eve
With the same purest lustre that the east
Worshipped. The river gently flows through fields
Where the broad-leaved corn spreads out, and loads
Its ear as when the Indian tilled the soil.
The dark green pine,—green in the winter's cold,
Still whispers meaning emblems, as of old;
The cricket chirps, and the sweet, eager birds
In the sad woods crowd their thick melodies;
But yet, to common eyes, life's poetry
Something has faded, and the cause of this
May be that man, no longer at the shrine
Of woman, kneeling with true reverence,
In spite of field, wood, river, stars and sea
Goes most disconsolate. A babble now,
A huge and wind-swelled babble, fills the place
Of that great adoration which of old
Man had for woman. In these days no more
Is love the pith and marrow of man's fate.

Thou who in early years feelest awake
To finest impulses from nature's breath,
And in thy walk hearest such sounds of truth
As on the common ear strike without heed,
Beware of men around thee. Men are foul,
With avarice, ambition and deceit;
The worst of all, ambition. This is life
Spent in a feverish chase for selfish ends,
Which has no virtue to redeem its toil
But one long, stagnant hope to raise the self.
The miser's life to this seems sweet and fair;
Better to pile the glittering coin, than seek
To overtop our brothers and our loves.
Merit in this? Where lies it, though thy name
Ring over distant lands, meeting the wind
Even on the extremest verge of the wide world.
Merit in this? Better be hurled abroad

On the vast whirling tide, than in thyself
Concentred, feed upon thy own applause.
Thee shall the good man yield no reverence;
But, while the idle, dissolute crowd are loud
In voice to send thee flattery, shall rejoice
That he has scaped thy fatal doom, and known
How humble faith in the good soul of things
Provides amplest enjoyment. O my brother,
If the Past's counsel any honor claim
From thee, go read the history of those
Who a like path have trod, and see a fate
Wretched with fears, changing like leaves at noon,
When the new wind sings in the white birch wood.
Learn from the simple child the rule of life,
And from the movements of the unconscious tribes
Of animal nature, those that bend the wing
Or cleave the azure tide, content to be,
What the great frame provides,—freedom and grace.
Thee, simple child, do the swift winds obey,
And the white waterfalls with their bold leaps
Follow thy movements. Tenderly the light
Thee watches, girding with a zone of radiance,
And all the swinging herbs love thy soft steps.'

DESCRIPTION OF ANGELA, FROM 'FESTUS.'

'I loved her for that she was beautiful,
And that to me she seemed to be all nature
And all varieties of things in one;
Would set at night in clouds of tears, and rise
All light and laughter in the morning; fear
No petty customs nor appearances,
But think what others only dreamed about;
And say what others did but think; and do
What others would but say; and glory in
What others dared but do; it was these which won me;
And that she never schooled within her breast
One thought or feeling, but gave holiday
To all; and that she told me all her woes
And wrongs and ills; and so she made them mine
In the communion of love; and we
Grew like each other, for we loved each other;

She, mild and generous as the sun in spring;
And I, like earth, all budding out with love.

* * *

The beautiful are never desolate:
For some one alway loves them; God or man;
If man abandons, God Himself takes them:
And thus it was. She whom I once loved died,
The lightning loathes its cloud; the soul its clay.
Can I forget that hand I took in mine,
Pale as pale violets; that eye, where mind
And matter met alike divine?—ah, no!
May God that moment judge me when I do!
Oh! she was fair; her nature once all spring
And deadly beauty, like a maiden sword,
Startlingly beautiful. I see her now!
Wherever thou art thy soul is in my mind;
Thy shadow hourly lengthens o'er my brain
And peoples all its pictures with thyself;
Gone, not forgotten; passed, not lost; thou wilt shine
In heaven like a bright spot in the sun!
She said she wished to die, and so she died,
For, cloudlike, she poured out her love, which was
Her life, to freshen this parched heart. It was thus;
I said we were to part, but she said nothing;
There was no discord; it was music ceased,
Life's thrilling, bursting, bounding joy. She sate,
Like a house-god, her hands fixed on her knee,
And her dark hair lay loose and long behind her,
Through which her wild bright eye flashed like a flint;
She spake not, moved not, but she looked the more,
As if her eye were action, speech, and feeling.
I felt it all, and came and knelt beside her,
The electric touch solved both our souls together;
Then came the feeling which unmakes, undoes;
Which tears the sealike soul up by the roots,
And lashes it in scorn against the skies.

* * *

It is the saddest and the sorest sight,
One's own love weeping. But why call on God?
But that the feeling of the boundless bounds
All feeling; as the welkin does the world;
It is this which ones us with the whole and God.

Then first we wept; then closed and clung together;
And my heart shook this building of my breast
Like a live engine booming up and down:
She fell upon me like a snow-wreath thawing.
Never were bliss and beauty, love and wo,
Ravelled and twined together into madness,
As in that one wild hour to which all else
The past, is but a picture. That alone
Is real, and forever there in front.

                    *   *   *

*   *   *   After that I left her,
And only saw her once again alive.'

———————

'Mother Saint Perpetua, the superior of the convent, was a tall woman, of about forty years, dressed in dark gray serge, with a long rosary hanging at her girdle; a white mob cap, with a long black veil, surrounded her thin wan face with its narrow hooded border. A great number of deep transverse wrinkles plowed her brow, which resembled yellowish ivory in color and substance. Her keen and prominent nose was curved like the hooked beak of a bird of prey; her black eye was piercing and sagacious; her face was at once intelligent, firm, and cold.

'For comprehending and managing the material interests of the society, Mother Saint Perpetua could have vied with the shrewdest and most wily lawyer. When women are possessed of what is called *business talent*, and when they apply thereto the sharpness of perception, the indefatigable perseverance, the prudent dissimulation, and above all, the correctness and rapidity of judgment at first sight, which are peculiar to them, they arrive at prodigious results.

'To Mother Saint Perpetua, a woman of a strong and solid head, the vast monied business of the society was but child's play. None better than she understood how to buy depreciated properties, to raise them to their original value, and sell them to advantage; the average purchase of rents, the fluctuations of exchange, and the current prices of shares in all the leading speculations, were perfectly familiar to her. Never had she directed her agents to make a single false speculation, when it had been the question how to invest funds, with which good souls were constantly endowing the society of Saint Mary. She had established in the house a degree of order, of discipline, and, above all, of economy, that were indeed remarkable; the constant aim of all her exertions being, not to enrich herself, but the community over which she presided; for the spirit of association, when it is directed to an object of *collective selfishness*, gives to corporations all the faults and vices of individuals.'

E.

The following is an extract from a letter addressed to me by one of the monks of the 19th century.* A part I have omitted, because it does not express my own view, unless such qualifications which I could not make, except by full discussion of the subject.

'Woman in the 19th century should be a pure, chaste, holy being.

This state of being in woman is no more attained by the expansion of her intellectual capacity, than by the augmentation of her physical force.

Neither is it attained by the increase or refinement of her love for man, or for any object whatever, or for all objects collectively; but

This state of being is attained by the reference of all her powers and all her actions to the source of Universal Love, whose constant requisition is a pure, chaste and holy life.

So long as woman looks to man (or to society) for that which she needs, she will remain in an indigent state, for he himself is indigent of it, and as much needs it as she does.

So long as this indigence continues, all unions or relations constructed between man and woman are constructed in indigence, and can produce only indigent results or unhappy consequences.

The unions now constructing, as well as those in which the parties constructing them were generated, being based on self-delight, or lust, can lead to no more happiness in the 20th, than is found in the 19th century.

It is not amended institutions, it is not improved education, it is not another selection of individuals for union, that can meliorate the sad result, but the *basis* of the union must be changed.

If in the natural order Woman and Man would adhere strictly to physiological or natural laws, in physical chastity, a most beautiful amendment of the human race, and human condition, would in a few generations adorn the world.

Still, it belongs to Woman in the spiritual order, to devote herself wholly to her eternal husband, and become the Free Bride of the One who alone can elevate her to her true position, and reconstruct her a pure, chaste, and holy being.'

F.

I have mislaid an extract from 'The Memoirs of an American Lady'* which I wished to use on this subject, but its import is, briefly, this:

Observing of how little consequence the Indian women are in youth, and how much in age, because in that trying life, good counsel and sagacity are more prized than charms, Mrs Grant expresses a wish that Reformers would take a hint from observation of this circumstance.

In another place she says: 'The misfortune of our sex is, that young women are not regarded as the material from which old women must be made.'

I quote from memory, but believe the weight of the remark is retained.

G.

EURIPIDES. SOPHOCLES.

As many allusions are made in the foregoing pages to characters of women drawn by the Greek dramatists, which may not be familiar to the majority of readers, I have borrowed from the papers of Miranda,* some notes upon them. I trust the girlish tone of apostrophizing rapture may be excused. Miranda was very young at the time of writing, compared with her present mental age. *Now*, she would express the same feelings, but in a worthier garb—if she expressed them at all.

'Iphigenia! Antigone! you were worthy to live! *We* are fallen on evil times, my sisters! our feelings have been checked; our thoughts questioned; our forms dwarfed and defaced by a bad nurture. Yet hearts, like yours, are in our breasts, living, if unawakened; and our minds are capable of the same resolves. You, we understand at once, those who stare upon us pertly in the street, we cannot—could never understand.

You knew heroes, maidens, and your fathers were kings of men. You believed in your country, and the gods of your country. A great occasion was given to each, whereby to test her character.

You did not love on earth; for the poets wished to show us the force of woman's nature, virgin and unbiassed. You were women; not wives, or lovers, or mothers. Those are great names, but we are glad to see *you* in untouched flower.

Were brothers so dear, then, Antigone? We have no brothers. We see no men into whose lives we dare look steadfastly, or to whose destinies we look forward confidently. We care not for their urns; what inscription could we put upon them? They live for petty successes; or to win daily the bread of the day. No spark of kingly fire flashes from their eyes.

None! are there *none*?

It is a base speech to say it. Yes! there are some such; we have sometimes caught their glances. But rarely have they been rocked in the same cradle as we, and they do not look upon us much; for the time is not yet come.

Thou art so grand and simple! we need not follow thee; thou dost not need our love.

But, sweetest Iphigenia; who knew *thee*, as to me thou art known. I was not born in vain, if only for the heavenly tears I have shed with thee. She will be grateful for them. I have understood her wholly; as a friend should, better than she understood herself.

With what artless art the narrative rises to the crisis. The conflicts in Agamemnon's mind, and the imputations of Menelaus give us, at once, the full image of him, strong in will and pride, weak in virtue, weak in the noble powers of the mind that depend on imagination. He suffers, yet it requires the presence of his daughter to make him feel the full horror of what he is to do.

'Ah me! that breast, those cheeks, those golden tresses!'*

It is her beauty, not her misery, that makes the pathos. This is noble. And then, too, the injustice of the gods, that she, this creature of unblemished loveliness, must perish for the sake of a worthless woman.* Even Menelaus feels it, the moment he recovers from his wrath.

> 'What hath she to do,
> The virgin daughter, with my Helena!
> *   *   Its former reasonings now
> My soul foregoes.   *   *   *   *
>   For it is not just
> That thou shouldst groan, but my affairs go pleasantly,
> That those of thy house should die, and mine see the light.'

Indeed the overwhelmed aspect of the king of men might well move him.

> *Men.* 'Brother, give me to take thy right hand,
> *Aga.*   I give it, for the victory is thine, and I am wretched.
>   I am, indeed, ashamed to drop the tear,
>   And not to drop the tear I am ashamed.'

How beautifully is Iphigenia introduced; beaming more and more softly on us with every touch of description. After Clytemnestra has given Orestes (then an infant,) out of the chariot, she says:

> 'Ye females, in your arms,
> Receive her, for she is of tender age.
> Sit here by my feet, my child,
> By thy mother, Iphigenia, and show
> These strangers how I am blessed in thee,
> And here address thee to thy father.
> *Iphi.*   Oh mother, should I run, wouldst thou be angry?
>   And embrace my father breast to breast?'

With the same sweet timid trust she prefers the request to himself, and as he holds her in his arms, he seems as noble as Guido's Archangel;* as if he never could sink below the trust of such a being!

The Achilles, in the first scene, is fine. A true Greek hero; not too good; all flushed with the pride of youth; but capable of god-like impulses. At first, he thinks only of his own wounded pride, (when he finds Iphigenia has been decoyed to Aulis under the pretext of becoming his wife;) but the grief of the queen soon makes him superior to his arrogant chafings. How well he says:—

> '*Far as a young man may*, I will repress
> So great a wrong.'

By seeing him here, we understand why he, not Hector, was the hero of the Iliad. The beautiful moral nature of Hector was early developed by close domestic ties, and the cause of his country. Except in a purer simplicity of speech and manner, he might be a modern and a christian. But Achilles is cast in the largest and most vigorous mould of the earlier day: his nature is one of the richest capabilities, and therefore less quickly unfolds its meaning. The impression it makes at the early period is only of power and pride; running as fleetly with his armor on, as with it off; but sparks of pure lustre are struck, at moments, from the mass of ore. Of this sort is his refusal to see the beautiful virgin he has promised to protect. None of the Grecians must have the right to doubt his motives. How wise and prudent, too, the advice he gives as to the queen's conduct! He will not show himself, unless needed. His pride is the farthest possible remove from vanity. His thoughts are as free as any in our own time.

> 'The prophet? what is he? a man
> Who speaks 'mong many falsehoods, but few truths,
> Whene'er chance leads him to speak true; when false,
> The prophet is no more.'

Had Agamemnon possessed like clearness of sight, the virgin would not have perished, but also, Greece would have had no religion and no national existence.

When, in the interview with Agamemnon, the Queen begins her speech, in the true matrimonial style, dignified though her gesture be, and true all she says, we feel that truth, thus sauced with taunts, will not touch his heart, nor turn him from his purpose. But when Iphigenia begins her exquisite speech, as with the breathings of a lute,

> 'Had I, my father, the persuasive voice
> Of Orpheus, &c.
>
>   Compel me not
> What is beneath to view. I was the first
> To call thee father; me thou first didst call
> Thy child: I was the first that on thy knees
> Fondly caressed thee, and from thee received
> The fond caress: this was thy speech to me:—
> "Shall I, my child, e'er see thee in some house
> Of splendor, happy in thy husband, live
> And flourish, as becomes my dignity?"
> My speech to thee was, leaning 'gainst thy cheek,
> (Which with my hand I now caress:) "And what
> Shall I then do for thee? shall I receive
> My father when grown old, and in my house
> Cheer him with each fond office, to repay
> The careful nurture which he gave my youth?"
> These words are in my memory deep impressed,
> Thou hast forgot them and will kill thy child.'

Then she adjures him by all the sacred ties, and dwells pathetically on the circumstance which had struck even Menelaus.

> 'If Paris be enamored of his bride,
> His Helen, what concerns it me? and how
> Comes he to my destruction?
>   Look upon me;
> Give me a smile, give me a kiss, my father;
> That if my words persuade thee not, in death
> I may have this memorial of thy love.'

Never have the names of father and daughter been uttered with a holier tenderness than by Euripides, as in this most lovely passage, or in the 'Supplicants,'* after the voluntary death of Evadne; Iphis says

> 'What shall this wretch now do? Should I return
> To my own house?—sad desolation there
> I shall behold, to sink my soul with grief.
> Or go I to the house of Capaneus?
> That was delightful to me, when I found
> My daughter there; but she is there no more:
> Oft would she kiss my cheek, with fond caress
> Oft soothe me. To a father, waxing old,

> Nothing is dearer than a daughter! sons
> Have spirits of higher pitch, but less inclined
> To sweet endearing fondness. Lead me then,
> Instantly lead me to my house, consign
> My wretched age to darkness, there to pine
> And waste away.
> > Old age,
> Struggling with many griefs, O how I hate thee!'

But to return to Iphigenia,—how infinitely melting is her appeal to Orestes, whom she holds in her robe.

> 'My brother, small assistance canst thou give
> Thy friends; yet for thy sister with thy tears
> Implore thy father that she may not die:
> Even infants have a sense of ills; and see,
> My father! silent though he be, he sues
> To thee: be gentle to me; on my life
> Have pity: thy two children by this beard
> Entreat thee, thy dear children: one is yet
> An infant, one to riper years arrived.'

The mention of Orestes, then an infant, all through, though slight, is of a domestic charm that prepares the mind to feel the tragedy of his after lot.* When the Queen says

> 'Dost thou sleep,
> My son? The rolling chariot hath subdued thee;
> Wake to thy sister's marriage happily.'

We understand the horror of the doom which makes this cherished child a parricide. And so when Iphigenia takes leave of him after her fate is by herself accepted.

Iphi. 'To manhood train Orestes,
Cly.   Embrace him, for thou ne'er shalt see him more.
Iphi. (*To Orestes.*) Far as thou couldst, thou didst assist thy friends.'

We know not how to blame the guilt of the maddened wife and mother. In her last meeting with Agamemnon, as in her previous expostulations and anguish, we see that a straw may turn the balance, and make her his deadliest foe. Just then, came the suit of Ægisthus, then, when every feeling was uprooted or lacerated in her heart.

Iphigenia's moving address has no further effect than to make her father turn at bay and brave this terrible crisis. He goes out, firm in resolve; and she and her mother abandon themselves to a natural grief.

Hitherto nothing has been seen in Iphigenia, except the young girl, weak, delicate, full of feeling and beautiful as a sunbeam on the full green tree. But, in the next scene, the first impulse of that passion which makes and unmakes us, though unconfessed even to herself, though hopeless and unreturned, raises her at once into the heroic woman, worthy of the goddess who demands her.

Achilles appears to defend her, whom all others clamorously seek to deliver to the murderous knife. She sees him, and fired with thoughts, unknown before, devotes herself at once for the country which has given birth to such a man.

> 'To be too fond of life
> Becomes not me; nor for myself alone,
> But to all Greece, a blessing didst thou bear me.
> Shall thousands, when their country's injured, lift
> Their shields; shall thousands grasp the oar, and dare,
> Advancing bravely 'gainst the foe, to die
> For Greece? And shall my life, my single life,
> Obstruct all this? Would this be just? What word
> Can we reply? Nay more, it is not right
> That he with all the Grecians should contest
> In fight, should die, *and for a woman*. No:
> More than a thousand women is one man
> Worthy to see the light of day.
>   * * *   for Greece I give my life.
> Slay me; demolish Troy: for these shall be
> Long time my monuments, my children these,
> My nuptials and my glory.'

This sentiment marks woman, when she loves enough to feel what a creature of glory and beauty a true *man* would be, as much in our own time as that of Euripides. Cooper* makes the weak Hetty say to her beautiful sister:

'Of course, I don't compare you with Harry. A handsome man is always far handsomer than any woman.' True, it was the sentiment of the age, but it was the first time Iphigenia had felt it. In Agamemnon she saw *her father*, to him she could prefer her claim. In Achilles she saw *a man*, the crown of creation, enough to fill the world with his presence, were all other beings blotted from its spaces.[†]

The reply of Achilles is as noble. Here is his bride, he feels it now, and all his vain vauntings are hushed.

> 'Daughter of Agamemnon, highly blessed
> Some god would make me, if I might attain
> Thy nuptials. Greece in thee I happy deem,
> And thee in Greece.   *   *
>   *   *   *   in thy thought
> Revolve this well; death is a dreadful thing.'

How sweet is her reply, and then the tender modesty with which she addresses him here and elsewhere as '*stranger*.'

> 'Reflecting not on any, thus I speak:
> Enough of wars and slaughters from the charms
> Of Helen rise; but die not thou for me,
> O Stranger, nor distain thy sword with blood,
> But let me save my country if I may.'

Achilles. 'O glorious spirit! nought have I 'gainst this
> To urge, since such thy will, for what thou sayst
> Is generous. Why should not the truth be spoken?'

But feeling that human weakness may conquer yet, he goes to wait at the altar, resolved to keep his promise of protection thoroughly.

In the next beautiful scene she shows that a few tears might overwhelm her in his absence. She raises her mother beyond weeping them, yet her soft purity she cannot impart.

> *Iphi.*   'My father, and thy husband do not hate:
> *Cly.*   For thy dear sake fierce contests must he bear.
> *Iphi.*   For Greece reluctant me to death he yields;
> *Cly.*   Basely, with guile unworthy Atreus' son.'[*]

[†] Men do not often reciprocate this pure love.

> 'Her prentice han' she tried on man,
> And then she made the lasses o',[*]

Is a fancy, not a feeling, in their more frequently passionate and strong, than noble or tender natures. [Fuller's note.]

This is truth incapable of an answer and Iphigenia attempts none.

She begins the hymn which is to sustain her,

> 'Lead me; mine the glorious fate,
> To o'erturn the Phrygian state.'*

After the sublime flow of lyric heroism, she suddenly sinks back into the tenderer feeling of her dreadful fate.

	'O my country, where these eyes
	Opened on Pelasgic* skies!
	O ye virgins, once my pride,
	In Mycenæ* who abide!
Chorus.	Why of Perseus name the town,
	Which Cyclopean ramparts crown!
Iphigenia.	Me you rear'd a beam of light,
	Freely now I sink in night.'

Freely; as the messenger afterwards recounts it.

* * *

> 'Imperial Agamemnon, when he saw
> His daughter, as a victim to the grave,
> Advancing, groan'd, and bursting into tears,
> Turned from the sight his head, before his eyes,
> Holding his robe. The virgin near him stood,
> And thus addressed him: "Father, I to thee
> Am present; for my country, and for all
> The land of Greece, I freely give myself
> A victim: to the altar let them lead me,
> Since such the oracle. If aught on me
> Depends, be happy, and obtain the prize
> Of glorious conquest, and revisit safe
> Your country. Of the Grecians, for this cause,
> Let no one touch me; with intrepid spirit
> Silent will I present my neck." She spoke,
> And all that heard revered the noble soul
> And virtue of the virgin.'

How quickly had the fair bud bloomed up into its perfection. Had she lived a thousand years, she could not have surpassed this. Goethe's Iphigenia, the mature woman, with its myriad delicate traits, never surpasses, scarcely equals what we know of her in Euripides.

Can I appreciate this work in a translation? I think so, impossible as it may seem to one who can enjoy the thousand melodies, and words in exactly the right place and cadence of the original. They say you can see the Apollo Belvidere* in a plaster cast, and I cannot doubt it, so great the benefit conferred on my mind, by a transcript thus imperfect. And so with these translations from the Greek. I can divine the original through this veil, as I can see the movements of a spirited horse by those of his coarse grasscloth muffler. Beside, every translator who feels his subject is inspired, and the divine Aura informs even his stammering lips.

Iphigenia is more like one of the women Shakspeare loved than the others; she is a tender virgin, ennobled and strengthened by sentiment more than intellect, what they call a woman *par excellence*.

Macaria is more like one of Massinger's women. She advances boldly, though with the decorum of her sex and nation:

> *Macaria.* 'Impute not boldness to me that I come
>   Before you, strangers; this my first request
>   I urge; for silence and a chaste reserve
>   Is woman's genuine praise, and to remain
>   Quiet within the house. But I come forth,
>   Hearing thy lamentations, Iolaus:
>   Though charged with no commission, yet perhaps,
>   I may be useful.' * *

Her speech when she offers herself as the victim, is reasonable, as one might speak to-day. She counts the cost all through. Iphigenia is too timid and delicate to dwell upon the loss of earthly bliss, and the due experience of life, even as much as Jeptha's* daughter did, but Macaria is explicit, as well befits the daughter of Hercules.

>   'Should *these* die, myself
>   Preserved, of prosperous future could I form
>   One cheerful hope?
>   A poor forsaken virgin who would deign
>   To take in marriage? Who would wish for sons
>   From one so wretched? Better then to die,
>   Than bear such undeserved miseries:
>   One less illustrious this might more beseem.

* * *

> I have a soul that unreluctantly
> Presents itself, and I proclaim aloud
> That for my brothers and myself I die.
> I am not fond of life, but think I gain
> An honorable prize to die with glory.'

Still nobler when Iolaus proposes rather that she shall draw lots with her sisters.

> '*By lot* I will not die, for to such death
> No thanks are due, or glory—name it not.
> If you accept me, if my offered life
> Be grateful to you, willingly I give it
> For these, but by constraint I will not die.'

Very fine are her parting advice and injunctions to them all:

> 'Farewell! revered old man, farewell! and teach
> These youths in all things to be wise, like thee,
> Naught will avail them more.'

Macaria has the clear Minerva eye: Antigone's is deeper, and more capable of emotion, but calm. Iphigenia's, glistening, gleaming with angel truth, or dewy as a hidden violet.

I am sorry that Tennyson,* who spoke with such fitness of all the others in his 'Dream of fair women,' has not of Iphigenia. Of her alone he has not made a fit picture, but only of the circumstances of the sacrifice. He can never have taken to heart this work of Euripides, yet he was so worthy to feel it. Of Jeptha's daughter, he has spoken as he would of Iphigenia, both in her beautiful song, and when

> 'I heard Him, for He spake, and grief became
> A solemn scorn of ills.
>
> It comforts me in this one thought to dwell
> That I subdued me to my father's will;
> Because the kiss he gave me, ere I fell,
> Sweetens the spirit still.
>
> Moreover it is written, that my race
> Hewed Ammon, hip and thigh from Arroer
> Or Arnon unto Minneth.* Here her face
> Glow'd as I look'd on her.

> She locked her lips; she left me where I stood;
>   "Glory to God," she sang, and past afar,
> Thridding the sombre boskage of the woods,
>   Toward the morning-star.'

In the 'Trojan dames' there are fine touches of nature with regard to Cassandra. Hecuba shows that mixture of shame and reverence, that prose kindred always do, towards the inspired child, the poet, the elected sufferer for the race.

When the herald announces that she is chosen to be the mistress of Agamemnon, Hecuba answers indignant, and betraying the involuntary pride and faith she felt in this daughter.

>   'The virgin of Apollo, whom the God,
>   Radiant with golden locks, allowed to live
>   In her pure vow of maiden chastity?
> *Tal.* With love the raptured virgin smote his heart.
> *Hec.* Cast from thee, O my daughter, cast away
>   Thy sacred wand, rend off the honored wreaths,
>   The splendid ornaments that grace thy brows.'

Yet the moment Cassandra appears, singing wildly her inspired song, Hecuba calls her

> 'My *frantic* child.'

Yet how graceful she is in her tragic phrenzy, the chorus shows—

> 'How sweetly at thy house's ills thou smil'st,
>   Chanting what haply thou wilt not show true?'

But if Hecuba dares not trust her highest instinct about her daughter, still less can the vulgar mind of the herald (a man not without tenderness of heart, but with no princely, no poetic blood,) abide the wild prophetic mood which insults his prejudices both as to country and decorums of the sex. Yet Agamemnon, though not a noble man, is of large mould and could admire this strange beauty which excited distaste in common minds.

> *Tal.* 'What commands respect, and is held high
>   As wise, is nothing better than the mean
>   Of no repute: for this most potent king

Of all the Grecians, the much honored son
Of Atreus, is enamored with his prize,
This frantic raver. I am a poor man,
Yet would I not receive her to my bed.'

Cassandra answers with a careless disdain,

'This is a busy slave.'

With all the lofty decorum of manners among the ancients,
how free was their intercourse, man to man, how full the
mutual understanding between prince and 'busy slave!' Not
here in adversity only, but in the pomp of power, it was so.
Kings were approached with ceremonious obeisance, but not
hedged round with etiquette, they could see and know their
fellows.

The Andromache here is just as lovely as that of the Iliad.

To her child whom they are about to murder, the same that
was frightened at the 'glittering plume.'

'Dost thou weep,
My son? Hast thou a sense of thy ill fate?
Why dost thou clasp me with thy hands, why hold
My robes, and shelter thee beneath my wings,
Like a young bird? No more my Hector comes,
Returning from the tomb; he grasps no more
His glittering spear, bringing protection to thee.'

* * *

* * 'O soft embrace,
And to thy mother dear. O fragrant breath!
In vain I swathed thy infant limbs, in vain
I gave thee nurture at this breast, and toiled,
Wasted with care. *If ever*, now embrace,
Now clasp thy mother; throw thine arms around
My neck and join thy cheek, thy lips to mine.'

As I look up I meet the eyes of Beatrice Cenci.* Beautiful
one, these woes, even, were less than thine, yet thou seemest to
understand them all. Thy clear melancholy gaze says, they, at
least, had known moments of bliss, and the tender relations of
nature had not been broken and polluted from the very first.
Yes! the gradations of wo are all but infinite: only good can be
infinite.

Certainly the Greeks knew more of real home intercourse, and more of woman than the Americans. It is in vain to tell me of outward observances. The poets, the sculptors always tell the truth. In proportion as a nation is refined, women *must* have an ascendancy, it is the law of nature.

Beatrice! thou wert not 'fond of life,' either, more than those princesses. Thou wert able to cut it down in the full flower of beauty, as an offering to *the best* known to thee. Thou wert not so happy as to die for thy country or thy brethren, but thou wert worthy of such an occasion.

In the days of chivalry woman was habitually viewed more as an ideal, but I do not know that she inspired a deeper and more home-felt reverence than Iphigenia in the breast of Achilles, or Macaria in that of her old guardian, Iolaus.

We may, with satisfaction, add to these notes the words to which Haydn has adapted his magnificent music in 'The Creation.'

'In native worth and honor clad, with beauty, courage, strength adorned, erect to heaven, and tall, he stands, a Man!—the lord and king of all! The large and arched front sublime of wisdom deep declares the seat, and in his eyes with brightness shines the soul, the breath and image of his God. With fondness leans upon his breast the partner for him formed, a woman fair, and graceful spouse. Her softly ·smiling virgin looks, of flowery spring the mirror, bespeak him love, and joy and bliss.'

Whoever has heard this music must have a mental standard as to what man and woman should be. Such was marriage in Eden, when 'erect to heaven *he* stood,' but since, like other institutions, this must be not only reformed, but revived, may be offered as a picture of something intermediate,—the seed of the future growth,—

H.

THE SACRED MARRIAGE.*

And has another's life as large a scope?
It may give due fulfilment to thy hope,
And every portal to the unknown may ope.

If, near this other life, thy inmost feeling
Trembles with fateful prescience of revealing
The future Deity, time is still concealing.

If thou feel thy whole force drawn more and more
To launch that other bark on seas without a shore;
And no still secret must be kept in store;

If meannesses that dim each temporal deed,
The dull decay that mars the fleshly weed,
And flower of love that seems to fall and leave no
  seed—

Hide never the full presence from thy sight
Of mutual aims and tasks, ideals bright,
Which feed their roots to-day on all this seeming blight.

Twin stars that mutual circle in the heaven,
Two parts for spiritual concord given,
Twin Sabbaths that inlock the Sacred Seven;

Still looking to the centre for the cause,
Mutual light giving to draw out the powers,
And learning all the other groups by cognizance of one
  another's laws:

The parent love the wedded love includes,
The one permits the two their mutual moods,
The two each other know mid myriad multitudes;

With child-like intellect discerning love,
And mutual action energizing love,
In myriad forms affiliating love.

A world whose seasons bloom from pole to pole,
A force which knows both starting-point and goal,
A Home in Heaven,—the Union in the Soul.

TO A FRIEND

Some dried grass-tufts from the wide flowery plain,
A mussel shell from the lone fairy shore,
Some antlers from tall woods which never more
To the wild deer a safe retreat can yield,
An eagle's feather which adorned a Brave,
Well-nigh the last of his despairing band,
For such slight gifts wilt thou extend thy hand
When weary hours a brief refreshment crave?
I give you what I can, not what I would,
If my small drinking-cup would hold a flood,
As Scandinavia sung those must contain
With which the giants gods may entertain;
In our dwarf day we drain few drops, and soon must
       thirst again.

Since you are to share with me such footnotes as may be made on the pages of my life during this summer's wanderings, I should not be quite silent as to this magnificent prologue to the, as yet, unknown drama. Yet I, like others, have little to say where the spectacle is, for once, great enough to fill the whole life, and supersede thought, giving us only its own presence. 'It is good to be here,' is the best as the simplest expression that occurs to the mind. [. . .]

But all great expression, which, on a superficial survey, seems so easy as well as so simple, furnishes, after a while, to the faithful observer its own standard by which to appreciate it. Daily these proportions widened and towered more and more upon my sight, and I got, at last, a proper foreground for these sublime distances. Before coming away, I think I really saw the full wonder of the scene. After awhile it so drew me into itself as to inspire an undefined dread, such as I never knew before, such as may be felt when death is about to usher us into a new existence. The perpetual trampling of the waters seized my senses. I felt that no other sound, however near, could be heard, and would start and look behind me for a foe. I realized the identity of that mood of nature in which these waters were poured down with such absorbing force, with that in which the Indian was shaped on the same soil. For continually upon my mind came, unsought and unwelcome, images, such as never haunted it before, of naked savages stealing behind me with uplifted tomahawks; again and again this illusion recurred, and even after I had thought it over, and tried to shake it off, I could not help starting and looking behind me.

As picture, the Falls can only be seen from the British side. There they are seen in their veils, and at sufficient distance to appreciate the magical effects of these, and the light and shade. From the boat, as you cross, the effects and contrasts are more melodramatic. On the road back from the whirlpool, we saw them as a reduced picture with delight. But what I liked best was to sit on Table Rock, close to the great fall. There all power of observing details, all separate consciousness, was quite lost.

Once, just as I had seated myself there, a man came to take

his first look. He walked close up to the fall, and, after looking at it a moment, with an air as if thinking how he could best appropriate it to his own use, he spat into it. [. . .]

Coming up the river St Clair, we saw Indians for the first time. They were camped out on the bank. It was twilight, and their blanketed forms, in listless groups or stealing along the bank, with a lunge and a stride so different in its wildness from the rudeness of the white settler, gave me the first feeling that I really approached the West.

The people on the boat were almost all New Englanders, seeking their fortunes. They had brought with them their habits of calculation, their cautious manners, their love of polemics. It grieved me to hear these immigrants who were to be the fathers of a new race, all, from the old man down to the little girl, talking not of what they should do, but of what they should get in the new scene. It was to them a prospect, not of the unfolding nobler energies, but of more ease, and larger accumulation. It wearied me, too, to hear Trinity and Unity* discussed in the poor, narrow doctrinal way on these free waters; but that will soon cease, there is not time for this clash of opinions in the West, where the clash of material interests is so noisy. They will need the spirit of religion more than ever to guide them, but will find less time than before for its doctrine. This change was to me, who am tired of the war of words on these subjects, and believe it only sows the wind to reap the whirlwind, refreshing, but I argue nothing from it; there is nothing real in the freedom of thought at the West, it is from the position of men's lives, not the state of their minds. So soon as they have time, unless they grow better meanwhile, they will cavil and criticise, and judge other men by their own standard, and outrage the law of love every way, just as they do with us. [. . .]

The fourth day on these waters, the weather was milder and brighter, so that we could now see them to some purpose. At night was clear moon, and, for the first time, from the upper deck, I saw one of the great steamboats come majestically up. It was glowing with lights, looking many-eyed and sagacious; in its heavy motion it seemed a dowager queen, and this motion, with its solemn pulse, and determined sweep, becomes these smooth waters, especially at night, as much as the dip of the sail-ship the long billows of the ocean.

But it was not so soon that I learned to appreciate the lake scenery; it was only after a daily and careless familiarity that I entered into its beauty, for nature always refuses to be seen by being stared at. Like Bonaparte, she discharges her face of all expression when she catches the eye of impertinent curiosity fixed on her. But he who has gone to sleep in childish ease on her lap, or leaned an aching brow upon her breast, seeking there comfort with full trust as from a mother, will see all a mother's beauty in the look she bends upon him. Later, I felt that I had really seen these regions, and shall speak of them again.

In the afternoon we went on shore at the Manitou islands,* where the boat stops to wood. No one lives here except wood-cutters for the steamboats. I had thought of such a position, from its mixture of profound solitude with service to the great world, as possessing an ideal beauty. I think so still, after seeing the woodcutters and their slovenly huts.

In times of slower growth, man did not enter a situation without a certain preparation or adaptedness to it. He drew from it, if not to the poetical extent, at least, in some proportion, its moral and its meaning. The woodcutter did not cut down so many trees a day, that the hamadryads* had not time to make their plaints heard; the shepherd tended his sheep, and did no jobs or chores the while; the idyl had a chance to grow up, and modulate his oaten pipe. But now the poet must be at the whole expense of the poetry in describing one of these positions; the worker is a true Midas to the gold he makes. The poet must describe, as the painter sketches Irish peasant girls and Danish fishwives, adding the beauty, and leaving out the dirt.

I come to the west prepared for the distaste I must experience at its mushroom growth. I know that where 'go ahead' is the only motto, the village cannot grow into the gentle proportions that successive lives, and the gradations of experience involuntarily give. In older countries the house of the son grew from that of the father, as naturally as new joints on a bough. And the cathedral crowned the whole as naturally as the leafy summit the tree. This cannot be here. The march of peaceful is scarce less wanton than that of warlike invasion. The old landmarks are broken down, and the land, for a season, bears none, except of the rudeness of conquest and the needs of the day, whose bivouac fires blacken the sweetest forest glades. I have come prepared to see all this, to dislike it, but not with stupid narrowness to distrust or defame. On the contrary, while I will not be so obliging as to confound ugliness with beauty, discord with harmony, and laud and be contented with all I meet, when it conflicts with my best desires and tastes, I trust by reverent faith to woo the mighty meaning of the scene, perhaps to foresee the law by which a new order, a new poetry is to be evoked from this chaos, and with a curiosity as ardent, but not so selfish as that of Macbeth, to call up the apparitions of future kings from the strange ingredients of the witch's caldron. Thus, I will not grieve that all the noble trees are gone already from this island to feed this caldron, but believe it will have Medea's virtue,* and reproduce them in the form of new intellectual growths, since centuries cannot again adorn the land with such.

On this most beautiful beach of smooth white pebbles, interspersed with agates and cornelians, for those who know how to find them, we stepped, not like the Indian, with some humble offering, which, if no better than an arrow-head or a little parched corn, would, he judged, please the Manitou,* who looks only at the spirit in which it is offered. Our visit was so far for a religious purpose that one of our party went to inquire the fate of some Unitarian tracts left among the woodcutters a year or two before. But the old Manitou, though, daunted like his children by the approach of the fire-ships which he probably considered demons of a new dynasty, he had suffered his woods to be felled to feed their pride, had been less patient of an encroachment, which did not to him seem so authorized by the law of the strongest, and had scattered those leaves as carelessly as the others of that year.

But S.* and I, like other emigrants, went not to give, but to get, to rifle the wood of flowers for the service of the fire-ship. We returned with a rich booty, among which was the uva ursi, whose leaves the Indians smoke, with the kinnick-kinnick, and which had then just put forth its highly-finished little blossoms, as pretty as those of the blueberry.

Passing along still further, I thought it would be well if the crowds assembled to stare from the various landings were still confined to the kinnick-kinnick, for almost all had tobacco written on their faces, their cheeks rounded with plugs, their eyes dull with its fumes. We reached Chicago on the evening of the sixth day, having been out five days and a half, a rather longer passage than usual at a favorable season of the year.

Chicago, June 20.

There can be no two places in the world more completely thoroughfares than this place and Buffalo. They are the two correspondent valves that open and shut all the time, as the life-blood rushes from east to west, and back again from west to east.

Since it is their office thus to be the doors, and let in and out, it would be unfair to expect from them much character of their own. To make the best provisions for the transmission of produce is their office, and the people who live there are such as are suited for this; active, complaisant, inventive, business people. There are no provisions for the student or idler; to know what the place can give, you should be at work with the rest, the mere traveller will not find it profitable to loiter there as I did.

Since circumstances made it necessary for me so to do, I read all the books I could find about the new region, which now began to become real to me. All the books about the Indians, a paltry collection, truly, yet which furnished material for many thoughts. The most narrow-minded and awkward recital still bears some lineaments of the great features of this nature, and the races of men that illustrated them. [. . .]

Schoolcraft's Algic Researches* is a valuable book, though a worse use could hardly have been made of such fine material. Had the mythological or hunting stories of the Indians been written down exactly as they were received from the lips of the narrators, the collection could not have been surpassed in interest, both for the wild charm they carry with them, and the light they throw on a peculiar modification of life and mind. As it is, though the incidents have an air of originality and pertinence to the occasion, that gives us confidence that they have not been altered, the phraseology in which they were expressed has been entirely set aside, and the flimsy graces, common to the style of annuals and souvenirs, substituted for the Spartan brevity and sinewy grasp of Indian speech. We can just guess what might have been there, as we can detect the fine proportions of the Brave whom the bad taste of some white patron has arranged in frock-coat, hat, and pantaloons.

The few stories Mrs Jameson* wrote out, though to these also a sentimental air has been given, offend much less in that way than is common in this book. What would we give for a completely faithful version of some among them. Yet with all these drawbacks we cannot doubt from internal evidence that they truly ascribe to the Indian a delicacy of sentiment and of fancy that justifies Cooper* in such inventions as his Uncas. It is a white man's view of a savage hero, who would be far finer in his natural proportions; still, through a masquerade figure, it implies the truth.

Irving's books* I also read, some for the first, some for the second time, with increased interest, now that I was to meet such people as he received his materials from. Though the books are pleasing from their grace and luminous arrangement, yet, with the exception of the Tour to the Prairies, they have a stereotype, second-hand air. They lack the breath, the glow, the charming minute traits of living presence. His scenery is only fit to be glanced at from dioramic distance; his Indians are academic figures only. He would have made the best of pictures, if he could have used his own eyes for studies and sketches; as it is, his success is wonderful, but inadequate. [. . .]

In Chicago I first saw the beautiful prairie flowers. They were in their glory the first ten days we were there—

'The golden and the flame-like flowers.'*

The flame-like flower I was taught afterwards, by an Indian girl, to call 'Wickapee;' and she told me, too, that its splendors had a useful side, for it was used by the Indians as a remedy for an illness to which they were subject.

Beside these brilliant flowers, which gemmed and gilt the grass in a sunny afternoon's drive near the blue lake, between the low oakwood and the narrow beach, stimulated, whether sensuously by the optic nerve, unused to so much gold and crimson with such tender green, or symbolically through some meaning dimly seen in the flowers, I enjoyed a sort of fairyland exultation never felt before, and the first drive amid the flowers gave me anticipation of the beauty of the prairies.

At first, the prairie seemed to speak of the very desolation of dullness. After sweeping over the vast monotony of the lakes to come to this monotony of land, with all around a limitless horizon,—to walk, and walk, and run, but never climb, oh! it was too dreary for any but a Hollander to bear. How the eye greeted the approach of a sail, or the smoke of a steamboat; it seemed that any thing so animated must come from a better land, where mountains gave religion to the scene.

The only thing I liked at first to do, was to trace with slow and unexpecting step the narrow margin of the lake. Sometimes a heavy swell gave it expression; at others, only its varied coloring, which I found more admirable every day, and which gave it an air of mirage instead of the vastness of ocean. Then there was a grandeur in the feeling that I might continue that walk, if I had any seven-leagued mode of conveyance to save fatigue, for hundreds of miles without an obstacle and without a change.

But after I had rode out, and seen the flowers and seen the sun set with that calmness seen only in the prairies, and the cattle winding slowly home to their homes in the 'island groves'—peacefullest of sights—I began to love because I began to know the scene, and shrank no longer from 'the encircling vastness.'

It is always thus with the new form of life; we must learn to look at it by its own standard. At first, no doubt my accustomed eye kept saying, if the mind did not, What! no distant mountains? what, no valleys? But after a while I would ascend the roof of the house where we lived, and pass many hours, needing no sight but the moon reigning in the heavens, or starlight falling upon the lake, till all the lights were out in the island grove of men beneath my feet, and felt nearer heaven that there was nothing but this lovely, still reception on the earth; no towering mountains, no deep tree-shadows, nothing but plain earth and water bathed in light.

Sunset, as seen from that place, presented most generally, low-lying, flaky clouds, of the softest serenity, 'like,' said S., 'the Buddhist tracts.'

One night a star shot madly from its sphere, and it had a fair chance to be seen, but that serenity could not be astonished.

Yes! it was a peculiar beauty of those sunsets and moonlights on the levels of Chicago which Chamonix or the Trossachs could not make me forget.

Notwithstanding all the attractions I thus found out by degrees on the flat shores of the lake, I was delighted when I found myself really on my way into the country for an excursion of two or three weeks. We set forth in a strong wagon, almost as large, and with the look of those used elsewhere for transporting caravans of wild beasts, loaded with every thing we might want, in case nobody would give it to us—for buying and selling were no longer to be counted on—with a pair of strong horses, able and willing to force their way through mud holes and amid stumps, and a guide, equally admirable as marshal and companion, who knew by heart the country and its history, both natural and artificial, and whose clear hunter's eye needed neither road nor goal to guide it to all the spots where beauty best loves to dwell.

Add to this the finest weather, and such country as I had never seen, even in my dreams, although these dreams had been haunted by wishes for just such an one, and you may judge whether years of dullness might not, by these bright days, be redeemed, and a sweetness be shed over all thoughts of the West.

The first day brought us through woods rich in the moccasin flower and lupine, and plains whose soft expanse was continually touched with expression by the slow moving clouds which

> 'Sweep over with their shadows, and beneath
> The surface rolls and fluctuates to the eye;
> Dark hollows seem to glide along and chase
> The sunny ridges,'

to the banks of the Fox river, a sweet and graceful stream. We reached Geneva just in time to escape being drenched by a violent thunder shower, whose rise and disappearance threw expression into all the features of the scene.

Geneva reminds me of a New England village, as indeed there, and in the neighborhood, are many New Englanders of an excellent stamp, generous, intelligent, discreet, and seeking to win from life its true values. Such are much wanted, and seem like points of light among the swarms of settlers, whose aims are sordid, whose habits thoughtless and slovenly.

With great pleasure we heard, with his attentive and affectionate congregation, the Unitarian clergyman, Mr Conant, and afterward visited him in his house, where almost everything bore traces of his own handywork or that of his father. He is just such a teacher as is wanted in this region, familiar enough with the habits of those he addresses to come home to their experience and their wants; earnest and enlightened enough to draw the important inferences from the life of every day.

A day or two we remained here, and passed some happy hours in the woods that fringe the stream, where the gentlemen found a rich booty of fish.

Next day, travelling along the river's banks, was an uninterrupted pleasure. We closed our drive in the afternoon at the house of an English gentleman, who has gratified, as few men do, the common wish to pass the evening of an active day amid the quiet influences of country life. He showed us a bookcase filled with books about this country; these he had collected for years, and become so familiar with the localities that, on coming here at last, he sought and found, at once, the very spot he wanted, and where he is as content as he hoped to be, thus realizing Wordsworth's description of the wise man, who 'sees what he foresaw.'

A wood surrounds the house, through which paths are cut in every direction. It is, for this new country, a large and handsome dwelling; but round it are its barns and farm yard, with cattle and poultry. These, however, in the framework of wood, have a very picturesque and pleasing effect. There is that mixture of culture and rudeness in the aspect of things as gives a feeling of freedom, not of confusion.

I wish it were possible to give some idea of this scene as viewed by the earliest freshness of dewy dawn. This habitation of man seemed like a nest in the grass, so thoroughly were the buildings and all the objects of human care harmonized with what was natural. The tall trees bent and whispered all around, as if to hail with sheltering love the men who had come to dwell among them.

The young ladies were musicians, and spoke French fluently, having been educated in a convent. Here in the prairie, they had learned to take care of the milk-room, and kill the rattle-snakes that assailed their poultry yard. Beneath the shade of heavy curtains you looked out from the high and large windows to see Norwegian peasants at work in their national dress. In the wood grew, not only the flowers I had before seen, and wealth of tall, wild roses, but the splendid blue spiderwort, that orna-ment of our gardens. Beautiful children strayed there, who were soon to leave these civilized regions for some really wild and western place, a post in the buffalo country. Their no less beautiful mother was of Welsh descent, and the eldest child bore the name of Gwynthleon. Perhaps there she will meet with some young descendants of Madoc,* to be her friends; at any rate, her looks may retain that sweet, wild beauty, that is soon made to vanish from eyes which look too much on shops and streets, and the vulgarities of city 'parties.'

Next day we crossed the river. We ladies crossed on a little foot-bridge, from which we could look down the stream, and see the wagon pass over at the ford. A black thunder cloud was coming up. The sky and waters heavy with expectation. The motion of the wagon, with its white cover, and the laboring horses, gave just the due interest to the picture, because it seemed as if they would not have time to cross before the storm came on. However, they did get across, and we were a mile or two on our way before the violent shower obliged us to take refuge in a solitary house upon the prairie. In this country it is as pleasant to stop as to go on, to lose your way as to find it, for the variety in the population gives you a chance for fresh enter-tainment in every hut, and the luxuriant beauty makes every path attractive. In this house we found a family 'quite above the common,' but, I grieve to say, not above false pride, for the father, ashamed of being caught barefoot, told us a story of a man, one of the richest men, he said, in one of the eastern cities, who went barefoot, from choice and taste.

Near the door grew a Provence rose, then in blossom. Other families we saw had brought with them and planted the locust. It was pleasant to see their old home loves, brought into con-nection with their new splendors. Wherever there were traces of this tenderness of feeling, only too rare among Americans, other things bore signs also of prosperity and intelligence, as if the ordering mind of man had some idea of home beyond a mere shelter, beneath which to eat and sleep.

No heaven need wear a lovelier aspect than earth did this afternoon, after the clearing up of the shower. We traversed the blooming plain, unmarked by any road, only the friendly track of wheels which tracked, not broke the grass. Our stations were not from town to town, but from grove to grove. These groves first floated like blue islands in the distance. As we drew nearer, they seemed fair parks, and the little log houses on the edge, with their curling smokes, harmonized beautifully with them.

One of these groves, Ross's grove, we reached just at sunset. It was of the noblest trees I saw during this journey, for the trees generally were not large or lofty, but only of fair proportions. Here they were large enough to form with their clear stems pillars for grand cathedral aisles. There was space enough for crimson light to stream through upon the floor of water which the shower had left. As we slowly plashed through, I thought I was never in a better place for vespers.

That night we rested, or rather tarried at a grove some miles beyond, and there partook of the miseries so often jocosely portrayed, of bedchambers for twelve, a milk dish for universal handbasin, and expectations that you would use and lend your 'hankercher' for a towel. But this was the only night, thanks to the hospitality of private families, that we passed thus, and it was well that we had this bit of experience, else might we have pronounced all Trollopian records* of the kind to be inventions of pure malice.

With us was a young lady who showed herself to have been bathed in the Britannic fluid,* wittily described by a late French writer, by the impossibility she experienced of accommodating herself to the indecorums of the scene. We ladies were to sleep in the bar-room, from which its drinking visitors could be ejected only at a late hour. The outer door had no fastening to prevent their return. However, our host kindly requested we would call him, if they did, as he had 'conquered them for us,' and would do so again. We had also rather hard couches; (mine was the supper table,) but we yankees, born to rove, were altogether too much fatigued to stand upon trifles, and slept as sweetly as we would in the 'bigly bower' of any baroness. But I think England sat up all night, wrapped in her blanket shawl, and with a neat lace cap upon her head; so that she would have looked perfectly the lady, if any one had come in; shuddering and listening. I know that she was very ill next day, in requital. She watched, as her parent country watches the seas, that nobody may do wrong in any case, and deserved to have met some interruption, she was so well prepared. However, there was none, other than from the nearness of some twenty sets of powerful lungs, which would not leave the night to a deadly stillness. In this house we had, if not good beds, yet good tea, good bread, and wild strawberries, and were entertained with most free communications of opinion and history from our hosts. Neither shall any of us have a right to say again that we cannot find any who may be willing to hear all we may have to say. 'All's fish that comes to the net,' should be painted on the sign at Papaw grove.

In the afternoon of this day we reached the Rock river, in whose neighborhood we proposed to make some stay, and crossed at Dixon's ferry.

This beautiful stream flows full and wide over a bed of rocks, traversing a distance of near two hundred miles, to reach the Mississippi. Great part of the country along its banks is the finest region of Illinois, and the scene of some of the latest romance of Indian warfare. To these beautiful regions Black Hawk returned with his band 'to pass the summer,' when he drew upon himself the warfare in which he was finally vanquished. No wonder he could not resist the longing, unwise though its indulgence might be, to return in summer to this home of beauty.

Of Illinois, in general, it has often been remarked that it bears the character of country which has been inhabited by a nation skilled like the English in all the ornamental arts of life, especially in landscape gardening. That the villas and castles seem to have been burnt, the enclosures taken down, but the velvet lawns, the flower gardens, the stately parks, scattered at graceful intervals by the decorous hand of art, the frequent deer, and the peaceful herd of cattle that make picture of the plain, all suggest more of the masterly mind of man, than the prodigal, but careless, motherly love of nature. Especially is this true of the Rock river country. The river flows sometimes through these parks and lawns, then betwixt high bluffs, whose grassy ridges are covered with fine trees, or broken with crumbling stone, that easily assumes the forms of buttress, arch and clustered columns. Along the face of such crumbling rocks, swallows' nests are clustered, thick as cities, and eagles and deer do not disdain their summits. One morning, out in the boat along the base of these rocks, it was amusing, and affecting too, to see these swallows put their heads out to look at us. There was something very hospitable about it, as if man had never shown himself a tyrant near them. What a morning that was! Every sight is worth twice as much by the early morning light. We borrow something of the spirit of the hour to look upon them.

The first place where we stopped was one of singular beauty, a beauty of soft, luxuriant wildness. It was on the bend of the river, a place chosen by an Irish gentleman, whose absenteeship seems of the wisest kind, since for a sum which would have been but a drop of water to the thirsty fever of his native land, he commands a residence which has all that is desirable, in its independence, its beautiful retirement, and means of benefit to others.

His park, his deer-chase, he found already prepared; he had only to make an avenue through it. This brought us by a drive, which in the heat of noon seemed long, though afterwards, in the cool of morning and evening, delightful, to the house. This is, for that part of the world, a large and commodious dwelling. Near it stands the log-cabin where its master lived while it was building, a very ornamental accessory.

In front of the house was a lawn, adorned by the most graceful trees. A few of these had been taken out to give a full view of the river, gliding through banks such as I have described. On this bend the bank is high and bold, so from the house or the lawn the view was very rich and commanding. But if you descended a ravine at the side to the water's edge, you found there a long walk on the narrow shore, with a wall above of the richest hanging wood, in which they said the deer lay hid. I never saw one, but often fancied that I heard them rustling, at daybreak, by these bright clear waters, stretching out in such smiling promise, where no sound broke the deep and blissful seclusion, unless now and then this rustling, or the plash of some fish a little gayer than the others; it seemed not necessary to have any better heaven, or fuller expression of love and freedom than in the mood of nature here.

Then, leaving the bank, you would walk far and far through long grassy paths, full of the most brilliant, also the most delicate flowers. The brilliant are more common on the prairie, but both kinds loved this place.

Amid the grass of the lawn, with a profusion of wild strawberries, we greeted also a familiar love, the Scottish harebell, the gentlest, and most touching form of the flower-world.

The master of the house was absent, but with a kindness beyond thanks had offered us a resting place there. Here we were taken care of by a deputy, who would, for his youth, have been assigned the place of a page in former times, but in the young west, it seems he was old enough for a steward. Whatever be called his function, he did the honors of the place so much in harmony with it, as to leave the guests free to imagine themselves in Elysium. And the three days passed here were days of unalloyed, spotless happiness.

There was a peculiar charm in coming here, where the choice of location, and the unobtrusive good taste of all the arrangements, showed such intelligent appreciation of the spirit of the scene, after seeing so many dwellings of the new settlers, which showed plainly that they had no thought beyond satisfying the grossest material wants. Sometimes they looked attractive, the little brown houses, the natural architecture of the country, in the edge of the timber. But almost always when you came near, the slovenliness of the dwelling and the rude way in which objects around it were treated, when so little care would have presented a charming whole, were very repulsive. Seeing the traces of the Indians, who chose the most beautiful sites for their dwellings, and whose habits do not break in on that aspect of nature under which they were born, we feel as if they were the rightful lords of a beauty they forbore to deform. But most of these settlers do not see it at all; it breathes, it speaks in vain to those who are rushing into its sphere. Their progress is Gothic, not Roman,* and their mode of cultivation will, in the course of twenty, perhaps ten, years, obliterate the natural expression of the country.

This is inevitable, fatal; we must not complain, but look forward to a good result. Still, in travelling through this country, I could not but be struck with the force of a symbol. Wherever the hog comes, the rattlesnake disappears; the omnivorous traveller, safe in its stupidity, willingly and easily makes a meal of the most dangerous of reptiles, and one whom the Indian looks on with a mystic awe. Even so the white settler pursues the Indian, and is victor in the chase. But I shall say more upon the subject by-and-by.

While we were here we had one grand thunder storm, which added new glory to the scene.

One beautiful feature was the return of the pigeons every afternoon to their home. Every afternoon they came sweeping across the lawn, positively in clouds, and with a swiftness and softness of winged motion, more beautiful than anything of the kind I ever knew. Had I been a musician, such as Mendelsohn, I felt that I could have improvised a music quite peculiar, from the sound they made, which should have indicated all the beauty over which their wings bore them. [. . .]

Leaving this place, we proceeded a day's journey along the beautiful stream, to a little town named Oregon. We called at a cabin, from whose door looked out one of those faces which, once seen, are never forgotten; young, yet touched with many traces of feeling, not only possible, but endured; spirited, too, like the gleam of a finely tempered blade. It was a face that suggested a history, and many histories, but whose scene would have been in courts and camps. At this moment their circles are dull for want of that life which is waning unexcited in this solitary recess.

The master of the house proposed to show us a 'short cut,' by which we might, to especial advantage, pursue our journey. This proved to be almost perpendicular down a hill, studded with young trees and stumps. From these he proposed, with a hospitality of service worthy an Oriental, to free our wheels whenever they should get entangled, also, to be himself the drag, to prevent our too rapid descent. Such generosity deserved trust; however, we women could not be persuaded to render it. We got out and admired, from afar, the process. Left by our guide—and prop! we found ourselves in a wide field, where, by playful quips and turns, an endless 'creek,' seemed to divert itself with our attempts to cross it. Failing in this, the next best was to whirl down a steep bank, which feat our charioteer performed with an air not unlike that of Rhesus,* had he but been as suitably furnished with chariot and steeds!

At last, after wasting some two or three hours on the 'short cut,' we got out by following an Indian trail,—Black Hawk's! How fair the scene through which it led! How could they let themselves be conquered, with such a country to fight for!

Afterwards, in the wide prairie, we saw a lively picture of nonchalance, (to speak in the fashion of dear Ireland.) There, in the wide sunny field, with neither tree nor umbrella above his head, sat a pedler, with his pack, waiting apparently for customers. He was not disappointed. We bought, what hold in regard to the human world, as unmarked, as mysterious, and as important an existence, as the infusoria to the natural, to wit, pins. This incident would have delighted those modern sages, who, in imitation of the sitting philosophers of ancient Ind, prefer silence to speech, waiting to going, and scornfully smile in answer to the motions of earnest life,

> 'Of itself will nothing come,
> That ye must still be seeking?'*

However, it seemed to me to-day, as formerly on these sublime occasions, obvious that nothing would come, unless something would go; now, if we had been as sublimely still as the pedler, his pins would have tarried in the pack, and his pockets sustained an aching void of pence!

Passing through one of the fine, park-like woods, almost clear from underbrush and carpeted with thick grasses and flowers, we met, (for it was Sunday,) a little congregation just returning from their service, which had been performed in a rude house in its midst. It had a sweet and peaceful air as if such words and thoughts were very dear to them. The parents had with them all their little children; but we saw no old people; that charm was wanting, which exists in such scenes in older settlements, of seeing the silver bent in reverence beside the flaxen head.

At Oregon, the beauty of the scene was of even a more sumptuous character than at our former 'stopping place.' Here swelled the river in its boldest course, interspersed by halcyon isles on which nature had lavished all her prodigality in tree, vine, and flower, banked by noble bluffs, three hundred feet high, their sharp ridges as exquisitely definite as the edge of a shell; their summits adorned with those same beautiful trees, and with buttresses of rich rock, crested with old hemlocks, which wore a touching and antique grace amid the softer and more luxuriant vegetation. Lofty natural mounds rose amidst the rest, with the same lovely and sweeping outline, showing everywhere the plastic power of water,—water, mother of beauty, which, by its sweet and eager flow, had left such lineaments as human genius never dreamt of.

Not far from the river was a high crag, called the Pine Rock, which looks out, as our guide observed, like a helmet above the brow of the country. It seems as if the water left here and there a vestige of forms and materials that preceded its course, just to set off its new and richer designs.

The aspect of this country was to me enchanting, beyond any I have ever seen, from its fullness of expression, its bold and impassioned sweetness. Here the flood of emotion has passed over and marked everywhere its course by a smile. The fragments of rock touch it with a wildness and liberality which give just the needed relief. I should never be tired here, though I have elsewhere seen country of more secret and alluring charms, better calculated to stimulate and suggest. Here the eye and heart are filled.

How happy the Indians must have been here! It is not long since they were driven away, and the ground, above and below, is full of their traces.

'The earth is full of men.'

You have only to turn up the sod to find arrowheads and Indian pottery. On an island, belonging to our host, and nearly opposite his house, they loved to stay, and, no doubt, enjoyed its lavish beauty as much as the myriad wild pigeons that now haunt its flower-filled shades. Here are still the marks of their tomahawks, the troughs in which they prepared their corn, their caches.

A little way down the river is the site of an ancient Indian village, with its regularly arranged mounds. As usual, they had chosen with the finest taste. It was one of those soft shadowy afternoons when we went there, when nature seems ready to weep, not from grief, but from an overfull heart. Two prattling, lovely little girls, and an African boy, with glittering eye and ready grin, made our party gay; but all were still as we entered their little inlet and trod those flowery paths. They may blacken Indian life as they will, talk of its dirt, its brutality, I will ever believe that the men who chose that dwelling-place were able to feel emotions of noble happiness as they returned to it, and so were the women that received them. Neither were the children sad or dull, who lived so familiarly with the deer and the birds, and swam that clear wave in the shadow of the Seven Sisters. The whole scene suggested to me a Greek splendor, a Greek sweetness, and I can believe that an Indian brave, accustomed to ramble in such paths, and be bathed by such sunbeams, might be mistaken for Apollo, as Apollo was for him by West.* Two of the boldest bluffs are called the Deer's Walk, (not because deer do *not* walk there,) and the Eagle's Nest. The latter I visited one glorious morning; it was that of the fourth of July, and certainly I think I had never felt so happy that I was born in America. Wo to all country folks that never saw this spot, never swept an enraptured gaze over the prospect that stretched beneath. I do believe Rome and Florence are suburbs compared to this capital of nature's art.

The bluff was decked with great bunches of a scarlet variety of the milkweed, like cut coral, and all starred with a mysterious-looking dark flower, whose cup rose lonely on a tall stem. [. . .]

Returning, the gay flotilla hailed the little flag which the children had raised from a log-cabin, prettier than any president ever saw, and drank the health of their country and all mankind, with a clear conscience.

Dance and song wound up the day. I know not when the

mere local habitation has seemed to me to afford so fair a chance of happiness as this. To a person of unspoiled tastes, the beauty alone would afford stimulus enough. But with it would be naturally associated all kinds of wild sports, experiments, and the studies of natural history. In these regards, the poet, the sportsman, the naturalist, would alike rejoice in this wide range of untouched loveliness.

Then, with a very little money, a ducal estate may be purchased, and by a very little more, and moderate labor, a family be maintained upon it with raiment, food and shelter. The luxurious and minute comforts of a city life are not yet to be had without effort disproportionate to their value. But, where there is so great a counterpoise, cannot these be given up once for all? If the houses are imperfectly built, they can afford immense fires and plenty of covering; if they are small, who cares?—with such fields to roam in. In winter, it may be borne; in summer, is of no consequence. With plenty of fish, and game, and wheat, can they not dispense with a baker to bring 'muffins hot' every morning to the door for their breakfast?

Here a man need not take a small slice from the landscape, and fence it in from the obtrusions of an uncongenial neighbor, and there cut down his fancies to miniature improvements which a chicken could run over in ten minutes. He may have water and wood and land enough, to dread no incursions on his prospect from some chance Vandal that may enter his neighborhood. He need not painfully economise and manage how he may use it all; he can afford to leave some of it wild, and to carry out his own plans without obliterating those of nature.

Here, whole families might live together, if they would. The sons might return from their pilgrimages to settle near the parent hearth; the daughters might find room near their mother. Those painful separations, which already desecrate and desolate the Atlantic coast,* are not enforced here by the stern need of seeking bread; and where they are voluntary, it is no matter. To me, too, used to the feelings which haunt a society of struggling men, it was delightful to look upon a scene where nature still wore her motherly smile and seemed to promise room not only for those favored or cursed with the qualities best adapting for the strifes of competition, but for the delicate, the thoughtful, even the indolent or eccentric. She did not say, Fight or starve; nor even, Work or cease to exist; but, merely showing that the apple was a finer fruit than the wild crab, gave both room to grow in the garden.

A pleasant society is formed of the families who live along the banks of this stream upon farms. They are from various parts of the world, and have much to communicate to one another. Many have cultivated minds and refined manners, all a varied experience, while they have in common the interests of a new country and a new life. They must traverse some space to get at one another, but the journey is through scenes that make it a separate pleasure. They must bear inconveniences to stay in one another's houses; but these, to the well-disposed, are only a source of amusement and adventure.

The great drawback upon the lives of these settlers, at present, is the unfitness of the women for their new lot. It has generally been the choice of the men, and the women follow, as women will, doing their best for affection's sake, but too often in heart-sickness and weariness. Beside it frequently not being a choice or conviction of their own minds that it is best to be here, their part is the hardest, and they are least fitted for it. The men can find assistance in field labor, and recreation with the gun and fishing-rod. Their bodily strength is greater, and enables them to bear and enjoy both these forms of life.

The women can rarely find any aid in domestic labor. All its various and careful tasks must often be performed, sick or well, by the mother and daughters, to whom a city education has imparted neither the strength nor skill now demanded.

The wives of the poorer settlers, having more hard work to do than before, very frequently become slatterns; but the ladies, accustomed to a refined neatness, feel that they cannot degrade themselves by its absence, and struggle under every disadvantage to keep up the necessary routine of small arrangements.

With all these disadvantages for work, their resources for pleasure are fewer. When they can leave the housework, they have not learnt to ride, to drive, to row, alone: their culture has too generally been that given to women to make them 'the ornaments of society.' They can dance, but not draw; talk

French, but know nothing of the language of flowers; neither in childhood were allowed to cultivate them, lest they should tan their complexions. Accustomed to the pavement of Broadway, they dare not tread the wildwood paths for fear of rattlesnakes!

Seeing much of this joylessness, and inaptitude, both of body and mind, for a lot which would be full of blessings for those prepared for it, we could not but look with deep interest on the little girls, and hope they would grow up with the strength of body, dexterity, simple tastes, and resources that would fit them to enjoy and refine the western farmer's life.

But they have a great deal to war with in the habits of thought acquired by their mothers from their own early life. Everywhere the fatal spirit of imitation, of reference to European standards, penetrates, and threatens to blight whatever of original growth might adorn the soil.

If the little girls grow up strong, resolute, able to exert their faculties, their mothers mourn over their want of fashionable delicacy. Are they gay, enterprising, ready to fly about in the various ways that teach them so much, these ladies lament that 'they cannot go to school, where they might learn to be quiet.' They lament the want of 'education' for their daughters, as if the thousand needs which call out their young energies, and the language of nature around, yielded no education.

Their grand ambition for their children, is to send them to school in some eastern city, the measure most likely to make them useless and unhappy at home. I earnestly hope that, ere long, the existence of good schools near themselves, planned by persons of sufficient thought to meet the wants of the place and time, instead of copying New York or Boston, will correct this mania. Instruction the children want to enable them to profit by the great natural advantages of their position; but methods copied from the education of some English Lady Augusta, are as ill suited to the daughter of an Illinois farmer, as satin shoes to climb the Indian mounds. An elegance she would diffuse around her, if her mind were opened to appreciate elegance; it might be of a kind new, original, enchanting, as different from that of the city belle as that of the prairie torch-flower from the shopworn article that touches the cheek of that lady within her bonnet.

To a girl really skilled to make home beautiful and comfortable, with bodily strength to enjoy plenty of exercise, the woods, the streams, a few studies, music, and the sincere and familiar intercourse, far more easily to be met here than elsewhere, would afford happiness enough. Her eyes would not grow dim, nor her cheeks sunken, in the absence of parties, morning visits, and milliner's shops.

As to music, I wish I could see in such places the guitar rather than the piano, and good vocal more than instrumental music.

The piano many carry with them, because it is the fashionable instrument in the eastern cities. Even there, it is so merely from the habit of imitating Europe, for not one in a thousand is willing to give the labor requisite to ensure any valuable use of the instrument.

But, out here, where the ladies have so much less leisure, it is still less desirable. Add to this, they never know how to tune their own instruments, and as persons seldom visit them who can do so, these pianos are constantly out of tune, and would spoil the ear of one who began by having any.

The guitar, or some portable instrument which requires less practice, and could be kept in tune by themselves, would be far more desirable for most of these ladies. It would give all they want as a household companion to fill up the gaps of life with a pleasant stimulus or solace, and be sufficient accompaniment to the voice in social meetings.

Singing in parts is the most delightful family amusement, and those who are constantly together can learn to sing in perfect accord. All the practice it needs, after some good elementary instruction, is such as meetings by summer twilight, and evening firelight naturally suggest. And, as music is an universal language, we cannot but think a fine Italian duet would be as much at home in the log cabin as one of Mrs Gore's novels.*

The sixth July we left this beautiful place. It was one of those rich days of bright sunlight, varied by the purple shadows of large sweeping clouds. Many a backward look we cast, and left the heart behind.

Our journey to-day was no less delightful than before, still all new, boundless, limitless. Kinmont says, that limits are sacred;

that the Greeks were in the right to worship a god of limits. I say, that what is limitless is alone divine, that there was neither wall nor road in Eden, that those who walked there lost and found their way just as we did, and that all the gain from the Fall was that we had a wagon to ride in. I do not think, either, that even the horses doubted whether this last was any advantage.

Everywhere the rattlesnake-weed grows in profusion. The antidote survives the bane. Soon the coarser plantain, the 'white man's footstep,' shall take its place.

We saw also the compass plant, and the western tea plant. Of some of the brightest flowers an Indian girl afterwards told me the medicinal virtues. I doubt not those students of the soil knew a use to every fair emblem, on which we could only look to admire its hues and shape.

After noon we were ferried by a girl, (unfortunately not of the most picturesque appearance) across the Kishwaukie, the most graceful stream, and on whose bosom rested many full-blown water-lilies, twice as large as any of ours. I was told that, *en revanche*,* they were scentless, but I still regret that I could not get at one of them to try.

Query, did the lilied fragrance which, in the miraculous times, accompanied visions of saints and angels, proceed from water or garden lilies?

Kishwaukie is, according to tradition, the scene of a famous battle, and its many grassy mounds contain the bones of the valiant. On these waved thickly the mysterious purple flower, of which I have spoken before. I think it springs from the blood of the Indians, as the hyacinth did from that of Apollo's darling.*

The ladies of our host's family at Oregon, when they first went there, after all the pains and plagues of building and settling, found their first pastime in opening one of these mounds, in which they found, I think, three of the departed, seated in the Indian fashion.

One of these same ladies, as she was making bread one winter morning, saw from the window a deer directly before the house. She ran out, with her hands covered with dough, calling the others, and they caught him bodily before he had time to escape.

Here (at Kishwaukie) we received a visit from a ragged and barefoot, but bright-eyed gentleman, who seemed to be the intellectual loafer, the walking Will's coffeehouse of the place. He told us many charming snake stories; among others, of himself having seen seventeen young ones reënter the mother snake, on the intrusion of a visitor.

This night we reached Belvidere, a flourishing town in Boon county, where was the tomb, now despoiled, of Big Thunder. In this later day we felt happy to find a really good hotel.

From this place, by two days of very leisurely and devious journeying, we reached Chicago, and thus ended a journey, which one at least of the party might have wished unending. [. . .]

At the hotel table were daily to be seen new faces, and new stories to be learned. And any one who has a large acquaintance may be pretty sure of meeting some of them here in the course of a few days.

Among those whom I met was Mrs Z., the aunt of an old schoolmate, to whom I impatiently hastened, as soon as the meal was over, to demand news of Mariana.* The answer startled me. Mariana, so full of life, was dead. That form, the most rich in energy and coloring of any I had ever seen, had faded from the earth. The circle of youthful associations had given way in the part, that seemed the strongest. What I now learned of the story of this life, and what was by myself remembered, may be bound together in this slight sketch.

At the boarding-school to which I was too early sent, a fond, a proud, and timid child, I saw among the ranks of the gay and graceful, bright or earnest girls, only one who interested my fancy or touched my young heart; and this was Mariana. She was, on the father's side, of Spanish Creole blood, but had been sent to the Atlantic coast, to receive a school education under the care of her aunt, Mrs Z.

This lady had kept her mostly at home with herself, and Mariana had gone from her house to a dayschool; but the aunt, being absent for a time in Europe, she had now been unfortunately committed for some time to the mercies of a boarding-school.

A strange bird she proved there,—a lonely swallow that could not make for itself a summer. At first, her schoolmates were captivated with her ways; her love of wild dances and sudden song, her freaks of passion and of wit. She was always new, always surprising, and, for a time, charming.

But, after awhile, they tired of her. She could never be depended on to join in their plans, yet she expected them to follow out hers with their whole strength. She was very loving, even infatuated in her own affections, and exacted from those who had professed any love for her, the devotion she was willing to bestow.

Yet there was a vein of haughty caprice in her character; a love of solitude, which made her at times wish to retire entirely, and at these times she would expect to be thoroughly understood, and let alone, yet to be welcomed back when she returned. She did not thwart others in their humors, but she never doubted of great indulgence from them.

Some singular habits she had which, when new, charmed, but, after acquaintance, displeased her companions. She had by nature the same habit and power of excitement that is described in the spinning dervishes of the East. Like them, she would spin until all around her were giddy, while her own brain, instead of being disturbed, was excited to great action. Pausing, she would declaim verse of others or her own; act many parts, with strange catch-words and burdens that seemed to act with mystical power on her own fancy, sometimes stimulating her to convulse the hearer with laughter, sometimes to melt him to tears. When her power began to languish, she would spin again till fired to recommence her singular drama, into which she wove figures from the scenes of her earlier childhood, her companions, and the dignitaries she sometimes saw, with fantasies unknown to life, unknown to heaven or earth.

This excitement, as may be supposed, was not good for her. It oftenest came on in the evening, and often spoiled her sleep. She would wake in the night, and cheat her restlessness by inventions that teazed, while they sometimes diverted her companions.

She was also a sleep-walker; and this one trait of her case did somewhat alarm her guardians, who, otherwise, showed the same profound stupidity as to this peculiar being, usual in the overseers of the young. They consulted a physician, who said she would outgrow it, and prescribed a milk diet.

Meantime, the fever of this ardent and too early stimulated nature was constantly increased by the restraints and narrow routine of the boarding school. She was always devising means to break in upon it. She had a taste which would have seemed ludicrous to her mates, if they had not felt some awe of her, from a touch of genius and power that never left her, for costume and fancy dresses, always some sash twisted about her, some drapery, something odd in the arrangement of her hair and dress, so that the methodical preceptress dared not let her go out without a careful scrutiny and remodelling, whose soberizing effects generally disappeared the moment she was in the free air.

At last, a vent for her was found in private theatricals. Play followed play, and in these and the rehearsals she found entertainment congenial with her. The principal parts, as a matter of course, fell to her lot; most of the good suggestions and arrangements came from her, and for a time she ruled masterly and shone triumphant.

During these performances the girls had heightened their natural bloom with artificial red; this was delightful to them—it was something so out of the way. But Mariana, after the plays were over, kept her carmine saucer on the dressing-table, and put on her blushes regularly as the morning.

When stared and jeered at, she at first said she did it because she thought it made her look prettier; but, after a while, she became quite petulant about it,—would make no reply to any joke, but merely kept on doing it.

This irritated the girls, as all eccentricity does the world in general, more than vice or malignity. They talked it over among themselves, till they got wrought up to a desire of punishing, once for all, this sometimes amusing, but so often provoking nonconformist.

Having obtained the leave of the mistress, they laid, with great glee, a plan one evening, which was to be carried into execution next day at dinner.

Among Mariana's irregularities was a great aversion to the meal-time ceremonial. So long, so tiresome she found it, to be seated at a certain moment, to wait while each one was served at so large a table, and one where there was scarcely any conversation; from day to day it became more heavy to her to sit there, or go there at all. Often as possible she excused herself on the ever-convenient plea of headache, and was hardly ever ready when the dinner-bell rang.

To-day it found her on the balcony, lost in gazing on the beautiful prospect. I have heard her say afterwards, she had rarely in her life been so happy,—and she was one with whom happiness was a still rapture. It was one of the most blessed summer days; the shadows of great white clouds empurpled the distant hills for a few moments only to leave them more golden; the tall grass of the wide fields waved in the softest breeze. Pure blue were the heavens, and the same hue of pure contentment was in the heart of Mariana.

Suddenly on her bright mood jarred the dinner bell. At first rose her usual thought, I will not, cannot go; and then the *must*, which daily life can always enforce, even upon the butterflies and birds, came, and she walked reluctantly to her room. She merely changed her dress, and never thought of adding the artificial rose to her cheek.

When she took her seat in the dining-hall, and was asked if she would be helped, raising her eyes, she saw the person who asked her was deeply rouged, with a bright glaring spot, perfectly round, in either cheek. She looked at the next, same apparition! She then slowly passed her eyes down the whole line, and saw the same, with a suppressed smile distorting every countenance. Catching the design at once, she deliberately looked along her own side of the table, at every schoolmate in turn; every one had joined in the trick. The teachers strove to be grave, but she saw they enjoyed the joke. The servants could not suppress a titter.

When Warren Hastings* stood at the bar of Westminster Hall—when the Methodist preacher walked through a line of men, each of whom greeted him with a brickbat or a rotten egg, they had some preparation for the crisis, and it might not be very difficult to meet it with an impassive brow. Our little girl was quite unprepared to find herself in the midst of a world which despised her, and triumphed in her disgrace.

She had ruled, like a queen, in the midst of her companions; she had shed her animation through their lives, and loaded them with prodigal favors, nor once suspected that a powerful favorite might not be loved. Now, she felt that she had been but a dangerous plaything in the hands of those whose hearts she never had doubted.

Yet, the occasion found her equal to it, for Mariana had the kind of spirit, which, in a better cause, had made the Roman matron truly say of her deathwound, 'It is not painful, Poetus.' She did not blench—she did not change countenance. She swallowed her dinner with apparent composure. She made remarks to those near her, as if she had no eyes.

The wrath of the foe of course rose higher, and the moment they were freed from the restraints of the dining-room, they all ran off, gaily calling, and sarcastically laughing, with backward glances, at Mariana, left alone.

She went alone to her room, locked the door, and threw herself on the floor in strong convulsions. These had sometimes threatened her life, as a child, but of later years, she had outgrown them. School-hours came, and she was not there. A little girl, sent to her door, could get no answer. The teachers became alarmed, and broke it open. Bitter was their penitence and that of her companions at the state in which they found her. For some hours, terrible anxiety was felt; but, at last, nature, exhausted, relieved herself by a deep slumber.

From this Mariana rose an altered being. She made no reply to the expressions of sorrow from her companions, none to the grave and kind, but undiscerning comments of her teacher. She did not name the source of her anguish, and its poisoned dart sank deeply in. It was this thought which stung her so. What, not one, not a single one, in the hour of trial, to take my part, not one who refused to take part against me. Past words of love, and caresses, little heeded at the time, rose to her memory, and gave fuel to her distempered thoughts. Beyond the sense of universal perfidy, of burning resentment, she could not get. And Mariana, born for love, now hated all the world.

The change, however, which these feelings made in her conduct and appearance bore no such construction to the careless observer. Her gay freaks were quite gone, her wildness, her invention. Her dress was uniform, her manner much subdued. Her chief interest seemed now to lie in her studies, and in music. Her companions she never sought, but they, partly from uneasy remorseful feelings, partly that they really liked her much better now that she did not oppress and puzzle them, sought her continually. And here the black shadow comes upon her life, the only stain upon the history of Mariana.

They talked to her, as girls, having few topics, naturally do, of one another. And the demon rose within her, and spontaneously, without design, generally without words of positive falsehood, she became a genius of discord among them. She fanned those flames of envy and jealousy which a wise, true word from a third will often quench forever; by a glance, or a seemingly light reply, she planted the seeds of dissension, till there was scarce a peaceful affection, or sincere intimacy in the circle where she lived, and could not but rule, for she was one whose nature was to that of the others as fire to clay.

It was at this time that I came to the school, and first saw Mariana. Me she charmed at once, for I was a sentimental child, who, in my early ill health, had been indulged in reading novels, till I had no eyes for the common greens and browns of life. The heroine of one of these, 'The Bandit's Bride,' I immediately saw in Mariana. Surely the Bandit's Bride had just such hair, and such strange, lively ways, and such a sudden flash of the eye. The Bandit's Bride, too, was born to be 'misunderstood' by all but her lover. But Mariana, I was determined, should be more fortunate, for, until her lover appeared, I myself would be the wise and delicate being who could understand her.

It was not, however, easy to approach her for this purpose. Did I offer to run and fetch her handkerchief, she was obliged to go to her room, and would rather do it herself. She did not like to have people turn over for her the leaves of the music book as she played. Did I approach my stool to her feet, she moved away, as if to give me room. The bunch of wild flowers which I timidly laid beside her plate was left there.

After some weeks my desire to attract her notice really preyed upon me, and one day meeting her alone in the entry, I fell upon my knees, and kissing her hand, cried, 'O Mariana, do let me love you, and try to love me a little.' But my idol snatched away her hand, and, laughing more wildly than the Bandit's Bride was ever described to have done, ran into her room. After that day her manner to me was not only cold, but repulsive; I felt myself scorned, and became very unhappy.

Perhaps four months had passed thus, when, one afternoon, it became obvious that something more than common was brewing. Dismay and mystery were written in many faces of the older girls; much whispering was going on in corners.

In the evening, after prayers, the principal bade us stay; and, in a grave, sad voice, summoned forth Mariana to answer charges to be made against her.

Mariana came forward, and leaned against the chimney-piece. Eight of the older girls came forward, and preferred against her charges, alas, too well-founded, of calumny and falsehood.

My heart sank within me, as one after the other brought up their proofs, and I saw they were too strong to be resisted. I could not bear the thought of this second disgrace of my shining favorite. The first had been whispered to me, though the girls did not like to talk about it. I must confess, such is the charm of strength to softer natures, that neither of these crises could deprive Mariana of hers in my eyes.

At first, she defended herself with self-possession and eloquence. But when she found she could no more resist the truth, she suddenly threw herself down, dashing her head, with all her force, against the iron hearth, on which a fire was burning, and was taken up senseless.

The affright of those present was great. Now that they had perhaps killed her, they reflected it would have been as well, if they had taken warning from the former occasion, and approached very carefully a nature so capable of any extreme. After awhile she revived, with a faint groan, amid the sobs of her companions. I was on my knees by the bed, and held her cold hand. One of those most aggrieved took it from me to beg her pardon, and say it was impossible not to love her. She made no reply.

Neither that night, nor for several days, could a word be obtained from her, nor would she touch food; but, when it was presented to her, or any one drew near for any cause, she merely turned away her head, and gave no sign. The teacher saw that some terrible nervous affection had fallen upon her, that she grew more and more feverish. She knew not what to do.

Meanwhile a new revolution had taken place in the mind of the passionate, but nobly-tempered child. All these months nothing but the sense of injury had rankled in her heart. She had gone on in one mood, doing what the demon prompted, without scruple and without fear.

But, at the moment of detection, the tide ebbed, and the bottom of her soul lay revealed to her eye. How black, how stained and sad. Strange, strange that she had not seen before the baseness and cruelty of falsehood, the loveliness of truth. Now, amid the wreck, uprose the moral nature which never before had attained the ascendant. 'But,' she thought, 'too late, sin is revealed to me in all its deformity, and, sin-defiled, I will not, cannot live. The mainspring of life is broken.'

And thus passed slowly by her hours in that black despair of which only youth is capable. In older years men suffer more dull pain, as each sorrow that comes drops its leaden weight into the past, and, similar features of character bringing similar results, draws up a heavy burden buried in those depths. But only youth has energy, with fixed unwinking gaze, to contemplate grief, to hold it in the arms and to the heart, like a child which makes it wretched, yet is indubitably its own.

The lady who took charge of this sad child had never well understood her before, but had always looked on her with great tenderness. And now love seemed, when all around were in greatest distress, fearing to call in medical aid, fearing to do without it, to teach her where the only balm was to be found that could have healed this wounded spirit.

One night she came in, bringing a calming draught. Mariana was sitting, as usual, her hair loose, her dress the same robe they had put on her at first, her eyes fixed vacantly upon the whited wall. To the proffers and entreaties of her nurse she made no reply.

The lady burst into tears, but Mariana did not seem even to observe it.

The lady then said, 'O my child, do not despair, do not think

that one great fault can mar a whole life. Let me trust you, let
me tell you the griefs of my sad life. I will tell to you, Mariana,
what I never expected to impart to any one.'

And so she told her tale: it was one of pain, of shame, borne,
not for herself, but for one near and dear as herself. Mariana
knew the lady, knew the pride and reserve of her nature; she
had often admired to see how the cheek, lovely, but no longer
young, mantled with the deepest blush of youth, and the blue
eyes were cast down at any little emotion. She had understood
the proud sensibility of the character. She fixed her eyes on
those now raised to hers, bright with fast falling tears. She
heard the story to the end, and then, without saying a word,
stretched out her hand for the cup.

She returned to life, but it was as one who has passed
through the valley of death. The heart of stone was quite
broken in her. The fiery life fallen from flame to coal. When
her strength was a little restored, she had all her companions
summoned, and said to them; 'I deserved to die, but a generous
trust has called me back to life. I will be worthy of it, nor ever
betray the truth, or resent injury more. Can you forgive the
past?'

And they not only forgave, but, with love and earnest tears,
clasped in their arms the returning sister. They vied with one
another in offices of humble love to the humbled one; and, let it
be recorded as an instance of the pure honor of which young
hearts are capable, that these facts, known to forty persons,
never, so far as I know, transpired beyond those walls.

It was not long after this that Mariana was summoned home.
She went thither a wonderfully instructed being, though in ways
those who had sent her forth to learn little dreamed of.

Never was forgotten the vow of the returning prodigal.
Mariana could not resent, could not play false. The terrible
crisis, which she so early passed through, probably prevented
the world from hearing much of her. A wild fire was tamed in
that hour of penitence at the boarding school, such as has
oftentimes wrapped court and camp in its destructive glow.

But great were the perils she had yet to undergo, for she was
one of those barks which easily get beyond soundings, and ride
not lightly on the plunging billow.

Her return to her native climate seconded the effects of inward revolutions. The cool airs of the north had exasperated nerves too susceptible for their tension. Those of the south restored her to a more soft and indolent state. Energy gave place to feeling, turbulence to intensity of character.

At this time love was the natural guest, and he came to her under a form that might have deluded one less ready for delusion.

Sylvain was a person well proportioned to her lot in years, family, and fortune. His personal beauty was not great, but of a noble character. Repose marked his slow gesture, and the steady gaze of his large brown eye, but it was a repose that would give way to a blaze of energy when the occasion called. In his stature, expression, and heavy coloring, he might not unfitly be represented by the great magnolias that inhabit the forests of that climate. His voice, like everything about him, was rich and soft, rather than sweet or delicate.

Mariana no sooner knew him than she loved, and her love, lovely as she was, soon excited his. But, oh! it is a curse to woman to love first, or most. In so doing she reverses the natural relations, and her heart can never, never be satisfied with what ensues.

Mariana loved first, and loved most, for she had most force and variety to love with. Sylvain seemed, at first, to take her to himself, as the deep southern night might some fair star. But it proved not so.

Mariana was a very intellectual being, and she needed companionship. This she could only have with Sylvain, in the paths of passion and action. Thoughts he had none, and little delicacy of sentiment. The gifts she loved to prepare of such for him, he took with a sweet, but indolent smile; he held them lightly, and soon they fell from his grasp. He loved to have her near him, to feel the glow and fragrance of her nature, but cared not to explore the little secret paths whence that fragrance was collected.

Mariana knew not this for a long time. Loving so much, she imagined all the rest, and, where she felt a blank, always hoped that further communion would fill it up. When she found this could never be; that there was absolutely a whole province of her being to which nothing in his answered, she was too deeply in love to leave him. Often after passing hours together, beneath the southern moon, when, amid the sweet intoxication of mutual love, she still felt the desolation of solitude, and a repression of her finer powers, she had asked herself, can I give him up? But the heart always passionately answered, no! I may be miserable with him, but I cannot live without him.

And the last miserable feeling of these conflicts was, that if the lover, soon to be the bosom friend, could have dreamed of these conflicts, he would have laughed, or else been angry, even enough to give her up.

Ah weakness of the strong. Of these strong only where strength is weakness. Like others she had the decisions of life to make, before she had light by which to make them. Let none condemn her. Those who have not erred as fatally, should thank the guardian angel who gave them more time to prepare for judgment, but blame no children who thought at arm's length to find the moon. Mariana, with a heart capable of highest Eros, gave it to one who knew love only as a flower or plaything, and bound her heartstrings to one who parted his as lightly as the ripe fruit leaves the bough. The sequel could not fail. Many console themselves for the one great mistake with their children, with the world. This was not possible to Mariana. A few months of domestic life she still was almost happy. But Sylvain then grew tired. He wanted business and the world; of these she had no knowledge, for them no faculties. He wanted in her the head of his house; she to make her heart his home. No compromise was possible between natures of such unequal poise, and which had met only on one or two points. Through all its stages she

> 'felt
> The agonizing sense
> Of seeing love from passion melt
> Into indifference;
> The fearful shame that, day by day,
> Burns onward, still to burn,
> To have thrown her precious heart away,
> And met this black return,'*

till death at last closed the scene. Not that she died of one downright blow on the heart. That is not the way such cases proceed. I cannot detail all the symptoms, for I was not there to watch them, and aunt Z. was neither so faithful an observer or narrator as I have shown myself in the school-day passages; but, generally, they were as follows.

Sylvain wanted to go into the world, or let it into his house. Mariana consented; but, with an unsatisfied heart, and no lightness of character, she played her part ill there. The sort of talent and facility she had displayed in early days, were not the least like what is called out in the social world by the desire to please and to shine. Her excitement had been muse-like, that of the improvisatrice, whose kindling fancy seeks to create an atmosphere round it, and makes the chain through which to set free its electric sparks. That had been a time of wild and exuberant life. After her character became more tender and concentrated, strong affection or a pure enthusiasm might still have called out beautiful talents in her. But in the first she was utterly disappointed. The second was not roused within her thought. She did not expand into various life, and remained unequal; sometimes too passive, sometimes too ardent, and not sufficiently occupied with what occupied those around her to come on the same level with them and embellish their hours.

Thus she lost ground daily with her husband, who, comparing her with the careless shining dames of society, wondered why he had found her so charming in solitude.

At intervals, when they were left alone, Mariana wanted to open her heart, to tell the thoughts of her mind. She was so conscious of secret riches within herself, that sometimes it seemed; could she but reveal a glimpse of them to the eye of Sylvain, he would be attracted near her again, and take a path where they could walk hand in hand. Sylvain, in these intervals, wanted an indolent repose. His home was his castle. He wanted no scenes too exciting there. Light jousts and plays were well enough, but no grave encounters. He liked to lounge, to sing, to read, to sleep. In fine, Sylvain became the kind, but preoccupied husband, Mariana, the solitary and wretched wife. He was off continually, with his male companions, on excursions or affairs of pleasure. At home Mariana found that neither her books nor music would console her.

She was of too strong a nature to yield without a struggle to so dull a fiend as despair. She looked into other hearts, seeking whether she could there find such home as an orphan asylum may afford. This she did rather because the chance came to her, and it seemed unfit not to seize the proffered plank, than in hope, for she was not one to double her stakes, but rather with Cassandra power to discern early the sure course of the game. And Cassandra whispered that she was one of those

'Whom men love not, but yet regret,'

And so it proved. Just as in her childish days, though in a different form, it happened betwixt her and these companions. She could not be content to receive them quietly, but was stimulated to throw herself too much into the tie, into the hour, till she filled it too full for them. Like Fortunio, who sought to do homage to his friends by building a fire of cinnamon, not knowing that its perfume would be too strong for their endurance, so did Mariana. What she wanted to tell, they did not wish to hear; a little had pleased, so much overpowered, and they preferred the free air of the street, even, to the cinnamon perfume of her palace.

However, this did not signify; had they staid, it would not have availed her! It was a nobler road, a higher aim she needed now; this did not become clear to her.

She lost her appetite, she fell sick, had fever. Sylvain was alarmed, nursed her tenderly; she grew better. Then his care ceased, he saw not the mind's disease, but left her to rise into health and recover the tone of her spirits, as she might. More solitary than ever, she tried to raise herself, but she knew not yet enough. The weight laid upon her young life was a little too heavy for it. One long day she passed alone, and the thoughts and presages came too thick for her strength. She knew not what to do with them, relapsed into fever, and died.

Notwithstanding this weakness, I must ever think of her as a fine sample of womanhood, born to shed light and life on some palace home. Had she known more of God and the universe, she would not have given way where so many have conquered. But peace be with her; she now, perhaps, has entered into a larger freedom, which is knowledge. With her died a great interest in life to me. Since her I have never seen a Bandit's

Bride. She, indeed, turned out to be only a merchant's.—Sylvain is married again to a fair and laughing girl, who will not die, probably, till their marriage grows a 'golden marriage.'

Aunt Z. had with her some papers of Mariana's, which faintly shadow forth the thoughts that engaged her in the last days. One of these seems to have been written when some faint gleam had been thrown across the path, only to make its darkness more visible. It seems to have been suggested by remembrance of the beautiful ballad, *Helen of Kirconnel Lee*, which once she loved to recite, and in tones that would not have sent a chill to the heart from which it came.

> 'Death
> Opens her sweet white arms, and whispers Peace;
> Come, say thy sorrows in this bosom! This
> Will never close against thee, and my heart,
> Though cold, cannot be colder much than man's.'

'I wish I were where Helen lies,'
  A lover in the times of old,
    Thus vents his grief in lonely sighs,
  And hot tears from a bosom cold.

But, mourner for thy martyred love,
  Could'st thou but know what hearts must feel,
    Where no sweet recollections move,
  Whose tears a desert fount reveal.

When 'in thy arms burd Helen fell,'
  She died, sad man, she died for thee,
    Nor could the films of death dispel
  Her loving eye's sweet radiancy.

Thou wert beloved, and she had loved,
  Till death alone the whole could tell,
    Death every shade of doubt removed,
  And steeped the star in its cold well.

On some fond breast the parting soul
  Relies,—earth has no more to give;
    Who wholly loves has known the whole,
  The wholly loved doth truly live.

But some, sad outcasts from this prize,
  Wither down to a lonely grave,

All hearts their hidden love despise,
And leave them to the whelming wave.

They heart to heart have never pressed,
Nor hands in holy pledge have given.
   By father's love were ne'er caressed,
Nor in a mother's eye saw heaven.

A flowerless and fruitless tree,
A dried up stream, a mateless bird,
   They live, yet never living be,
They die, their music all unheard.

I wish I were where Helen lies,
For there I could not be alone;
   But now, when this dull body dies,
The spirit still will make its moan.

Love passed me by, nor touched my brow;
Life would not yield one perfect boon;
   And all too late it calls me now,
O all too late, and all too soon.

If thou couldst the dark riddle read
Which leaves this dart within my breast,
   Then might I think thou lov'st indeed,
Then were the whole to thee confest.

Father, they will not take me home,
To the poor child no heart is free;
   In sleet and snow all night I roam;
Father,—was this decreed by thee?

I will not try another door,
To seek what I have never found;
   Now, till the very last is o'er,
Upon the earth I'll wander round.

I will not hear the treacherous call
That bids me stay and rest awhile,
   For I have found that, one and all,
They seek me for a prey and spoil.

They are not bad, I know it well;
I know they know not what they do;
   They are the tools of the dread spell
Which the lost lover must pursue.

In temples sometimes she may rest,
In lonely groves, away from men,
    There bend the head, by heats distrest,
Nor be by blows awoke again.

Nature is kind, and God is kind,
And, if she had not had a heart,
    Only that great discerning mind,
She might have acted well her part.

But oh this thirst, that none can still,
Save those unfounden waters free;
    The angel of my life should fill
And soothe me to Eternity!

It marks the defect in the position of woman that one like
Mariana should have found reason to write thus. To a man of
equal power, equal sincerity, no more!—many resources would
have presented themselves. He would not have needed to seek,
he would have been called by life, and not permitted to be
quite wrecked through the affections only. But such women as
Mariana are often lost, unless they meet some man of sufficiently
great soul to prize them. [. . .]

MACKINAW.

Late at night we reached this island, so famous for its beauty,
and to which I proposed a visit of some length. It was the last
week in August, when a large representation from the Chippewa
and Ottawa tribes are here to receive their annual payments
from the American government. As their habits make travelling
easy and inexpensive to them, neither being obliged to wait for
steamboats, or write to see whether hotels are full, they come
hither by thousands, and those thousands in families, secure
of accommodation on the beach, and food from the lake, to
make a long holiday out of the occasion. There were near two
thousand encamped on the island already, and more arriving
every day.

As our boat came in, the captain had some rockets let off.
This greatly excited the Indians, and their yells and wild cries

resounded along the shore. Except for the momentary flash of the rockets, it was perfectly dark, and my sensations as I walked with a stranger to a strange hotel, through the midst of these shrieking savages, and heard the pants and snorts of the departing steamer, which carried away all my companions, were somewhat of the dismal sort; though it was pleasant, too, in the way that everything strange is; everything that breaks in upon the routine that so easily incrusts us.

I had reason to expect a room to myself at the hotel, but found none, and was obliged to take up my rest in the common parlor and eating-room, a circumstance which ensured my being an early riser.

With the first rosy streak, I was out among my Indian neighbors, whose lodges honeycombed the beautiful beach, that curved away in long, fair outline on either side the house. They were already on the alert, the children creeping out from beneath the blanket door of the lodge; the women pounding corn in their rude mortars, the young men playing on their pipes. I had been much amused, when the strain proper to the Winnebago courting flute was played to me on another instrument, at any one fancying it a melody; but now, when I heard the notes in their true tone and time, I thought it not unworthy comparison, in its graceful sequence, and the light flourish, at the close, with the sweetest bird-songs; and this, like the bird-song, is only practised to allure a mate. The Indian, become a citizen and a husband, no more thinks of playing the flute than one of the 'settled down' members of our society would of choosing the 'purple light of love' as dye-stuff for a surtout.

Mackinaw has been fully described by able pens, and I can only add my tribute to the exceeding beauty of the spot and its position. It is charming to be on an island so small that you can sail round it in an afternoon, yet large enough to admit of long secluded walks through its gentle groves. You can go round it in your boat; or, on foot, you can tread its narrow beach, resting, at times, beneath the lofty walls of stone, richly wooded, which rise from it in various architectural forms. In this stone, caves are continually forming, from the action of the atmosphere; one of these is quite deep, and with a fragment left at its mouth, wreathed with little creeping plants, that looks, as you sit within, like a ruined pillar.

The arched rock surprised me, much as I had heard of it, from the perfection of the arch. It is perfect whether you look up through it from the lake, or down through it to the transparent waters. We both ascended and descended, no very easy matter, the steep and crumbling path, and rested at the summit, beneath the trees, and at the foot upon the cool mossy stones beside the lapsing wave. Nature has carefully decorated all this architecture with shrubs that take root within the crevices, and small creeping vines. These natural ruins may vie for beautiful effect with the remains of European grandeur, and have, beside, a charm as of a playful mood in nature.

The sugar-loaf rock, is a fragment in the same kind as the pine rock we saw in Illinois. It has the same air of a helmet, as seen from an eminence at the side, which you descend by a long and steep path. The rock itself may be ascended by the bold and agile. Half way up is a niche, to which those, who are neither, can climb by a ladder. A very handsome young officer and lady who were with us did so, and then, facing round, stood there side by side, looking in the niche, if not like saints or angels wrought by pious hands in stone, as romantically, if not as holily, worthy the gazer's eye.

The woods which adorn the central ridge of the island are very full in foliage, and, in August, showed the tender green and pliant leaf of June elsewhere. They are rich in beautiful mosses and the wild raspberry.

From Fort Holmes, the old fort, we had the most commanding view of the lake and straits, opposite shores, and fair islets. Mackinaw, itself, is best seen from the water. Its peculiar shape is supposed to have been the origin of its name, Michilimackinac, which means the Great Turtle. One person whom I saw, wished to establish another etymology, which he fancied to be more refined; but, I doubt not, this is the true one, both because the shape might suggest such a name, and that the existence of an island in this commanding position, which did so, would seem a significant fact to the Indians. [. . .]

It is crowned most picturesquely, by the white fort, with its gay flag. From this, on one side, stretches the town. How pleasing a sight, after the raw, crude, staring assemblage of houses, everywhere else to be met in this country, an old French town, mellow in its coloring, and with the harmonious effect of a slow growth, which assimilates, naturally, with objects round it. The people in its streets, Indian, French, half-breeds, and others, walked with a leisure step, as of those who live a life of taste and inclination, rather than of the hard press of business, as in American towns elsewhere.

On the other side, along the fair, curving beach, below the white houses scattered on the declivity, clustered the Indian lodges, with their amber brown matting, so soft, and bright of hue, in the late afternoon sun. The first afternoon I was there, looking down from a near height, I felt that I never wished to see a more fascinating picture. It was an hour of the deepest serenity; bright blue and gold, rich shadows. Every moment the sunlight fell more mellow. The Indians were grouped and scattered among the lodges; the women preparing food, in the kettle or frying-pan, over the many small fires; the children, half-naked, wild as little goblins, were playing both in and out of the water. Here and there lounged a young girl, with a baby at her back, whose bright eyes glanced, as if born into a world of courage and of joy, instead of ignominious servitude and slow decay. Some girls were cutting wood, a little way from me, talking and laughing, in the low musical tone, so charming in the Indian women. Many bark canoes were upturned upon the beach, and, by that light, of almost the same amber as the lodges. Others, coming in, their square sails set, and with almost arrowy speed, though heavily laden with dusky forms, and all the apparatus of their household. Here and there a sail-boat glided by, with a different, but scarce less pleasing motion.

It was a scene of ideal loveliness, and these wild forms adorned it, as looking so at home in it. All seemed happy, and they were happy that day, for they had no firewater to madden them, as it was Sunday, and the shops were shut.

From my window, at the boarding house, my eye was constantly attracted by these picturesque groups. I was never tired of seeing the canoes come in, and the new arrivals set up their temporary dwellings. The women ran to set up the tent-poles, and spread the mats on the ground. The men brought the chests, kettles, &c.; the mats were then laid on the outside, the cedar boughs strewed on the ground, the blanket hung up for a door, and all was completed in less than twenty minutes. Then they began to prepare the night meal, and to learn of their neighbors the news of the day.

The habit of preparing food out of doors, gave all the gipsy charm and variety to their conduct. Continually I wanted Sir Walter Scott to have been there. If such romantic sketches were suggested to him, by the sight of a few gipsies, not a group near one of these fires but would have furnished him material for a separate canvass. I was so taken up with the spirit of the scene, that I could not follow out the stories suggested by these weather-beaten, sullen, but eloquent figures.

They talked a great deal, and with much variety of gesture, so that I often had a good guess at the meaning of their discourse. I saw that, whatever the Indian may be among the whites, he is anything but taciturn with his own people. And he often would declaim, or narrate at length, as indeed it is obvious, that these tribes possess great power that way, if only from the fables taken from their stores, by Mr Schoolcraft.

I liked very much to walk or sit among them. With the women I held much communication by signs. They are almost invariably coarse and ugly, with the exception of their eyes, with a peculiarly awkward gait, and forms bent by burthens. This gait, so different from the steady and noble step of the men, marks the inferior position they occupy. I had heard much eloquent contradiction of this. Mrs Schoolcraft had maintained to a friend, that they were in fact as nearly on a par with their husbands as the white woman with hers. 'Although,' said she, 'on account of inevitable causes, the Indian woman is subjected to many hardships of a peculiar nature, yet her position, compared with that of the man, is higher and freer than that of the white woman.' Why will people look only on one side? They either exalt the Red man into a Demigod or degrade him into a beast. They say that he compels his wife to do all the drudgery, while he does nothing but hunt and amuse himself; forgetting that, upon his activity and power of endurance as a hunter, depends the support of his family; that this is labor of the most fatiguing kind, and that it is absolutely necessary that he should keep his frame unbent by burdens and unworn by toil, that he may be able to obtain the means of subsistence. I have witnessed scenes of conjugal and parental love in the Indian's wigwam from which I have often, often thought the educated white man, proud of his superior civilization, might learn an useful lesson. When he returns from hunting, worn out with fatigue, having tasted nothing since dawn, his wife, if she is a good wife, will take off his moccasins and replace them with dry ones, and will prepare his game for their repast, while his children will climb upon him, and he will caress them with all the tenderness of a woman; and in the evening the Indian wigwam is the scene of the purest domestic pleasures. The father will relate for the amusement of the wife, and for the instruction of the children, all the events of the day's hunt, while they will treasure up every word that falls, and thus learn the theory of the art, whose practice is to be the occupation of their lives.

Mrs Grant* speaks thus of the position of woman amid the Mohawk Indians:

'Lady Mary Montague* says, that the court of Vienna was the paradise of old women, and that there is no other place in the world where a woman past fifty excites the least interest. Had her travels extended to the interior of North America, she would have seen another instance of this inversion of the common mode of thinking. Here a woman never was of consequence, till she had a son old enough to fight the battles of his country. From that date she held a superior rank in society; was allowed to live at ease, and even called to consultations on national affairs. In savage and warlike countries, the reign of beauty is very short, and its influence comparatively limited. The girls in childhood had a very pleasing appearance; but excepting their fine hair, eyes, and teeth, every external grace was soon banished by perpetual drudgery, carrying burdens too heavy to be borne, and other slavish employments considered beneath the dignity of the men. These walked before erect and graceful, decked with ornaments which set off to advantage the symmetry of their well-formed persons, while the poor women followed, meanly attired, bent under the weight of the children and utensils, which they carried everywhere with them, and disfigured and degraded by ceaseless toils. They were very early married, for a Mohawk had no other servant but his wife, and, whenever he commenced hunting, it was requisite he should have some one to carry his load, cook his kettle, make his moccasins, and, above all, produce the young warriors who were to succeed him in the honors of the chase and of the tomahawk. Wherever man is a mere hunter, woman is a mere slave. It is domestic intercourse that softens man, and elevates woman; and of that there can be but little, where the employments and amusements are not in common; the ancient Caledonians honored the fair; but then it is to be observed, they were fair huntresses, and moved in the light of their beauty to the hill of roes; and the culinary toils were entirely left to the rougher sex. When the young warrior made his appearance, it softened the cares of his mother, who well knew that, when he grew up, every deficiency in tenderness to his wife would be made up in superabundant duty and affection to her. If it were possible to carry filial veneration to excess, it was done here; for all other charities were absorbed in it. I wonder this system of depressing the sex in their early years, to exalt them when all their juvenile attractions were flown, and when mind alone can distinguish them, has not occurred to our modern reformers. The Mohawks took good care not to admit their women to share their prerogatives, till they approved themselves good wives and mothers.'

The observations of women upon the position of woman are always more valuable than those of men; but, of these two, Mrs Grant's seems much nearer the truth than Mrs Schoolcraft's, because, though her opportunities for observation did not bring her so close, she looked more at both sides to find the truth.

Carver,* in his travels among the Winnebagoes, describes two queens, one nominally so, like Queen Victoria; the other invested with a genuine royalty, springing from her own conduct.

In the great town of the Winnebagoes, he found a queen presiding over the tribe, instead of a sachem.* He adds, that, in some tribes, the descent is given to the female line in preference to the male, that is, a sister's son will succeed to the authority, rather than a brother's son.

The position of this Winnebago queen, reminded me forcibly of Queen Victoria's.

'She sat in the council, but only asked a few questions, or

gave some trifling directions in matters relative to the state, for women are never allowed to sit in their councils, except they happen to be invested with the supreme authority, and then it is not customary for them to make any formal speeches, as the chiefs do. She was a very ancient woman, small in stature, and not much distinguished by her dress from several young women that attended her. These, her attendants, seemed greatly pleased whenever I showed any tokens of respect to their queen, especially when I saluted her, which I frequently did to acquire her favor.'

The other was a woman, who being taken captive, found means to kill her captor, and make her escape, and the tribe were so struck with admiration at the courage and calmness she displayed on the occasion, as to make her chieftainess in her own right.

Notwithstanding the homage paid to women, and the consequence allowed her in some cases, it is impossible to look upon the Indian women, without feeling that they *do* occupy a lower place than women among the nations of European civilization. The habits of drudgery expressed in their form and gesture, the soft and wild but melancholy expression of their eye, reminded me of the tribe mentioned by Mackenzie,* where the women destroy their female children, whenever they have a good opportunity; and of the eloquent reproaches addressed by the Paraguay woman to her mother, that she had not, in the same way, saved her from the anguish and weariness of her lot.

More weariness than anguish, no doubt, falls to the lot of most of these women. They inherit submission, and the minds of the generality accommodate themselves more or less to any posture. Perhaps they suffer less than their white sisters, who have more aspiration and refinement, with little power of self-sustenance. But their place is certainly lower, and their share of the human inheritance less.

Their decorum and delicacy are striking, and show that when these are native to the mind, no habits of life make any difference. Their whole gesture is timid, yet self-possessed. They used to crowd round me, to inspect little things I had to show them, but never press near; on the contrary, would reprove and keep off the children. Anything they took from my hand, was held with care, then shut or folded, and returned with an air of lady-like precision. They would not stare, however curious they might be, but cast sidelong glances.

A locket that I wore, was an object of untiring interest; they seemed to regard it as a talisman. My little sun-shade was still more fascinating to them; apparently they had never before seen one. For an umbrella they entertain profound regard, probably looking upon it as the most luxurious superfluity a person can possess, and therefore a badge of great wealth. I used to see an old squaw, whose sullied skin and coarse, tanned locks, told that she had braved sun and storm, without a doubt or care, for sixty years at the least, sitting gravely at the door of her lodge, with an old green umbrella over her head, happy for hours together in the dignified shade. For her happiness pomp came not, as it so often does, too late; she received it with grateful enjoyment.

One day, as I was seated on one of the canoes, a woman came and sat beside me, with her baby in its cradle set up at her feet. She asked me by a gesture, to let her take my sun-shade, and then to show her how to open it. Then she put it into her baby's hand, and held it over its head, looking at me the while with a sweet, mischievous laugh, as much as to say, 'you carry a thing that is only fit for a baby;' her pantomime was very pretty. She, like the other women, had a glance, and shy, sweet expression in the eye; the men have a steady gaze. [. . .]

It is also evident that, as Mrs Schoolcraft says, the women have great power at home. It can never be otherwise, men being dependent upon them for the comfort of their lives. Just so among ourselves, wives who are neither esteemed nor loved by their husbands, have great power over their conduct by the friction of every day, and over the formation of their opinions by the daily opportunities so close a relation affords, of perverting testimony and instilling doubts. But these sentiments should not come in brief flashes, but burn as a steady flame, then there would be more women worthy to inspire them. This power is good for nothing, unless the woman be wise to use it aright. Has the Indian, has the white woman, as noble a feeling of life and its uses, as religious a self-respect, as worthy a field of thought and action, as man? If not, the white woman, the Indian woman, occupies an inferior position to that of man. It is not so much a question of power, as of privilege.

The men of these subjugated tribes, now accustomed to drunkenness and every way degraded, bear but a faint impress of the lost grandeur of the race. They are no longer strong, tall, or finely proportioned. Yet as you see them stealing along a height, or striding boldly forward, they remind you of what *was* majestic in the red man.

On the shores of lake Superior, it is said, if you visit them at home, you may still see a remnant of the noble blood. The Pillagers—(Pilleurs)—a band celebrated by the old travellers, are still existant there.

'Still some, "the eagles of their tribe," may rush.'*

I have spoken of the hatred felt by the white man for the Indian: with white women it seems to amount to disgust, to loathing. How I could endure the dirt, the peculiar smell of the Indians, and their dwellings, was a great marvel in the eyes of my lady acquaintances; indeed, I wonder why they did not quite give me up, as they certainly looked on me with great distaste for it. 'Get you gone, you Indian dog,' was the felt, if not the breathed, expression towards the hapless owners of the soil. All their claims, all their sorrows quite forgot, in abhorrence of their dirt, their tawny skins, and the vices the whites have taught them.

A person who had seen them during great part of a life, expressed his prejudices to me with such violence, that I was no longer surprised that the Indian children threw sticks at him, as he passed. A lady said, 'do what you will for them, they will be ungrateful. The savage cannot be washed out of them. Bring up an Indian child and see if you can attach it to you.' The next moment, she expressed, in the presence of one of those children whom she was bringing up, loathing at the odor left by one of her people, and one of the most respected, as he passed through the room. When the child is grown she will consider it basely ungrateful not to love her, as it certainly will not; and this will be cited as an instance of the impossibility of attaching the Indian.

Whether the Indian could, by any efforts of love and intelligence from the white man, have been civilized and made a valuable ingredient in the new state, I will not say; but this we are sure of; the French Catholics, at least, did not harm them, nor disturb their minds merely to corrupt them. The French they loved. But the stern Presbyterian, with his dogmas and his task-work, the city circle and the college, with their niggard concessions and unfeeling stare, have never tried the experiment. It has not been tried. Our people and our government have sinned alike against the first-born of the soil, and if they are the fated agents of a new era, they have done nothing—have invoked no god to keep them sinless while they do the hest of fate.

Worst of all, when they invoke the holy power only to mask their iniquity; when the felon trader, who, all the week, has been besotting and degrading the Indian with rum mixed with red pepper, and damaged tobacco, kneels with him on Sunday before a common altar, to tell the rosary which recalls the thought of him crucified for love of suffering men, and to listen to sermons in praise of 'purity'!! [. . .]

The Chippewas have lately petitioned the state of Michigan, that they may be admitted as citizens; but this would be vain, unless they could be admitted, as brothers, to the heart of the white man. And while the latter feels that conviction of superiority, [. . .] he had need to be very good, and very wise, not to abuse his position. But the white man, as yet, is a half-tamed pirate, and avails himself, as much as ever, of the maxim, 'Might makes right.' All that civilization does for the generality, is to cover up this with a veil of subtle evasions and chicane, and here and there to rouse the individual mind to appeal to heaven against it. [. . .]

SAULT ST MARIE

Nine days I passed alone at Mackinaw, except for occasional visits from kind and agreeable residents at the fort, and Mr and Mrs A. Mr A., long engaged in the fur-trade, is gratefully remembered by many travellers. From Mrs A., also, I received kind attentions, paid in the vivacious and graceful manner of her nation.

The society at the boarding house entertained, being of a kind entirely new to me. There were many traders from the remote stations, such as La Pointe, Arbre Croche,—men who had become half wild and wholly rude, by living in the wild; but good-humored, observing, and with a store of knowledge to impart, of the kind proper to their place.

There were two little girls here, that were pleasant companions for me. One gay, frank, impetuous, but sweet and winning. She was an American, fair, and with bright brown hair. The other, a little French Canadian, used to join me in my walks, silently take my hand, and sit at my feet when I stopped in beautiful places. She seemed to understand without a word; and I never shall forget her little figure, with its light, but pensive motion, and her delicate, grave features, with the pale, clear complexion and soft eye. She was motherless, and much left alone by her father and brothers, who were boatmen. The two little girls were as pretty representatives of Allegro and Penseroso, as one would wish to see.

I had been wishing that a boat would come in to take me to the Sault St Marie, and several times started to the window at night in hopes that the pant and dusky-red light crossing the waters belonged to such an one; but they were always boats for Chicago or Buffalo, till, on the 28th of August, Allegro, who shared my plans and wishes, rushed in to tell me that the General Scott had come, and, in this little steamer, accordingly, I set off the next morning.

I was the only lady, and attended in the cabin by a Dutch girl and an Indian woman. They both spoke English fluently, and entertained me much by accounts of their different experiences.

The Dutch girl told me of a dance among the common people at Amsterdam, called the shepherd's dance. The two leaders are dressed as shepherd and shepherdess; they invent to the music all kinds of movements, descriptive of things that may happen in the field, and the rest were obliged to follow. I have never heard of any dance which gave such free play to the fancy as this. French dances merely describe the polite movements of society; Spanish and Neapolitan, love; the beautiful Mazurkas,

&c., are warlike or expressive of wild scenery. But in this one is great room both for fun and fancy.

The Indian was married, when young, by her parents, to a man she did not love. He became dissipated, and did not maintain her. She left him, taking with her their child; for whom and herself she earns a subsistence by going as chambermaid in these boats. Now and then, she said, her husband called on her, and asked if he might live with her again; but she always answered, no. Here she was far freer than she would have been in civilized life.

I was pleased by the nonchalance of this woman, and the perfectly national manner she had preserved after so many years of contact with all kinds of people. The two women, when I left the boat, made me presents of Indian work, such as travellers value, and the manner of the two was characteristic of their different nations. The Indian brought me hers, when I was alone, looked bashfully down when she gave it, and made an almost sentimental little speech. The Dutch girl brought hers in public, and, bridling her short chin with a self-complacent air, observed she had *bought* it for me. But the feeling of affectionate regard was the same in the minds of both.

Island after island we passed, all fairly shaped and clustering friendly, but with little variety of vegetation.

In the afternoon the weather became foggy, and we could not proceed after dark. That was as dull an evening as ever fell.

The next morning the fog still lay heavy, but the captain took me out in his boat on an exploring expedition, and we found the remains of the old English fort on Point St Joseph's. All around was so wholly unmarked by anything but stress of wind and weather, the shores of these islands and their woods so like one another, wild and lonely, but nowhere rich and majestic, that there was some charm in the remains of the garden, the remains even of chimneys and a pier. They gave feature to the scene.

Here I gathered many flowers, but they were the same as at Mackinaw.

The captain, though he had been on this trip hundreds of times, had never seen this spot, and never would, but for this fog, and his desire to entertain me. He presented a striking instance how men, for the sake of getting a living, forget to live. It is just the same in the most romantic as the most dull and vulgar places. Men get the harness on so fast, that they can never shake it off, unless they guard against this danger from the very first. In Chicago, how many men, who never found time to see the prairies or learn anything unconnected with the business of the day, or about the country they were living in!

So this captain, a man of strong sense and good eyesight, rarely found time to go off the track or look about him on it. He lamented, too, that there had been no call which induced him to develop his powers of expression, so that he might communicate what he had seen, for the enjoyment or instruction of others.

This is a common fault among the active men, the truly living, who could tell what life is. It should not be so. Literature should not be left to the mere literati—eloquence to the mere orator. Every Cæsar should be able to write his own commentary. We want a more equal, more thorough, more harmonious development, and there is nothing to hinder from it the men of this country, except their own supineness, or sordid views. [. . .]

Although I have little to tell, I feel that I have learnt a great deal of the Indians, from observing them even in this broken and degraded condition. There is a language of eye and motion which cannot be put into words, and which teaches what words never can. I feel acquainted with the soul of this race; I read its nobler thought in their defaced figures. There *was* a greatness, unique and precious, which he who does not feel will never duly appreciate the majesty of nature in this American continent. [. . .]

In the boat many signs admonished that we were floating eastward. A shabbily dressed phrenologist laid his hand on every head which would bend, with half-conceited, half-sheepish expression, to the trial of his skill. Knots of people gathered here and there to discuss points of theology. A bereaved lover was seeking religious consolation in—Butler's Analogy,* which he had purchased for that purpose. However, he did not turn over many pages before his attention was drawn aside by the gay glances of certain damsels that came on board at Detroit, and, though Butler might afterwards be seen sticking from his pocket, it had not weight to impede him from many a feat of lightness and liveliness. I doubt if it went with him from the boat. Some there were, even, discussing the doctrines of Fourier. It seemed pity they were not going to, rather than from, the rich and free country where it would be so much easier, than with us, to try the great experiment of voluntary association, and show, beyond a doubt, that 'an ounce of prevention is worth a pound of cure,' a maxim of the 'wisdom of nations,' which has proved of little practical efficacy as yet.

Better to stop before landing at Buffalo, while I have yet the advantage over some of my readers.

REVIEW OF
MEMOIRS AND ESSAYS ILLUSTRATIVE OF ART, SCIENCE AND SOCIAL MORALS
BY MRS JAMESON
No. 64 of Wiley & Putnam's Library of Choice Reading.

Mrs Jameson* appears to be growing more and more desperately modest, if we may judge from her motto:

> What if the little rain should say,
> 'So small a drop as I
> Can ne'er refresh the thirsty plain,
> I'll tarry in the sky?'

and other superfluous doubts and disclaimers proffered in the course of the volume. We thought the time was gone by when it was necessary to plead 'request of friends' for printing, and that it was understood now-a-days that from the facility of getting thoughts into print, literature has become not merely an archive for the preservation of great thoughts, but a means of general communication between all classes of minds, and all grades of culture. If writers write much that is good, and write it well, they are read much and long; if the reverse, people simply pass them by, and go in search of what is more interesting. There needs be no great fuss about publishing or not publishing. Those who forbear may, rather, be considered the vain ones, who wish to be distinguished among the crowd. Especially this extreme modesty looks superfluous in a person who knows her thoughts have been received with interest for ten or twelve years back. We do not like this from Mrs Jameson, because we think she would be amazed if others spoke of her as this humble little flower, doubtful whether it ought to raise its head to light. She should leave such affectations to her Aunts; they were the fashion in their day. [. . .]

[Nonetheless] 'Woman's Mission and Woman's Position' is an excellent paper, in which plain truths are spoken with an honorable straight-forwardness and a great deal of good feeling. We despise the woman who, knowing such facts, is afraid to speak of them, yet we honor one, too, that does do the plain right thing, for she exposes herself to the assaults of vulgarity in a way painful to a person who has not strength to find repose and shelter in her motives. We recommend this paper to the consideration of all those, the unthinking, wilfully unseeing million, who are in the habit of talking of 'Woman's sphere' as if it really was, at present, for the majority, one of protection and the gentle offices of home. The rhetorical gentlemen and silken dames who, quite forgetting their washer-women, their seamstresses, and the poor hirelings for the sensual pleasures of man that jostle them daily in the streets, talk as if Woman need to be fitted for no other chance than that of growing like a cherished flower in the garden of domestic love, are requested to look at this paper, in which the state of women, both in the Manufacturing and Agricultural districts of England, is exposed with eloquence and just inferences drawn.

This, then, is what I mean when I speak of the anomalous condition of women in these days. I would point out as a primary source of incalculable mischief, the contradiction between her assumed and her real position, between what is called her proper sphere by the laws of God and Nature, and what has become her real sphere by the law of necessity, and through the complex relations of artificial existence. In the strong language of Carlyle I would say that 'here is a LIE, standing up in the midst of society'—I would say 'down with it, even to the ground;' for while this perplexing and barbarous anomaly exists, fretting like an ulcer at the very heart of society, all new specifics and palliatives are in vain. The question must be settled one way or another; either let the man in all the relations of life be held the natural guardian of the woman—constrained to fulfill that trust—responsible to society for her well-being and her maintenance; or, if she be liable to be thrust from the sanctuary of home to provide for herself through the exercise of such faculties as God has given her, let her at least have fair play; let it not be avowed in the same breath that protection is necessary to her, and that it is refused to her; and while we send her forth into the desert, and bind the burthen on her back, and put the staff in her hand—let not her steps be beset, her limbs fettered, and her eyes blindfolded.   Amen.

The sixth and last of these papers 'On the relative social position of Mothers and Governesses' exhibits in true and full colors a state of things in England beside which the custom in some parts of China, of drowning female infants, looks mild, generous and refined. An accursed state of things, beneath whose influence nothing can and nothing ought to thrive. Though this paper, of which we have not patience to speak farther at this moment, is valuable from putting the facts into due relief, it is very inferior to the other, and shows the want of thoroughness and depth in Mrs Jameson's intellect. She has taste, feeling and knowledge, but she cannot think out a subject thoroughly, and is unconsciously tainted and hampered by conventionalities. Her advice to the governesses reads like a piece of irony, but we believe it was not meant as such.—Advise them to be burnt at the stake at once rather than to this slow process of petrifaction. She is as bad as the reports of the 'Society for the relief of distressed and dilapidated Governesses.' We have no more patience. We must go to England ourselves and see these victims under the water torture. Till then—à Dieu.

REVIEW OF
THE WRONGS OF AMERICAN WOMEN
AND
THE DUTY OF AMERICAN WOMEN*

The same day brought us a copy of Mr Burdett's little book, in which the sufferings and difficulties that beset the large class of women who must earn their subsistence in a city like New-York are delineated with so much simplicity, feeling and exact adherence to the facts—and a printed circular containing proposals for immediate practical adoption of the plan more fully described in a book published some weeks since under the title 'The Duty of American Women to their Country,' which was ascribed alternately to Mrs Stone and Miss Catherine Beecher,* but of which we understand both those ladies decline the responsibility. The two matters seemed linked with one another by natural piety.* Full acquaintance with the wrong must call forth all manner of inventions for its redress.

The Circular, in showing the vast want that already exists of good means for instructing the children of this nation, especially in the West, states also the belief that among women, as being less immersed in other cares and toils, from the preparation it gives for their task as mothers, and from the necessity in which a great proportion stand of earning a subsistence somehow, at least during the years which precede marriage, if they *do* marry, must the number of teachers wanted be found, which is estimated already at *sixty thousand*.

We cordially sympathize with these views.

Much has been written about Woman's keeping within her sphere, which is defined as the domestic sphere. As a little girl she is to learn the lighter family duties, while she acquires that limited acquaintance with the realm of literature and science that will enable her to superintend the instruction of children in their earliest years. It is not generally proposed that she should be sufficiently instructed and developed to understand the pursuits or aims of her future husband; she is not to be a helpmeet to him, in the way of companionship or counsel, except in the care of his house and children. Her youth is to be passed partly in learning to keep house and the use of the needle, partly in the social circle where her manners may be formed, ornamental accomplishments perfected and displayed, and the husband found who shall give her the domestic sphere for which exclusively she is to be prepared.

Were the destiny of Woman thus exactly marked out, did she invariably retain the shelter of a parent's or a guardian's roof till she married, did marriage give her a sure home and protector, were she never liable to be made a widow, or, if so, sure of finding immediate protection from a brother or new husband, so that she might never be forced to stand alone one moment, and were her mind given for this world only, with no faculties capable of eternal growth and infinite improvement, we would still demand for her a far wider and more generous culture than is proposed by those who so anxiously define her sphere. We would demand it that she might not ignorantly or frivolously thwart the designs of her husband, that she might be the respected friend of her sons no less than her daughters, that she might give more refinement, elevation and attraction to the society which is needed to give the characters of *men* polish and plasticity—no less so than to save them from vicious and sensual habits. But the most fastidious critic of the departure of Woman from her sphere, can scarcely fail to see at present that a vast proportion of the sex, if not the better half, do not, CANNOT, have this domestic sphere. Thousands and scores of thousands in this country no less than in Europe are obliged to maintain themselves alone. Far greater numbers divide with their husbands the care of earning a support for the family. In England, now, the progress of society has reached so admirable a pitch that the position of the sexes is frequently reversed, and the husband is obliged to stay at home and 'mind the house and bairns' while the wife goes forth to the employment she alone can secure.

We readily admit that the picture of this is most painful— that Nature made entirely an opposite distribution of functions between the sexes. We believe the natural order to be the best, and that, if it could be followed in an enlightened spirit, it would bring to Woman all she wants, no less for her immortal than her mortal destiny. We are not surprised that men, who do not look deeply or carefully at causes or tendencies, should be led by disgust at the hardened, hackneyed characters which the present state of things too often produces in women to such conclusions as they are. We, no more than they, delight in the picture of the poor woman digging in the mines in her husband's clothes. We, no more than they, delight to hear their voices shrilly raised in the market-place, whether of apples or celebrity. But we see that at present they must do as they do for bread. Hundreds and thousands must step out of that hallowed domestic sphere, with no choice but to work or steal, or belong to men, not as wives, but as the wretched slaves of sensuality.

And this transition state, with all its revolting features, indicates, we do believe, the approach of a nobler era than the world has yet known. We trust that by the stress and emergencies of the present and coming time, the minds of women will be formed to more reflection and higher purposes than heretofore—their intent powers developed, their characters strengthened and eventually beautified and harmonized. Should the state of society then be such that each may remain, as Nature seems to have intended, the tutelary genius of a home, while men manage the out-door business of life, both may be done with a wisdom, a mutual understanding and respect unknown at present. Men will be no less the gainers by this than women, finding in pure and more religious marriages the joys of friendship and love combined—in their mothers and daughters better instruction, sweeter and nobler companionship, and in society at large an excitement to their finer powers and feelings unknown at present except in the region of the fine arts.

Blest be the generous, the wise among them who seek to forward hopes like these, instead of struggling against the fiat of Providence and the march of Fate to bind down rushing Life to the standard of the Past. Such efforts are vain, but those who make them are unhappy and unwise.

It is not, however, to such that we address ourselves, but to those who seek to make the best of things as they are, while they also strive to make them better. Such persons will have seen enough of the state of things in London, Paris, New-York, and manufacturing regions everywhere, to feel that there is an imperative necessity for opening more avenues of employment to women, and fitting them better to enter them, rather than keeping them back. Women have invaded many of the trades and some of the professions. Sewing, to the present killing extent, they cannot long bear. Factories seem likely to afford them permanent employment. In the culture of fruit, flowers and vegetables, even in the sale of them, we rejoice to see them engaged. In domestic service they will be aided, but can never be supplanted, by machinery. As much room as there is here for woman's mind and woman's labor will always be filled. A few have usurped the martial province, but these must always be few; the nature of woman is opposed to war. It is natural enough to see 'Female Physicians,' and we believe that the lace cap and work-bag are as much at home here as the wig and gold-headed cane. In the priesthood they have from all time shared more or less—in many eras more than at the present. We believe there has been no female lawyer, and probably will be none. The pen, many of the fine arts they have made their own, and, in the more refined countries of the world, as writers, as musicians, as painters, as actors, women occupy as advantageous ground as men. Writing and music may be esteemed professions for them more than any other.

But there are two others where the demand must invariably be immense, and for which they are naturally better fitted than men, for which we should like to see them better prepared and better rewarded than they are. These are the professions of nurse* to the sick and of teacher. The first of these professions we have warmly desired to see dignified. It is a noble one, now most unjustly regarded in the light of menial service. It is one which no menial, no servile nature can fitly occupy. We were rejoiced when an intelligent lady of Massachusetts made the refined heroine of a little romance select that calling. This lady (Mrs George Lee)* has looked on society with unusual largeness of spirit and healthiness of temper. She is well acquainted with the world of conventions, but, sees beneath it the world of nature. She is a generous writer and unpretending, as the generous are wont to be. We do not recall the name of the tale, but the circumstance above mentioned marks its temper. We hope to see the time when the refined and cultivated will choose this profession and learn it, not only through experience under the direction of the doctor, but by acquainting themselves with the laws of matter and of mind, so that all they do shall be intelligently done, and afford them the means of developing intelligence as well as the nobler, tenderer feelings of humanity; for even the last part of the benefit they cannot receive if their work be done in a selfish or mercenary spirit.

The other profession is that of teacher, for which women are peculiarly adapted by their nature, superiority in tact, quickness of sympathy, gentleness, patience, and a clear and animated manner in narration or description. To form a good teacher should be added to this sincere modesty combined with firmness, liberal views with a power and will to liberalize them still further, a good method and habits of exact and thorough investigation. In the two last requisites women are generally deficient, but there are now many shining examples to prove that if they are immethodical and superficial as teachers it is because it is the custom so to teach them, and that when aware of these faults they can and will correct them.

The profession is of itself an excellent one for the improvement of the teacher during that interim between youth and maturity when the mind needs testing, tempering, and to review and rearrange the knowledge it has acquired. The natural method of doing this for one's self is to attempt teaching others; those years also are the best of the practical teacher. The teacher should be near the pupil both in years and feelings—no oracle, but the elder brother or sister of the pupil. More experience and years form the lecturer and the director of studies, but injure the powers as to familiar teaching.

These are just the years of leisure in the lives even of those women who are to enter the domestic sphere, and this calling most of all compatible with a constant progress as to qualifications for that.

Viewing the matter thus it may well be seen that we should hail with joy the assurance that sixty thousand *female* teachers are wanted, and more likely to be, and that a plan is projected which looks wise, liberal and generous, to afford the means of those whose hearts answer to this high calling obeying their dictates. [. . .]

As to finding abundance of teachers, who that reads this little book of Mr Burdett's, or the account of the compensation of female labor in New-York, and the hopeless, comfortless, useless, pernicious lives those who have even the advantage of getting work must live with the sufferings and almost inevitable degradation to which those who cannot are exposed, but must long to snatch such as are capable of this better profession, and among the multitude there must be many who are or could be made so, from their present toils and make them free and the means of freedom and growth to others.

To many books on such subjects, among others to 'Woman in the Nineteenth Century,' the objection has been made that they exhibit ills without specifying any practical means for their remedy. The writer of the last named essay does indeed think that it contains one great rule which, if laid to heart, would prove a practical remedy for many ills, and of such daily and hourly efficacy in the conduct of life that any extensive observance of it for a single year would perceptibly raise the tone of thought, feeling and conduct throughout the civilized world. But to those who ask not only such a principle, but an external method for immediate use, we say, there is one proposed that looks noble and promising, the proposers offer themselves to the work with heart and hand, with time and purse: Go ye and do likewise. [. . .]

When I wrote last I could not finish with London, and there remain yet two or three things I wish to speak of before passing to my impressions of this wonder-full Paris.

I visited the model-prison at Pentonville;* but though in some respects an improvement upon others I have seen—though there was the appearance of great neatness and order in the arrangements of life—kindness and good judgment in the discipline of the prisoners—yet there was also an air of bleak forlornness about the place, and it fell far short of what my mind demands of such abodes considered as Redemption schools. But as the subject of prisons is now engaging the attention of many of the wisest and best, and the tendency is in what seems to me the true direction, I need not trouble myself to make crude and hasty suggestions;* it is a subject to which persons who would be of use should give the earnest devotion of calm and leisurely thought.

The same day I went to see an establishment which gave me unmixed pleasure; it is a bathing establishment put at a very low rate to enable the poor to avoid one of the worst miseries of their lot, and which yet promises *to pay*. Joined with this is an establishment for washing clothes, where the poor can go and hire, for almost nothing, good tubs, water ready heated, the use of an apparatus for rinsing, drying and ironing, all so admirably arranged that a poor woman can in three hours get through an amount of washing and ironing that would, under ordinary circumstances, occupy three or four days. Especially the drying closets I contemplated with great satisfaction, and hope to see in our own country the same arrangements throughout the cities and even in the towns and villages.—Hanging out the clothes is a great exposure for women, even when they have a good place for it, but when, as is so common in cities, they must dry them in the house, how much they suffer! In New-York I know those poor women who take in washing endure a great deal of trouble and toil from this cause; I have suffered myself from being obliged to send back what had cost them so much toil, because it had been, perhaps inevitably, soiled in the drying or ironing, or filled with the smell of their miscellaneous cooking. In London it is much worse. An eminent physician told me he knew of two children whom he considered to have died because their mother, having but one room to live in, was obliged to wash and dry clothes close to their bed when they were ill. The poor people in London naturally do without washing all they can, and beneath that perpetual fall of soot the result may be guessed. All but the very poor in England put out their washing, and this custom ought to be universal in civilized countries, as it can be done much better and quicker by a few regular laundresses than by many families, and 'the washing day' is so malignant a foe to the peace and joy of households that it ought to be effaced from the calendar. But, as long as we are so miserable as to have any very poor people in this world, *they* cannot put out their washing, because they cannot earn enough money to pay for it, and, preliminary to something better, washing establishments like this of London are desirable.

One arrangement that they have here in Paris will be a good one, even when we cease to have any very poor people, and, please Heaven, also to have any very rich. These are the *Crèches*—houses where poor women leave their children to be nursed during the day while they are at work. I have not yet been to see one of these, and must postpone speaking of them more fully to another letter.

I must mention that the superintendent of the washing establishment observed, with a legitimate triumph, that it had been built without giving a single dinner or printing a single puff*— an extraordinary thing, indeed, for England!

Review of *CONSUELO*:

BY GEORGE SAND

in two volumes, translated by Francis G. Shaw.
Boston: William D. Ticknor & Co. 1846.*

We greet with delight the conclusion of this translation which will make Consuelo accessible to the American reader. To the translator it has been a labor of love, the honorable and patient employment of leisure hours, and accordingly shows a very superior degree of fidelity and spirit to those which are undertaken for money, often by people who are not prepared for the task, but forced to it by their necessities, and who feel that they must go through it in the shortest possible time. Among such we must notice one from Dumas now going the rounds where the translator is even so ignorant as to use the verb *learn* instead of *teach*, a vulgarity very common among the worse educated people of this country, and which they should not be exposed to find authenticated by any kind of book. It is, however, no matter how the scene painting of Dumas is rendered, compared with the admirable style of Sand, the best living French writer, and in some respects the best living prose writer. [. . .]

The work itself cannot fail of innumerable readers, and a great influence, for it counts many of the most significant pulse-beats of the time. Apart from its range of character and fine descriptions, it records some of the mystical apparitions and attempts to solve some of the problems of the time. How to combine the benefits of the religious life with those of the artist life in an existence more simple, more full, more human in short, than either of the two hitherto known by these names has been. This problem is but poorly solved in the 'Countess of Rudolstadt,' the sequel to Consuelo. It is true, as the English reviewer says, that George Sand is a far better poet than philosopher, and that the chief use she can be of in these matters is by her great range of observation and fine intuitions to help to develop the thoughts of the time a little way farther. But the sincerity, the reality of all he can obtain from this writer will be highly valued by the earnest man.

In one respect the book is entirely successful, in showing how inward purity and honor may preserve a woman from bewilderment and danger, and secure her a genuine independence. Whoever aims at this is still considered by unthinking or prejudiced minds as wishing to despoil the female character of its natural and peculiar loveliness. It is supposed that delicacy must imply weakness, and that only an Amazon can stand upright and have sufficient command of her faculties to confront the shock of adversity or resist the allurements of tenderness. Miss Bremer, Dumas, and the Northern novelist, Andersen,* make women who have a tendency to the intellectual life of an artist fail and suffer the penalties of arrogant presumption, in the very first steps of a career to which an inward vocation called them in preference to the usual home duties. Yet nothing is more obvious than that the circumstances of the time do, more and more frequently, call women to such lives, and that, if guardianship is absolutely necessary to women, many must perish for the want of it. There is, then, reason to hope that God may be a sufficient guardian to those who dare to rely on Him, and if the heroines of the novelists we have named ended as they did, it was for want of the purity of ambition and simplicity of character which do not permit such as Consuelo to be either unsexed and depraved, or unresisting victims and breaking reeds if left alone in the storm and crowd of life. To many women this picture will prove a true Consuelo, (consolation) and we think even very prejudiced men will not read it without being charmed with the expansion, sweetness and genuine force of a female character such as they have not met, but must, when painted, recognize as possible, and may be led to review their opinions, and, perhaps, to elevate and enlarge their hopes as to 'woman's sphere' and 'woman's mission.' If such insist on what they have heard of the private life of this writer and refuse to believe that any good thing can come out of Nazareth,* we reply that we do not know the true facts as to the history of George Sand, there has been no memoir or notice of her published on which any one can rely, and we have seen too much of life to accept the monsters of gossip in reference to any one. But we know, through her works, that, whatever the stains on her life and reputation may have been, there is in her a soul so capable of goodness and honor as to depict them most successfully in her ideal forms.—It is her works and not her private life that we are considering. Of her works we have means of judging—of herself not; but among those who have passed unblamed through the walks of life, we have not often found a nobleness of purpose and feeling, a sincere religious hope to be compared with the spirit that breathes through the pages of Consuelo.

The experiences of the artist life, the grand and penetrating remarks upon music, make the book a precious acquisition to all whose hearts are fashioned to understand such things. We suppose that we receive here not only the mind of the writer but of Liszt, with whom she has publicly corresponded in 'Letters of a Traveller.' None could more avail us, for 'in him, also, is a spark of the divine fire,' as Beethoven said of Schubert. We may thus consider that we have in this book the benefit of the most electric nature, the finest sensibility, and the boldest spirit of investigation combined, expressing themselves in a little world of beautiful or picturesque forms.

Although there are grave problems discussed, and sad and searching experiences described in this work, yet its spirit is, in the main, hopeful, serene, almost glad. It is the spirit inspired from a near acquaintance with the higher life of Art. Seeing there something really achieved and completed corresponding with the soul's desires, faith is enlivened as to the eventual fulfilment of those desires, and we feel a certainty that the existence which looks at present so marred and fragmentary shall yet end in harmony. The shuttle is at work, and the threads are gradually added that shall bring out the pattern and prove that what seems at present confusion is really the way and means to order and beauty. [. . .]

AGLAURON AND LAURIE
(EXCERPTS)*

[*Editor's note: Emily, the spoilt youngest child of a marriage between a self-centred father and an ineffectual mother, was engaged and married at 15 to Leven, a much older man. Her parents were delighted by the social* kudos *of the match, but Emily, though uneducated and naïve, becomes increasingly convinced of the hollowness of her marriage. Here she relates her story to her acquaintance Aglauron*]:

'You know', she said, 'my past history: all do so here, I know, though they do not talk loudly of it. You and all others have probably blamed me. You know not, you cannot guess, the anguish, the struggles of my childish mind when it first opened to the meaning of those words, love, and marriage, and life. When I was bound to Mr Leven by a vow which from my heedless lips was mockery of all thought, all holiness, I had never known a duty, I had never felt the pressure of a tie. Life had been so far, a sweet, voluptuous dream, and I thought of this seemingly so kind and amiable person, as a new and devoted ministrant to me, of its pleasures.

'But I was scarcely in his power when I awoke, I perceived the unfitness of the tie, its closeness revolted me. I had no timidity: I had always been accustomed to indulge all my feelings, and I displayed them now. Leven, irritated, asserted his mastery: this drove me wild; I soon hated him, and despised too his insensitivity to all which I thought most beautiful. From all his faults, and the imperfection of our relation, grew up in my mind a knowledge of what the time might be to me; it is astonishing how the thought grew upon me day by day. I had not been married more than three months before I knew what it would be to love, and I longed to be free to do so. I had never known what it was to be resisted, and the thought never came to me that I could now, and for all my life, be bound by so early a mistake. I thought only of expressing my resolve to be free.'

[*Emily announces to her father that she wishes to dissolve her mar-*

riage and return to his house. Her parents and Leven are mortified.
A female confessor, Almeira, persuades Emily of the damage she is
doing, and she agrees to return to Leven on an entirely nonsexual
basis]:

'How I was repulsed, how disappointed, you know, or could
devine [*sic*] if you did not. For all but me have been trained to
bear the burden from their youth up, and accustomed to have
the individual will fettered, for the advantage of society. For the
same reason you cannot guess the silent fury that filled my mind
when I at last found that I struggled in vain, that I must remain
in the bondage I had ignorantly put on.

'My affections were totally alienated from my family, for I felt
they had known what I had not, and had neither put me on
my guard, nor guarded me against precipitation whose consequences must be fatal. I saw indeed that they did not look on
life as I did,—and could be content without being happy: but
this observation was far from making me love them more. I felt
alone, bitterly, contemptuously alone. I hated men, who had
made the laws that bound me. I did not believe in God, for why
had he permitted the dart to enter so unprepared a breast? I
determined never to submit, though I disdained to struggle,
since struggle was in vain.—In passive, lonely, wretchedness I
would pass my days. I would not feign what I did not feel, nor
take the hand which had poisoned for me the cup of life before
I had sipped the first drops.

'A friend, the only one I have ever known, taught me other
thoughts. She taught me that others, perhaps all others were
victims, as much as myself. She taught me that if all the wrecked
submitted to be drowned, the world would be a desert. She
taught me to pity others,—even those I myself was paining [?]:
for she shewed [*sic*] me that they had sinned in ignorance, and
that I had no right to make them suffer so long as I myself did,
merely because they were the causes of my suffering.

'She shewed me by her own pure example, what were duty
and benevolence and employment to the soul, even when baffled
and sickened in its dearest wishes. That example was not wholly
lost; I forced my parents, at least, from their pain; and, without
falsehood, became less cruel and more calm.

'Yet the kindness, the calmness, have never gone deep. I have been forced to live out of myself: and life, busy or idle, is still most bitter to the homeless heart. I cannot be like Almeira, I am more ardent: and Aglauron, you see I might now be happy.'

She looked towards V. I followed her eye, and was well-nigh melted by the beauty of his gaze.

'The question in my mind, is', she resumed, 'have I not a right to fly? To leave this vacant life, and a tie which, but for worldly circumstances, presses as heavily on Leven as on myself. I shall mortify him, but that is a trifle, compared to actual misery. I shall grieve my parents, but if they were truly such, would they not grieve still more that I should reject the real life of mutual love? I have already sacrificed enough: shall I sacrifice the happiness of one I could really bless for those who do not know one native heart-beat of my life?'

V. kissed her hand.

'And yet', said she, sighing, 'it does not always look so. We must leave the world, it will not tolerate us. Can I make V. happy in solitude? And what would Almeira think? Often it seems that she would feel that now I do love, and could make a green spot in the desert of life over which she mourned, she would rejoice to have me do so. Then again something whispers she might have objections to make, and I wish, oh I long to know them. For I feel that this is the great crisis of my life, and that if I do not act wisely, now I have thought and felt, it will be un- pardonable. In my first error, I was ignorant what I wished,— but now I know, and ought not to be weak or deluded.'

I said, 'Have you no religious scruples? Do you never think of your vow as sacred?'

'Never!' She replied with flashing eyes. 'Shall the woman be bound by the folly of the child? No, I have never once con- sidered myself as Leven's wife. If I have lived in his house, it was to make the best of what was left, as Almeira advised. But what I feel, he knows perfectly. I have never deceived him. Yet oh! I hazard all, all! and should I be again ignorant, again deceived,—[. . .]

'[T]hese laws, this society, are so strange, I can make nothing of them. In music I am at home. Why is not all life a music? We instantly know when we are going wrong there [. . .] Why am I not at liberty to declare unblushingly to all men that I will leave the man whom I do not love, and go with him I do love? That is the only way that would suit me. I cannot see clearly to take any other course.' [. . .]

[*On Aglauron's advice, Emily sends V. away for a trial period of a year, to see if she can reconcile herself with her marital duties. Within this year Leven dies, and Emily is free to marry V. But her restlessness remains:*]

Her strong nature found him too much hers, and too little his own. He satisfied her as little as Leven had done, though always lovely and dear. She saw with keen anguish, though this time without bitterness, that we are never wise enough to be sure any measure will fulfill our expectations. [. . .]

A DIALOGUE*

My cup already doth with light o'errun.
  Descend, fair sun;
I am all crimsoned for the bridal hour,
  Come to thy flower.

Ah, if I pause, my work will not be done,
  On I must run,
The mountains wait.—I love thee, lustrous flower,
  But give to love no hour.

EXPLANATORY NOTES

5 *Frailty, thy name is WOMAN: Hamlet*, I. ii. 146; *The Earth waits for her Queen*: this unattributed epigraph was widely taken to mean that Fuller thought of herself as the messianic queen. Of the earlier version of *Woman*, 'The Great Lawsuit', Sophia Peabody Hawthorne, wife of the novelist, wrote to her mother: 'What do you think of the speech which Queen Margaret Fuller has made from the throne?'

6 *Siquis tamen, Hercule . . . Assensere Dei*: 'If any God dissent, and judge too great | The sacred honors of the heavenly seat, | Even he shall own his deeds deserve the sky, | Even he, reluctant, shall at length comply, | Th' assembled powers assent.' (trans. by John Gay (1685–1732) of this passage from Book IX of Ovid's *Metamorphoses*, appended by Fuller to first appearance of the quotation in 'The Great Lawsuit').

The candlestick set in a low place . . . hill: a paraphrase of Matt. 5: 14–15 (from the Sermon on the Mount): 'Ye are the light of the world. A city that is set on a hill cannot be hid. Neither do men light a candle, and put it under a bushel, but on a candlestick; and it giveth light to all that are in the house.'

7 *Prometheus*: in Greek myth, a Titan who championed humankind, stealing fire from the gods, and in some stories actually making man out of clay.

8 *Be ye perfect*: the text of Fuller's 'sermon', from Matt. 5: 48 (the Sermon on the Mount): 'Be ye therefore perfect, even as your Father which is in heaven is perfect.'

Lamb: possibly Isaiah 53:5: 'He is brought as a lamb to the slaughter, and as a sheep before her shearers is dumb, so he openeth not his mouth.'

9 *an earnest mind of a foreign land*: identified in a note by Fuller as 'St Martin'. Louis Claude de Saint-Martin (1743–1803), a Catholic mystic, published as 'the unknown philosopher' and preached throughout the Continent and England. Saint-Martin hypothesized an ideal society in which spiritual 'divine commissioners' would rule.

9 *Crawford's Orpheus*: Thomas Crawford (1813–57), an American sculptor who worked in Rome. He and his wife Louisa Ward Crawford were to become part of Fuller's circle of American acquaintances during her Roman years.

'Orphic sayings'—'Orphics': Amos Bronson Alcott (1799–1888), whom Thomas Carlyle called 'the potato Quixote', was a Connecticut Yankee of atypically impractical stripe. His 'Orphic sayings', published in *The Dial* under Fuller's editorship, gained him the reputation of a head-in-the-clouds philosopher. Indeed, his daughter, the writer Louisa May Alcott, took a leaf out of Aristophanes' *The Clouds* by describing her father as 'a man up in a balloon, with his family and friends holding the ropes which confine him to earth and trying to haul him down'.

10 *Persephone*: queen of Hades.

. . . from the far-shining view: the poem is Fuller's.

Bacon: Francis Bacon (1561–1626), Lord Verulam, British statesman, essayist, and empiricist philosopher.

Syren coast: the Sirens, in Greek myth, were sea nymphs, part woman and part bird, whose singing enticed mariners to their deaths.

11 *Béranger*: Pierre-Jean de Béranger (1780–1857), French poet, author of 'La Liberté'. The quotation which follows is a paraphrase of the final words of the French democratic leader Mme Roland (Manon [Marie-Jeanne Philpon] Roland 1754–93) on mounting the scaffold to the guillotine: 'O liberty: what crimes are committed in thy name!'

12 *Father, forgive them . . . they do*: Luke 23: 34.

13 *'. . . Che contrista uno spirito immortal.'*: Fuller's note identifies this as a poem by Alessandro Manzoni (1785–1883), the Italian romantic novelist and poet. The quotation is from 'Coro Dell' Atto Secundo', *Il Conte di Carmagnola*, canto 45.

Cato: Marcus Porcius ('the Elder'), 234–149 BC, Roman soldier, statesman, and writer; famous for his oratory against Carthage in the Senate during the Punic Wars, when he harped constantly on the phrase 'Delenda est Carthago' ('Carthage must be destroyed').

Landor: Walter Savage Landor (1775–1864), English poet and prose writer.

Sterling's: John Sterling (1806–44), English poet and playwright.

14 *Carabbas*: the Marquis of Carabbas, the fictional title which the hero of *Puss in Boots* invents for himself.

14 *Jacobins*: the extreme revolutionary group associated with Robespierre's Reign of Terror in France, 1793–4.

15 *Schiller's 'Dignity of Woman'*: Johann Christoph Friedrich von Schiller (1759–1805), German poet, dramatist and historian. His philosophical lyric poetry includes *Würde der Frauen*, to which Fuller refers.

Deutsche Schnellpost: a German immigrants' newspaper published in New York. In August 1845 Fuller was to translate, for her *Tribune* readers, a letter from the Paris correspondent of the *Deutsche Schnellpost*. Featured in a front-page article, this would be one of the earliest mentions of Marx and Engels in an American periodical.

an article in the Democratic Review: 'The Legal Wrongs of Women', *United States Magazine and Democratic Review*, 14 (May 1844), 477–83.

16 *J. Q. Adams . . . Phocion*: John Quincy Adams (1767–1848), sixth president of the United States. *Phocion*: (*c.* 402–317 BC) pupil of Plato, and leader of the aristocratic party in Athens, who countered the oratory of Demosthenes and the growing influence of Macedon under Philip the Great. Fuller implies that Adams likewise resisted the populist politics of Andrew Jackson, seventh president of the United States.

21 *Miranda*: usually taken to be Fuller herself. However, Fuller suggested playfully in a letter written after the publication of 'The Great Lawsuit' that the world should consider the character of Miranda there to be no more or less the real Margaret than that of Mariana in *Summer on the Lakes* (see p. 174 of this volume). Different characters might represent different aspects of her own personality, she said. The American critic Elaine Showalter thinks that 'Miranda' means not the passive 'one to be wondered at', as in Latin, but the active 'seeing one', as in Spanish. She also believes that the reference to *The Tempest* is deliberate. This was a play with great resonance for a gifted woman who had learned what wizardry of knowledge she possessed largely from her father. Like Prospero, Timothy Fuller isolated his daughter on an island of anomaly, making her a fish out of water, a learned lady. Miranda speaks the language her father taught her and has no conversation with other women; she does not even remember her mother. Showalter calls Fuller 'a motherless Miranda trying to give birth to herself'. I think the case is a little more complicated. To accept that Fuller viewed herself as motherless would be to confirm a patriarchal view of

who mattered in her life, whose language was her native tongue. Fuller was not literally motherless, and indeed her mother was her preferred parent, I think—much more of a presence in her life than her frequently absent father. Indeed, Fuller's mother outlived her.

23 *... and spin her own free hours*: Ben Jonson, 'On Lucy, Countess of Bedford', *Epigrammes* LXXVI, ll. 7–16.

24 *Theseus ... wed the Amazonian Queen*: Theseus, hero of Greek mythology, attacked the Amazons and abducted one of them, Antiope, who bore him a son, Hippolytus. However, he repudiated her in favour of Phaedra.

Hercules ... fit guerdon: in fleeing from Aetolia after he accidentally murdered his father-in-law's favourite page, Hercules and his bride Deianeira had to cross the River Evenus. The centaur Nessus offered to carry Deianeira to the other shore, but attempted to violate her. Hercules killed him with an arrow, and as the centaur died he gave his blood to Deianeira, treacherously promising that it had the power to keep Hercules faithful to her. When Hercules embarked on his final adventure, involving the rescue of his former love Iole, he sent to Deianeira for a white tunic. Deianeira, fearful of her rival's attractions, soaked the tunic in the centaur's blood before sending it to Hercules. When Hercules put the tunic on, he was devoured by fire.

Richter: Jean (Johann) Paul Friedrich Richter (1763–1825), German Romantic poet, novelist, and essayist. Richter's view that the phenomena of nature symbolized higher realities resembled the Transcendentalists' convictions, and Fuller was much attracted by his idealism.

25 *Penelope*: in Greek myth, the faithful wife of Odysseus (Ulysses).

Countess Emily Plater: Emilija Plater (1806–31), Lithuanian nationalist and rebel. Born in Vilnius, she modelled herself on Joan of Arc, attempting to free Lithuania of Russian rule as Joan had fought to free France from Norman-English enclaves. She organized a regiment of riflemen, cavalry, and peasants armed with scythes in a failed attempt to seize the military academy at Daugavpils (Latvia). Subsequently she fought with regular insurgent units against the Russians at Ukmerge, Kaunas, and Vilnius, being appointed company commander with the rank of captain. When the rebels were defeated, she refused to surrender and escaped dressed as a peasant woman. While trying to reach Poland, where the fight against the Russians was continuing, she fell ill and died. Fuller had read the account of her life (which misrepresented her nationality) 'Emily Plater, the Polish Heroine', in the *United States Magazine and Democratic Review*, 11 (July 1842), 23–33.

26 *making him accuse her . . . God*: Genesis 3: 11–12: 'And he [God] said, "Who told thee that thou wast naked? Hast thou eaten of the tree, whereof I commanded thee that thou shouldest not eat?" And the man said, "The woman whom thou gavest to be with me, she gave me of the tree, and I did eat."'

27 *Semiramis*: Sammuramat (*c.*800 BC), Assyrian queen, who is said to have ruled for over forty years until overthrown by her son. The actual queen Sammuramat is connected by historians with the legend of Semiramis, daughter of a goddess, who irrigated Babylon and fought military campaigns as far away as India.

Aspasia: Aspasia of Miletos (5th cent. BC). Unconfined by the laws restricting native Athenian women to their homes, she gathered together philosophers, artists, and statesmen in the manner re-created two thousand years later by the ladies of the French salons. Socrates, Plato, and the ruler Pericles were among her frequent guests. Aspasia married Pericles and collaborated with him to destroy the power of the aristocracy, who had her charged in court with atheism and procuring. Pericles defended her, breaking into tears, and she was acquitted.

Eloisa: Héloise (1101–64), French abbess, best known for her letters to the abbot Peter Abelard (1079–1142). As a scholastic philosopher Abelard had been Héloise's teacher at the University of Paris. They married secretly after their son was born, but Héloise's uncle, the canon Fulbert, ordered Abelard to be castrated. He entered the Abbey of St Denis, and Héloise followed him into the cloister, becoming Abbess of Paraclete, a Benedictine convent founded by Abelard. The letters concern not only the couple's abiding love for each other, but their intense interest in spiritual questions and their great learning.

that he . . . could be ungrateful: possibly a reference to the later stories about Sappho's supposed suicide. She was said to have had herself thrown over a cliff for the unrequited love of a man called Phaon.

Tasso's prison bars: the Italian poet Torquato Tasso (1544–95) was cast into a madhouse in 1579 after verbally abusing his former patron, Duke Alfonso II of Ferrara. Both Goethe and Byron used Tasso as a subject.

28 *Mrs Carter and Madame Dacier*: Elizabeth Carter (1717–1806), English translator, poet, and editor, friend of Dr Johnson and member of the group of intellectual women popularly known as bluestockings. Anne Lefevre Dacier (1654–1720), whose translations of the *Iliad* (1699) and the *Odyssey* (1708) first made Homer widely known in France.

'*. . . but roughly since I heard thee last.*': from William Cowper (1731–1800), 'On the Receipt of My Mother's Picture out of Norfolk.'

29 '*. . . of Heaven and home.*': from William Wordsworth (1770–1850), 'To a Skylark'.

ignis fatuus: will o' the wisp.

Rosicrucian lamp: referring to an occult secret society (Rosicrucian Order, Ancient Mystic Order Rosae Crucis), founded in the seventeenth century and still active in America. When the founder's tomb was opened 120 years after burial, the body was allegedly in excellent preservation and the lamps surrounding the corpse were still burning.

Sita in the Ramayana: in the Hindu epic myth the *Ramayana*, Sita, the wife of Rama, insisted on accompanying her husband into his exile when he was forced to renounce the throne. Abducted by the evil Ravana in his skyborne chariot, she retained her chastity, which she proved after her liberation from Ravana by a test of fire.

Isis: the chief goddess of ancient Egypt. Isis taught women to grind corn, spin flax, and weave cloth, and instructed men how to cure disease; by instituting marriage, she also originated family life. When Osiris was killed by their evil brother Set, Isis joined the fragments together and performed, for the first time, the rites of embalming which would give him eternal life. See Fuller's Appendix A for further details.

Ceres and Proserpine: Ceres, Roman goddess of agriculture, under whose name the Romans subsumed the worship of the Greek corn-goddess Demeter. Proserpine (Persephone in Greek myth) was her daughter.

Diana: in Roman myth, virgin goddess of the hunt and the moon (Greek Artemis). *Minerva*: Roman warrior-goddess of wisdom (Greek Athene). *Vesta*: Roman goddess of the hearth, centre of a cult in Rome, served by her prestigious priestesses the Vestal Virgins. Fuller lays stress on the virginal ('self-sufficing') character of all three goddesses.

30   *Etruria*: ancient Italian state, precursor of Rome, originally the whole of north Italy from the Tiber to the Alps. Its independence came to an end in 309 BC. Since Etruscan remains largely undeciphered, knowledge about Etruria is necessarily speculative. The Etruscan nation was a loose agglomeration of clans, and it is unclear what source Fuller used for her claim about priestess and warrior queens. It does seem that two of the three principal Etruscan gods were female: goddesses roughly corresponding to the Roman deities Juno and Minerva.

  Brutus and Portia: Marcus Junius Brutus (*c.*84–42 BC), one of Julius Caesar's assassins, killed himself after his defeat by Mark Anthony. His wife Portia committed suicide by swallowing live coals. The quotations which follow are from Shakespeare's *Julius Caesar*.

31   *Cato's daughter*: Marcus Porcius ('Cato the Younger'), 95–46 BC, Roman statesman, soldier and Stoic philosopher, great-grandson of Cato the Elder (see note to p. 13).

  Ovid: Publius Ovidius Naso (43 BC–AD 17?), Roman poet.

32   *Sparta*: ancient Greek city, rival of Athens. Greek writers of the fifth century BC contrasted the restricted, private life of Athenian women with the greater freedom and public participation of Spartan women.

  'Honor gone . . . been born.': unidentified.

  Cassandra . . . Macaria: *Cassandra*: daughter of Priam, king of Troy; prophetess given the gift of foresight by Apollo. When she resisted the god, however, he added a curse to this blessing: her predictions would never be believed. *Iphigenia* was the daughter of Agamemnon and Clytemnestra, and was sacrificed by her father at Aulis in order to ensure the success of the Greek expedition to Troy. The story forms the subject of Euripides' play *Iphigenia at Aulis*, discussed by Fuller in Appendix 4. *Antigone*: protagonist of a tragedy by Sophocles, defied her uncle Creon, who had ordered that her brother, the rebel Polynices, should not be accorded funeral rites. Antigone was herself executed by being walled up alive in a cave. *Macaria*: in Euripides' *Children of Heracles*, daughter of Heracles, who offers herself as a sacrifice to ensure an Athenian victory.

  Sibylline priestesses: priestesses of Apollo, whose most famous sanctuary was at Delphi in ancient Greece.

  victory wore a female form: Nike, the winged Greek goddess of victory.

33 *Heine*: Heinrich Heine (1797–1856), German lyrical and satirical poet, journalist, and critic. *Dame du Comptoir*: female sales clerk. Heine means that the attractive image of the Virgin 'sells' Catholicism to the gullible.

Petrarch's Hymn to the Madonna: Petrarch (Francesco Petrarca) (1304–74), Italian poet and scholar.

34 *Lady Teresa's Bridal*: not St Theresa of Avila (1515–82), Spanish Carmelite nun and mystic, but an unknown Infanta or princess, a sister of King Alfonso of Leon in north-west Spain.

altvater: 'old father'.

35 *Drachenfels*: 'Dragon's Rock', mountain on the Rhine, home of the dragon killed by the German epic hero Siegfried.

36 *Xenophon*: Greek historian (*c.*430–354 BC). His *Economics* (the word derives from the Greek *oikos*, house, and *nomos*, law, rule, management) is a dialogue on domestic and estate management. The *Cyropaedia* is ostensibly the story of the youth of Cyrus the Great, founder of the Persian empire, but less a literal biography than a compilation of Xenophon's theories about education, written to rebut the principles in Plato's *Republic*. Several pages from the *Cyropaedia*, including the story of Panthea, are reproduced at pp. 54 ff.

Iphigenia say to Achilles: reference to Euripides' *Iphigenia at Aulis* (see note to p. 32).

37 *Pompadour and Du Barry*: Jeanne Antoinette Poisson, Marquise de Pompadour (1721–64), French courtesan, mistress of Louis XV. Marie Jeanne Gomard de Vaubernier, Comtesse du Barry (1743–93), mistress of Louis XV, successor to Madame Pompadour; executed on the guillotine.

Ximena: wife of the legendary Spanish hero El Cid.

worthless favorite of a worthless queen: probably the young guardsman Manuel de Godoy, lover of Queen Maria Louisa, wife of the ineffectual Charles IV of Spain (ruled 1788–1808). Gaining influence in the absence of a strong king, Godoy collaborated with Napoleon for self-advancement but was disgraced by the Spanish defeat at Trafalgar, the cession of Louisiana, and the eventual invasion of Spain by Napoleon's forces. Fuller apparently means that, despite the strict Spanish precautions to preserve wifely fidelity, an adventurer was able to worm his way into the favour of the highest lady in the land.

38 *'Vor dem Sklaven . . . erzittert nicht.'*: Schiller, 'Die Worte des Glaubens', str. 2.

38 *Swedenborg's*: Emanuel Swedenborg (1688–1722), Swedish scientist, theologian and philosopher, whose theosophic system inspired the founding of the New Jerusalem Church.

no marrying nor giving in marriage: 'For in the resurrection they neither marry, nor are given in marriage', Matt. 22: 30.

Jene... verklarten Leib: 'Those heavenly figures | Are not concerned about being husband or wife, | And neither clothes nor drapery | Surround the transfigured body.' Unidentified.

39 *magnanimity*: Fuller condemns Elizabeth's lack of 'magnanimity', but it is worth remembering that Elizabeth's succession to the English throne in 1558 had been challenged by Mary's Catholic supporters, that Mary was herself a claimant to the English throne in an unsettled and bloody period, and that Mary had encouraged a series of conspiracies with Spanish help, resulting in Parliament's demand for her execution.

40 *Mr Prescott... 'Malinche'*: William Hickling Prescott (1796–1859), American author of *History of the Conquest of Mexico* (1843), which contains the story of the Spanish conquistador Hernando Cortés (1485–1547) and his Indian guide and mistress Malinche, whom he baptized 'Marina'.

Queen Anne: (1665–1714), who became Queen of England in 1702. Anne was largely uninterested in the arts, which flourished regardless in her reign, but she did patronize such architects as Sir Christopher Wren.

'We will die for our King, Maria Theresa': the Austrian empress Maria Theresa (1717–80), mother of Marie Antoinette (and fifteen other children). After her brother's death, her father, Charles VI, the last Habsburg prince, passed a statute called the 'Pragmatic Sanction' which allowed the throne to pass to the female line. Maria, his eldest daughter, succeeded to the throne at the age of 23. She unified the far-flung parts of the Austro-Hungarian empire under a reformed and centralized government, initiated the Seven Years' War in order to regain lands lost to Prussia and Russia, and encouraged the artistic and architectural development of Vienna.

Spenser... fairest type: references to *The Faerie Queene* by the English poet Edmund Spenser (*c.*1552–99). Britomart is a female knight symbolizing chastity; Belphœbe represents Queen Elizabeth as a young woman; Florimel embodies the beneficent charms of womankind; and Una personifies truth.

40   *Ford and Massinger*: John Ford (1586–*c*.1640) and Philip
      Massinger (1583–1640), English dramatists. Besides his best-
      known play, *'Tis Pity She's a Whore*, which is unlikely to be the
      one Fuller praises, Ford wrote *The Queen, or the Excellency of the
      Sea*, *The Lady's Trial* (1639), and *The Broken Heart* (1633) (to
      which Fuller returns on p. 41); he also collaborated on *The
      Witch of Edmonton* (*c*.1621). Massinger's plays *The Virgin Martyr*
      (1620) and *The Maid of Honour* (1621) concern spiritual heroines
      facing ethical dilemmas.

      *Imogen ... Desdemona ... Rosalind ... Portia ... Isabella ... Cor-
      delia*: female characters in Shakespeare's plays *Cymbeline*, *Othello*,
      As You Like It, *The Merchant of Venice*, *Measure for Measure*,
      and *King Lear* (respectively).

41   '... *Loved I not honor more.*': From Richard Lovelace (1618–58),
      'To Lucasta, Going to the Wars'.

      the Commonwealth's man: unidentified, presumably a supporter of
      the Commonwealth in the English Civil War, executed on the
      Restoration of King Charles II after 1660.

      Colonel Hutchinson: John Hutchinson (1615–64), English Puritan
      and signer of Charles I's death warrant. His wife Lucy's *Memoirs
      of the Life of Colonel Hutchinson* was written soon after her
      husband's death, but not published until 1806.

      Donne: from John Donne (1575–1631), 'The Exstacie'.

      Lord Herbert: Edward, Lord Herbert of Cherbury (1583–1648),
      brother of the poet George Herbert, from his poem 'An Ode
      upon a Question Moved, Whether Love should continue forever'.
      Fuller wrote an imaginary dialogue between the two Herberts,
      published in her *Papers on Literature and Art* (1846).

      Penthea ... Calanthe: Calanthe (or Calautha) dies of a broken
      heart after being told of her father's, brother's and friend's
      deaths; Penthea is driven mad by a forced marriage, and dies.

      '*If thou art false ... itself.*': *Othello*, III. iii. 278.

42   *Calderon's Justina*: Character in *El Magico Prodigioso* (1637) by
      the Spanish playwright Pedro Calderón de la Barca (1600–81).

43   *Dante ... Beatrice*: Dante Alighieri (1265–1321), author of *The
      Divine Comedy*, married his childhood fiancée Gemma Donati
      after the death in 1290 of his muse and courtly love Beatrice
      Portinari.

      Boccaccio: Giovanni Boccaccio (1313–75), Italian writer and poet.

45 *Roland and his wife*: see note to Béranger, p. 11, for Mme Roland. Her husband, Roland de la Platière (1734–93), whom she married in 1780, was Minister of the Interior in 1792; both were involved in revolutionary politics, siding with the Girondins against Danton and Robespierre. Roland de la Platière committed suicide on learning of his wife's execution.

46 *Godwin...Mary Wolstonecraft* [*sic*]: William Godwin (1756–1836), English political philosopher, husband of the philosopher and radical Mary Wollstonecraft (1759–97), who wrote *A Vindication of the Rights of Woman* (1792). Wollstonecraft died of puerperal fever after the birth in 1797 of their daughter, Mary. Godwin's posthumous memoir of Wollstonecraft actually did a great deal to harm her reputation, revealing the earlier birth of an illegitimate daughter, Fanny (what Fuller calls 'all that was repulsive in her own past history'). Many writers on the Woman Question in the nineteenth century were therefore loath to claim her as an intellectual forebear. Wollstonecraft was more politically minded than Fuller, making the demand for the vote which Fuller never explicitly stipulates. But her feminism resembled Fuller's in that she regarded the task less as formal equality with men than as a 'revolution in female manners', a radical transformation of women to reach their full potential. George Eliot compared the two in an essay published in 1855, five years after Fuller's death. The biographical parallels, which Eliot largely omits, are as moving as the intellectual ones that she identifies are striking. They include both women's attempts to provide for their siblings on the meagre wages paid in the only professions open to women; their extensive travels; and the possibly illegitimate birth of Fuller's own child, Nino, four years after she wrote this passage condemning Wollstonecraft's transgression.

George Sand: Amantine-Lucile-Aurore Dupin, Baroness Dudevant (1804–76). Although Sand's heroines are capable and high-minded, she was far from being an overt feminist in her political writings, later mocking the women who sought the vote in the 1848 revolution. 'In effect, what is the liberty that a woman can seize? Adultery,' she wrote to the Central Committee in that year. Chafing against an unfortunate early marriage from which there was no divorce possible under the Napoleonic Code, she was widely slandered in America for her affairs with the poet Alfred de Musset and the composer Frédéric Chopin. In contrast to her dismissal of Wollstonecraft, Fuller is less ready to condemn Sand: she looked on her as someone who had carried out that most important task, to act out one's nature despite the world's restrictions. This predisposition to look sympathetically on the Frenchwoman was fulfilled when the two met in 1847 at Sand's Paris residence. Fuller wrote to her friend Elizabeth Hoar: '[I]t made me very happy to see such a woman, so large and so developed a character, and everything that *is* good in it so *really* good. I loved, shall always love her . . . I never liked a woman better.' See also Fuller's review of Sand's *Consuelo* for the *New York Daily Tribune*, reproduced on pp. 215–17 of this volume.

46 *Marguerite . . . St Leon*: characters in Godwin's novel *St Leon* (1799).

47 *Simon and Indiana*: *Indiana* (1832), (Oxford World's Classics, 1994, trs. Sylvia Raphael) the first novel published by 'George Sand', an instant popular and critical success, concerns the conflict between marital duty and spontaneous love. *Simon* (1836) revolves around the debate between eighteenth-century rationalism, republican idealism, and nineteenth-century romanticism.

Elizabeth Barrett: from the *Poems* (1844) of Elizabeth Barrett (later Browning) (1806–61), later to be Fuller's close friend in Florence during 1849–50. There is some irony in Fuller's preference for Barrett as more high-minded than Sand, since Barrett would shortly elope with Robert Browning, to the unending condemnation of her family: her father and brothers refused to have anything more to do with her. After Fuller's death in 1850 Barrett Browning was dismissive of her erstwhile friend's political radicalism and her written work, writing of Fuller's death and the loss in the shipwreck of her manuscript history of the Roman Revolution: 'I believe nothing was finished; nor, if finished, could the work have been otherwise than deeply coloured by those blood colours of Socialistic views, which would have drawn the wolves on her, with a still more howling enmity, both in England and America. Therefore it was better for her to go.'

48 *La Roche Mauprat*: Sand's *Mauprat* (1837). Its heroine, Edmée de Mauprat, is thought to have been the model for Dostoevsky's series of virtuous women who reform fallen men, such as Sonia in *Crime and Punishment*.

49 *Shelley*: the poet Percy Bysshe Shelley (1792–1822). Probably the first half of this sentence ('Shelley feared not to be fettered') refers to Shelley's willingness to marry Harriet Westbrook in August 1811, despite his atheism and his rejection of the insti-

tution of marriage. Subsequently he rejected Harriet in favour of
Mary Godwin (see note to p. 46 above), with whom he eloped in
1814: hence the second half of the sentence, 'unless so to be was
to be false'.

49 *the calumniated authoress of the 'Rights of Woman'*: Fuller's implicit
approval of Shelley's behaviour contrasts with her continuing
condemnation of Mary Godwin's mother, Mary Wollstonecraft,
and suggests Fuller was not immune from double standards. It is
particularly ironic that Shelley imbibed his views on marriage as a
readily dissoluble bond from Godwin, who held that marriage
was a compact of equals, without any religious sanction behind it,
and that it could, like any contract, be ended by mutual consent.

Goodwyn Barmby: John Goodwyn Barmby (1820–81), Christian
socialist.

50 *William and Mary Howitt*: William Howitt (1792–1879), Quaker
poet and author of *The Rural and Domestic Life of Germany* (1842);
Mary Botham Howitt (1799–1888), Quaker poet and political
activist, author of the popular poem 'The Spider and the Fly'.
Mary Howitt was later a member (with Barbara Bodichon, Anna
Jameson and other nineteenth-century English feminists) of
the committee which, in 1856, would present to Parliament a
26,000-signature petition to gain married women the right to
control their own earnings and property. I am unable to identify
the reference in the next paragraph to the 'vulgar apparition'
which has marred Fuller's good opinion of Mary Howitt, or the
source of the tale of 'L'Amie Inconnue'.

51 *Goetz Von Berlichingen*: play by Goethe (1773) about a historical
German knight.

Manzoni thus dedicates his Adelchi: for Manzoni, see note to
p. 13. In 1808 he had married Henriette Blondel, daughter of a
banker of Geneva. The tragedy *Adelchi* was published in 1822.
His wife did not die until 1833, so this dedication (referring as it
does to a 'monument' and 'the memory of so many virtues') must
be from a later edition.

Count Zinzendorf: Nicolaus Ludwig, Graf von Zinzendorf (1700–
60), husband of Erdmute, confidante and collaborator in all his
work. Zinzendorf was a German religious and social reformer
who established the Moravian Brethren, on whose behalf he
travelled to America and elsewhere.

52 *'Daughter of God and Man, accomplished Eve!'*: Milton, *Paradise
Lost*, iv. 660.

52 *An observer*: Fuller notes this as 'Spangenberg'. August Gottlieb
    Spangenberg (1704–92), Zinzendorf's successor as bishop of the
    German Moravians.

54 *Xenophon*: from his *Cyropaedia*.

59 *the Banquet*: Plato's dialogue, also known as 'The Symposium'.

    the Economics: by Xenophon.

60 *Montague* [*sic*]: Lady Mary Wortley Montagu (1689–1762),
    English traveller, writer, and feminist, sister of the novelist Henry
    Fielding. She eloped with Edward Wortley Montagu, ambassador
    to Turkey between 1716–18, and wrote a series of brilliant
    letters about Turkish life and culture. From Turkey she also
    brought back knowledge of innoculation against smallpox, a pro-
    cedure which she introduced to England.

    Somerville: Mary Fairfax Somerville (1780–1872), Scottish
    mathematician who had no formal education beyond a single year
    of boarding school at the age of 10. At 15 she decided to study
    algebra, geometry, and classics, much against the will of most of
    her family, and later of her first husband, her cousin Samuel
    Greig. His death within three years of their marriage left her
    free to study mathematics, and at 33 she won a prize in a
    mathematical journal. Her second husband, the surgeon William
    Somerville, encouraged her work and introduced her to London
    intellectual circles, where she presented papers to the Royal
    Society, translated Laplace's texts, and was elected to honorary
    membership of the Society.

    De Stael's name: Anne Louise Germaine Necker (1766–1817),
    Baroness de Staël, French novelist, literary critic, and political
    writer. Although here Fuller implicitly condemns de Staël's
    affairs, most famously with the writer Benjamin Constant, the
    example of this foremost European woman of intellect and action
    inspired Fuller in the absence of American models. The rest-
    lessness which Fuller suffered at home in Cambridge, while all
    her male contemporaries were at university, was writ large in de
    Staël's heroine Corinne (in the novel of that name, published in
    1807). Indeed, Fuller was called 'a New England Corinne'.

61 *Lady Jane Grey*: (1537–54) English claimant to the throne,
    executed after her nine-day reign. Educated, like Elizabeth I, by
    the tutors hired by Henry VIII's wife Catherine Parr, she was
    proficient in Greek, Hebrew, Latin, Italian, and French at the
    age of 15.

62 *mental and moral Ishmaelites*: outcasts, from Ishmael, son of the patriarch Abraham's concubine Hagar, who was cast out with his mother after the birth of a legitimate son, Isaac, to Abraham's wife Sarah (Gen. 16, 17, 21).

the Aunt ... actual parents: Fuller may well be thinking of her own niece Greta, born on her birthday in 1844 to her tubercular sister Ellen and Ellen's irresponsible husband, the poet Ellery Channing.

63 *the Martha*: 'But Martha was cumbered about much serving, and came to him [Jesus], and said, Lord, dost thou not care that my sister hath left me to serve alone? bid her therefore that she help me.' (Luke 10: 40).

Urania: Greek muse of astronomy.

64 *Persican Sibyl ... Canova*: *Persican* or *Persian Sibyl*, eldest of the Sibyls (see notes to p. 32). Painted on the ceiling of the Sistine Chapel by Michelangelo. *St Theresa of Avila* (1515–82), Spanish Carmelite nun and mystic. *Leonora d'Este*, Tasso's patroness (see note to p. 27), a princess of the powerful d'Este family of Ferrara. *Electra*, the sister of Iphigenia (see notes for p. 32). Clytemnestra, mother of Iphigenia and wife of Agamemnon, had Agamemnon slain by her lover Aegisthus to avenge Iphigenia's sacrifice by Agamemnon. In turn Electra urged her brother Orestes to avenge their father's death by killing Clytemnestra and Aegisthus. *Antonio Canova* (1757–1822), Italian sculptor.

Iphigenia in Aulis: apparently a mistake: Fuller means Euripides' *Iphigenia in Tauris*. Later versions of the Iphigenia legend recount that the goddess Artemis took pity on the girl and snatched her up at the moment of the sacrifice. She was spirited away to Tauris and made priestess of the Artemis cult there, serving for over twenty years (till roughly the age of 40, since she was a maiden at the time of the sacrifice at Aulis).

65 *Chrysalid*: variant of 'chrysalis', that is, pupa or cocoon.

Vittoria Colonna: Italian poet (1490–1549), who wrote over a hundred elegies to her husband after his death from battle wounds in 1525. Thirteen years after his death she began a long platonic friendship with Michelangelo, with whom she exchanged sonnets and letters.

Mrs Jameson: Anna Murphy Brownell Jameson (1794–1860), Irish author. Fuller's iconography of women of achievement here had been prefigured by Jameson's *Memoirs of the Loves of the Poets: Biographical Sketches of Women Celebrated in Ancient and Modern Poetry* (1829), *Memoirs of Celebrated Female Sovereigns*, and *Characteristics of Women* (1832) (on the women in Shakespeare's plays, later retitled *Women of Shakespeare* or *The Heroines of Shakespeare*). Jameson also travelled widely, supporting herself and her family by the pen after her separation from her husband. Although a frequent collaborator with the Cult of True Womanhood, Jameson was outspoken in condemning male hypocrisy about prostitution.

65 *Joanna Southcott*: English religious leader (1750–1814), originally a Methodist, who prophesied the imminent second coming of Christ. At 64 she announced that she was to bear the second Christ by virgin birth, but died shortly afterwards. At the time of her death there were about 100,000 Southcottians.

Mother Anne Lee: Ann Lee (1736–84), English-born founder of the American Shaker movement. After the deaths of all four of her children in infancy, she became convinced of the evil of carnal relations, which were banned in Shaker communities. Presenting herself as the female religious principle, of which Christ had embodied the male, she increased the number of Shakers through promotion of frugality and industry.

Ecstatica, Dolorosa: fictional names of female mystics or seers (see also p. 67).

66 *as described by De Maistre*: probably an allusion to the *Soirées de Saint-Petersbourg* by Joseph de Maistre (1753–1821), French conservative political theorist appointed envoy to St Petersburg in 1802; but possibly a reference from his younger brother Xavier's *Les prisonniers du Caucase* (1825) or *La jeune Sibérienne* (1825).

Behmen . . . St Simon: Jacob *Behmen* or Boehme (1575–1624), German mystic. Claude-Henri de Rouvroy, Comte *Saint-Simon* (1760–1825), French socialist of aristocratic birth, best known as a theorist of modern industrial society, but also the author of *Nouveau Christianisme* (1825). In this, his last work, Saint-Simon argued for a new religion, Christian in spirit, to inspire a modern earthly paradise in which all wants would be fulfilled by the forces of science and industry.

Plato . . . treats woman in the Republic as property: a debatable reading of Plato's idea of the community of wives. The highest class in his Republic, the guardians, practise communal marriage and child-rearing in order to free themselves for ruling the state; but women are eligible to be trained up as guardians, although Plato doubts that the best woman will ever be as good as the best man.

67 *hérissé*: ruffled, unnerved.

Mademoiselle Rachel: pseudonym of Élisa Félix (1821–58), French tragic actress. The daughter of a poor Jewish merchant, she sang on the streets for money as a child. But by the time of her premature death from tuberculosis, she was recognized as the possessor of an unrivalled technique in the great classic tragedies of Racine and Corneille, and the most accomplished actress of her day.

La Rochefoucauld: François, Duc de la Rochefoucauld (1613–80), French writer of maxims. The 'modern La Rochefoucauld' may be the critic Jules Gabriel Janin (1804–74), who championed Rachel in the *Journal des débats*.

Guercino: Giovanni Francesco Barbieri (1591–1666), Italian painter.

Ecstatica: 'the one in ecstasy', prototypical seer in a trance. Mesmerism enjoyed a tremendous vogue in the nineteenth century, and Fuller showed her own fascination with it in a lengthy account of the Seeress of Prevorst in *Summer on the Lakes* (not reproduced in this volume; see also p. 6). The fictional character of Verena Tarrant in Henry James's *The Bostonians* (1886) is such a female seer, and her protector, Olive Chancellor, is often taken to be an unflattering portrait of Fuller.

68 '. . . *Its hymn to the Gods,*': unidentified.

Trojan Dames: *The Trojan Women* by Euripides; all the quotations which follow are from the play. Hecuba was the Queen of Troy, widow of King Priam, and mother of Cassandra.

69 *raptus*: 'being taken', rapture.

Seeress of Prevorst: Friederike Hauffe, a psychic whose case is described in *Die Seherin von Prevorst* (1829) by the German poet and doctor Justinus Kerner.

70 *Fenelon learns from Guyon*: François Fénélon (1651–1715), French prelate and author; Jeanne Marie (de Bouvier de la Mothe) Guyon (1648–1717), religious thinker who developed the doctrine of Quietism, which preached complete unconcern, even for salvation. Arrested in 1687, Guyon was freed with the assistance of Louis XIV's unacknowledged wife Mme de

Maintenon and won the backing of powerful figures at court, including the Abbé (later Archbishop) Fénélon.

70 *Isabella's jewels*: Queen Isabella of Castile was said to have sold her jewels in order to finance Columbus's expedition. Hence, America ought to make good the debt to a woman, Fuller says, by giving its women greater opportunities.

Another Isabella: Isabella II (1830–1904), queen of Spain from 1843 until her abdication in 1870 after a turbulent and capricious reign.

Bourbon . . . Guelph: the Bourbons were the French royal family between 1589 and 1792, the powers in Spain between 1700 and 1931, and the rulers of Naples between 1735 and 1806, and again from 1815 to 1860. The Guelphs originated as dukes of Saxony and Bavaria in the twelfth century.

71 *Lady's Book*: this unattributed quote probably refers to the long-running and influential magazine *Godey's Lady's Book*, edited by the conservative feminist Sarah Josepha (Buell) Hale (1788–1879).

72 *Angelina Grimké*: (1805–79), younger of the two abolitionist and feminist sisters. Born in South Carolina, she and her elder sister Sarah (1792–1873) left the South out of hatred for slavery. When the sisters began to campaign publicly for abolition and to address mixed-sex audiences—challenging the convention against women speaking in public except to all-female groups—they got a hostile and sometimes violent reception from politicians, press, fellow abolitionists, and clergy in the North. But their persistence put heart into the nascent Woman Question movement, to which they also contributed through Sarah's *Letters on the Equality of the Sexes* and *The Condition of Women* (1838).

Abby Kelley: (1811–67), American abolitionist who, like the Grimké sisters, was progressively drawn into women's issues as she encountered hostility from male abolitionists and the press to women's public participation. Abby Kelley's violation of proper womanly silence at the 1840 meeting of the Connecticut Anti-Slavery Society provoked the male chairman to rage: 'I will not sit in a chair where women bear rule. I vacate this chair. No woman shall speak or vote where I am moderator. I will not countenance such an outrage on decency . . . It is woman's business to take care of children in the nursery. She has no business to come into this meeting, and by speaking and voting lord it over men. Where woman's enticing eloquence is heard men are incapable of right and efficient action. She beguiles and blinds man by her smiles and her bland and winning voice.'

72 *The late Dr Channing*: William Ellery Channing (1780–1842), Boston clergyman and anti-slavery writer, for whom Fuller had worked briefly as an unpaid assistant and translator. His nephew, William Henry Channing (1810–84), was to be one of the three editors of Fuller's *Memoirs* after her death. Another nephew, the poet Ellery Channing (1817–1901), was Fuller's brother-in-law (see note to p. 62).

73 *Harriet Martineau*: (1802–76), English traveller and successful political essayist, an acquaintance of Fuller's youth. Martineau was later to condemn as 'gorgeous pedants' Fuller and her students in the 1839–44 Boston Conversations, college-level lectures for women (who were at that time largely denied university education). This snide account probably represented a delayed revenge for Fuller's mixed review of Martineau's *Society in America* in a letter written at the time of the book's American publication in 1837. Martineau's resentment did not dim over the years, and she slandered Fuller in these self-serving terms: 'She [Fuller] was not only completely spoiled in conversation and manners: she made false estimates of the objects and interests of human life. She was not content with pursuing, and inducing others to pursue, a metaphysical idealism destructive of all genuine feeling and sound activity; she mocked at objects and efforts of a higher order than her own, and despised those who, like myself, could not adopt her scale of valuation.'

Kinmont: Alexander Kinmont, Scottish writer on slavery in America. In her review of *The Narrative of Frederick Douglas*, published in the *New York Daily Tribune* on 10 June 1845, Fuller noted that both Kinmont and Dr Channing believed in negro emancipation because they 'thought that the African race had in them a peculiar element, which, if it could be assimilated with those imported among us from Europe, would give to genius a development, and to the energies of character a balance and harmony, beyond what has been seen heretofore in the history of the world.' Both men likewise believed in the admixture of 'female' qualities to 'male' ones in employment and public life through the emancipation of women.

74 *two articles headed 'Femality'*: 'V.', 'Femality', *Pathfinder*, 18 Mar. 1843, pp. 35–6, 51–2.

'. . . *keep thy vow.*': William Wordsworth, 'Liberty'.

75 *sets Hercules spinning*: Hercules was condemned to a year's slavery by the oracle of Apollo at Delphi, as penance for killing the innocent son of a treacherous king. He was bought for three talents by Omphale, queen of Lydia, who set him to spinning wool.

76 *Linnæus*: Carol Linnaeus (later von Linné) (1707–78), who originated the scientific classificatory system for all plants and animals which bears his name.

Often in my contemplation... flashes of light: unidentified quotations.

Jove sprang from Rhea, Pallas from Jove: in Greek myth, the Titan Rhea, daughter of Uranus (Sky) and Gaea (Earth), was the mother of the supreme God Zeus (Jove or Jupiter in Roman myth). Fuller's point is that the highest classical deity, unlike the Christian God, was not seen as timeless and self-engendered, but rather as born of a female. Conversely, Pallas Athene (Roman Minerva), the virgin goddess of wisdom and courage, had no mother, but sprang fully formed from the head of her father Zeus.

77 *Proclus*: (AD 410–85), Neoplatonist philosopher who influenced later Christian thought. Like most of the Neoplatonists, he excelled in elaborate metaphysical speculation.

Titanic: not in the prevalent modern sense of 'enormous', but rather referring to the period of the Titans in Greek myth. Ancestors of the more civilized Olympian gods, the Titans committed horrendously bloody deeds, typified by Cronos's emasculation and murder of his father Uranus.

78 *written of a sister*: for example, Wordsworth's 'To My Sister' and Byron's 'Epistle to Augusta'. Fuller took her own role as eldest sister of seven surviving children very seriously, tutoring four of her younger siblings and trying over and over to find a placement for her youngest brother Lloyd, who had learning difficulties. For most of her adult life after the death of her father in 1835, Fuller acted as surrogate father to her youngest brothers and sister, her nearest brothers, five and seven years younger, having left New England to seek their fortunes in the South and West. It was not until 1848 that she was able to found her own family, only two years before she, her husband, and their infant son were drowned.

Southey's Kehama: Robert Southey (1774–1843), English poet laureate, author of *The Curse of Kehama* (1810).

79 *Alcibiades with his phials*: (*c.*450–404 BC), opportunistic Athenian
    politician and general, lover in his youth of the philosopher
    Socrates and renowned for his beauty and audacity. One of his
    would-be admirers, Anytus, invited Alcibiades to a dinner party;
    Alcibiades refused, but got drunk at home with friends and led a
    procession to Anytus's house, where he ordered his slaves to
    carry off half of the gold and silver drinking cups (*phiales*).
    Anytus was philosophical about the outrage, remarking to his
    guests that it would have been more in Alcibiades's character to
    have taken the lot. The parallel is unclear. Perhaps Fuller means
    that the father in her story would have wanted to do the taking
    (of a wife) rather than be taken for the security he could provide
    (just as Alcibiades resented Anytus's overtures and humiliated
    him for them).

80 *Quakerism . . . equality with man*: the founder of the Religious
    Society of Friends (Quakers), George Fox, published in 1656 a
    defence of the spiritual equality of women. His wife Margaret
    Fell wrote her justification of female preaching, *Womens Speaking*,
    during her imprisonment in 1666. She lambasted the Church's
    prohibition against women's ordination and preaching as deeply
    evil: 'and if the seed of the Woman speak not, the Seed of the
    Serpent speaks: for God hath put enmity between the two seeds,
    and it is manifest that those that speak against the Woman and
    her Seeds speaking, speak out of the enmity of the Serpent's
    seed. All this opposing and gainsaying of Women's Speaking
    hath risen out of the bottomless Pit.' When Fuller wrote, Quaker-
    ism was in a rather sterile period before a time of renewed
    social and political action: hence, perhaps, her criticism that 'its
    scope is too narrow'. Indeed, some nineteenth-century American
    Quakers (Hicksites) disagreed with the Society's long-standing
    tradition of female ministry. Nevertheless, many of the most
    prominent advocates of the rights of women and slaves were
    Quakers, such as Sarah Grimké. It is a little difficult to see what
    similar practical effect the Swedenborgians had!

    Charles Fourier: (1772–1837), French utopian socialist whose
    writings inspired the founding in 1840 of Brook Farm, the ex-
    perimental community near Boston which Hawthorne depicted in
    The Blithedale Romance (1852), and which Fuller occasionally
    visited, trying to establish her brother Lloyd in a place there.
    Fourier wrote: 'The degree of emancipation of women is the
    natural measure of general emancipation.' To Fourier marriage
    or sexual partnership was more than a mirror of social progress,

as the Enlightenment had held: it was actually the cause of social evolution. 'Social progress and changes of period are brought about by virtue of the progress of women towards liberty, and social retrogression occurs as a result of a diminution in the liberty of women.'

82 *Frau Aja . . . Lili*: some women in the life of Goethe, from whose works, conversations, and letters Fuller had already translated two books, despite polite Bostonian censure of Goethe for his illicit relations with a common-law wife, Christiane Vulpius. First his mother, *Frau Aja*, Katharina Elisabeth Textor, whose own poetic, imaginative disposition greatly influenced her eldest and only surviving son. Next *the wise and gentle maiden*, possibly Friderike Brion, daughter of the pastor of Sesenheim, an Alsatian village near Strasburg, where Goethe was studying law in 1770; Goethe described this idyllic but unfulfilled love in *Dichtung und Wahrheit*. Third, *his sister*, Cornelia, the only other child of the family who survived to adulthood. Fourth, *Duchess Amelia*, wife of Duke Ernst August of Weimar and mother of Goethe's employer, Duke Karl August; ruled for seventeen years as regent after her husband's death and until her son's accession in September 1775, during which time she fostered the arts. Finally, *Lili* Schoenemann, daughter of a wealthy Frankfurt banker, to whom Goethe was briefly engaged in 1775.

Margaret: (Gretchen), Faust's lover in the verse play by Goethe (1808), personification of womanly love.

Mater Dolorosa: Mary, Mother of Sorrows.

Mater Gloriosa: Mary, Mother of Glory.

Leonora: in Goethe's *Torquato Tasso*. For the historical Leonora d'Este, see note to p. 64.

Iphigenia: in Goethe's play *Iphigenie auf Tauris*.

83 *Wilhelm Meister's Apprenticeship and Wandering Years*: *Wilhelm Meisters Lehrjahre* and *Wanderjahre*, Goethe's influential *Bildungs-romane* or novels of development of character.

the child of his degrading connection: Wieland (b. 1789), son of Goethe and Christiane Vulpius, Goethe's common-law wife from 1788 until their marriage in 1806.

Henri Blaze: (1813–88), French literary critic.

84 *'So let me seem . . . forever young.'*: from *Wilhelm Meisters Lehrjahre*, book VIII, chap. 2.

85 *upon his canvas*: from this point the text is newly written, with no
     use of the material from her early 'Great Lawsuit' except for the
     four paragraphs marked on p. 117. The writing now becomes
     much less consciously literary and more politically minded. In
     particular, Fuller becomes very bold indeed about prostitution,
     and quite frank about marriage and sexuality.

     Miss Edgeworth: Maria Edgeworth (1767–1849), Anglo-Irish
     novelist, who defended women's right to education and her own
     work as a literary translator in *Letters to Literary Ladies* (1793), but
     was best known for her novels such as *Castle Rackrent* (1800).
     At the age of 10 Fuller had fought back against her father's
     prohibition of all except historical novels, writing in a letter of
     December 1820: 'I wish I could be wiser, but that person *is*
     illiberal who condemns Scotts and Edgeworths novels.'

86 *Mrs Jameson*: see note to p. 65.

88 *Paladin . . . Poet*: Paladin, originally one of the emperor
     Charlemagne's twelve champions, but later any heroic knight.
     Fuller means 'the Paladin' and 'the Poet' as archetypes of courtly
     ideals.

89 *Bacchanals*: (Bacchantes, or Maenads), female devotees of the
     Roman wine-god Bacchus (Greek Dionysus), who whipped them-
     selves in a frenzy of lust and murderous fury during their rituals.

     Circe: in the *Odyssey*, an enchantress whose potions (hence
     Fuller's reference to a cup) turned all who landed on her island
     to animals. She changed Odysseus's companions into swine.

90 *Nestorian Sage*: from Nestor, the wise old counsellor of the *Iliad*
     and *Odyssey*. The poem is by Fuller.

91 *marriage* de convenance: marriage of convenience or expediency,
     for example one undertaken to enrich or ennoble the families.

     Sidney: Sir Philip Sidney (1554–86), English poet and statesman.

     Lady Russell: probably Rachel (1636–1723), second daughter of
     the fourth earl of Southampton, wife of the statesman Lord
     William Russell, with whom she lived on terms of great mutual
     respect and affection until his execution on a trumped-up treason
     charge in 1683. Lady Russell had a wide circle of distinguished
     acquaintances; her letters, published in 1773, were thought a
     model of clarity and style. One commentator, Joel Myerson,
     thinks this is a reference to the would-be marriage-arranger
     Lady Russell in Jane Austen's *Persuasion*, who 'attempts to force
     a loveless union', but that is to miss the point of the passage

entirely. The Lady Russell to whom Fuller refers is *contrasted* with English peeresses who take a conniving view of marriage, as the idealistic poets Milton and Sidney are opposed to the stew of sensuality which London has become. Clearly Fuller's Lady Russell must be one who took a high view of marriage. That Fuller was familiar with Rachel, Lady Russell, as an exemplar for wives is shown in the quotation on p. 95; again on p. 110, Lady Russell is invoked as a power for good.

93 '*. . . last thee long*': unidentified.

Duessa . . . trod: allegorical figures from Spenser's *Faerie Queene* (on Una see note to p. 40). Duessa embodies the perfidy of the Roman Catholic Church.

Mr Adams: John Quincy Adams (see note to p. 16). Fuller's father Timothy, as a congressman, was one of Adams's most loyal supporters, and expected an ambassadorship as a reward. This would have allowed Margaret to travel and continue her education in Europe; but the election of Andrew Jackson in 1828 put paid to those hopes. Timothy Fuller had already left Congress in 1825 and returned to his law practice in Cambridge, but further retrenchment was to follow. When Jackson was re-elected in 1832, Timothy Fuller, now entirely disillusioned with politics, retired to the country, taking his family with him. The period which followed was the nadir of Fuller's existence: isolated from Boston intellectual life by her residence in rural Groton, immersed in the heavy housework required for a family of nine, obliged to tutor her four youngest siblings at her father's behest. It is little wonder that she idealizes Adams and the period his presidency represented in her life, when the congressman's family lived in some style—though most historians' view of John Quincy Adams has been less adulatory. Although public-spirited and capable, he alienated politicians and people alike by his forbidding manner and his support for a series of unpopular measures; few presidents (at least in the nineteenth century) have been as vilified and frequently attacked. As Secretary of State under President James Monroe, he was the actual author of the 'Monroe Doctrine', by which America asserted its right to intervene in any country in Latin America. It is ironic that Fuller, who would live through and detest the French invasion which overthrew the Roman Republic in 1849, could so strongly support an imperialist at this earlier point in her political development.

my father: John Adams (1735–1826), second president of the United States.

94   *a mother*: Abigail Smith Adams (1744–1818), known for her
     letters, written in an excellent style, which give much valuable
     detail about the revolutionary period.

95   *her husband without a head*: John Adams refers to his anti-British
     activity before and during the American Revolution. The parallel
     is with Lord Russell's execution for alleged treason (see note to
     p. 91).

     Journal and Correspondence of Miss Adams... [Fuller's footnote]:
     published by Wiley and Putnam, New York, 1841. John Adams's
     letter is dated 12 July 1820.

96   '... *Eve.'*: the first quotation is from Book IV, l. 660 of Milton's
     Paradise Lost, the second from Book IX, l. 291.

98   *Mrs Child...Amelia Norman*: Lydia Maria (Francis) Child
     (1802–80), whom Fuller had known from her youth, progressed,
     as did so many early nineteenth-century American women, from
     abolitionism to concern for women's emancipation. A novelist,
     pamphleteer, and, essayist, she championed the case of Amelia
     Norman, who was acquitted of the charge of publicly stabbing
     her seducer.

     Eugène Sue: (1804–57), French popular novelist, author of
     Mysteries of Paris and *The Wandering Jew*.

99   '... *that he knows.'*: unidentified.

     Fleur de Marie...La Louve...Rigolette...Matilda: the first three
     are characters in Sue's *Mysteries of Paris*, the last the heroine of
     his novel *Matilda*.

     Sir Charles Grandison: hero of the novel *The History of Sir Charles
     Grandison* (1754) by Samuel Richardson (1689–1761).

100 *Madame Necker de Saussure* [Fuller's footnote]: Albertine Necker
     de Saussure (d. 1817), cousin, intimate friend, and biographer of
     Mme de Staël (see note to p. 60), not to be confused with
     Mme de Staël's more famous mother, Mme Suzanne (Curchod)
     Necker (d. 1794), reformer and founder of a literary salon. The
     sexual repugnance which Mme Necker de Saussure identifies
     in arranged marriages figures in Fuller's story 'Aglauron and
     Laurie', reproduced on pp. 218–21 of this volume.

102 *Los Exaltados...Exaltadas*: ('the exalted men'), Spanish liberal
     political party. Fuller makes a surprisingly modern point about
     gender bias in language through her reminder of the need to
     specifically include women as 'Las Exaltadas', even though it is
     grammatically correct to use the masculine ending for a mixed
     male and female group.

103 *D'Israeli*: Benjamin Disraeli (1804–81), later Conservative prime minister, published the autobiographical novel *The Young Duke* in 1831.

104 *The Whole Duty of Woman*: William Kenrick (1725?–79), *The Whole Duty of a Woman, by a Lady* (1753, first published in America in 1783).

The Study of the Life of Woman, by Madame Necker de Saussure: see note to p. 100. Perhaps the final volume, *Observations on the Life of a Woman*, of the English edition (published 1839–43) of *L'Éducation progressive; ou, Étude du cours de la vie, par Mme Necker de Saussure* (Paris, 1828–32).

105 *Cette vie… notre cœur*: 'This life only has value if it serves towards the moral education of our heart.' Which of Mme de Staël's works this comes from is not identified. It may possibly be from Mme Necker de Saussure's *Notice sur le caractère et les écrits de Mme de Staël*, in Mme de Staël's *Oeuvres complètes*, volume I of the seventeen volumes published 1820–1.

106 *Sir A. Mackenzie*: Alexander Mackenzie (*c.*1755–1820), Scottish explorer of northern and western Canada.

107 *Brunhilda*: Brunnhilde (Norse Brynhild), in the medieval German epic *Das Nibelungenlied*. Originally Brynhild was a Valkyrie, in Norse myth, a goddess, dispenser of the destiny of warriors, she who chooses which will die, and which of those will be admitted to Valhalla. The god Odin punished her for thwarting the victory of his chosen hero, Hjalmgunnar, by pricking her with a magic thorn which sent her into a deep slumber, and then by enclosing her in a castle surrounded by sheets of fire. She could only be rescued by the hero Sigurd (Siegfried in the *Nibelungenlied*), who rode his horse through the flames.

108 *Miss Sedgwick*: Catherine Maria Sedgwick (1789–1867), American writer. A letter of 12 April 1840 reveals that Fuller was reading Sedgwick's sketches of the Indians (in *Hope Leslie*, New York, 1827) and *Tales and Sketches* (Philadelphia, 1835).

109 *Miss Martineau and Miss Barrett*: see notes for pp. 73 and 47. Elizabeth Barrett's invalidism before her marriage to Robert Browning is well known. Harriet Martineau was an invalid between 1839 and 1844, during which time she wrote two novels, *Deerbrook* (1839) and *The Hour and the Man*, about the Haitian slave leader Toussaint l'Ouverture.

110 *O'Connell*: Daniel O'Connell (1775–1847), Irish nationalist

leader jailed for organizing a meeting at Tara's Hill which urged repeal of the Act of Union between Great Britain and Ireland. Fuller was sympathetic to Irish home rule, as was her employer, the *New York Tribune* editor Horace Greeley, who sponsored the publication of *Woman in the Nineteenth Century*. Despite a certain genteel condescension, her *Tribune* pieces on the character of the Irish, the autobiography of Frederick Douglas, and United States cultural imperialism share a common radical theme with *Woman*: the right to self-development. Fuller denounces the supposed 'laziness' of the Irish, 'contentment' of the slave, and 'superiority' of the white race as lies—and she never has much patience with lies. Her defence of the Irish—'fundamentally one of the best nations of the world'—drew angry correspondence, at a time when Americans felt themselves to be overwhelmed by a flood of Irish immigrants, but Fuller remained convinced of the need for an independent Irish republic.

the annexation of Texas: Texas had been an independent republic since 1836, but in 1845 it was added to the Union as a slave state, upsetting the balance between slave and free states so laboriously carved out in the Missouri Compromise of 1820. Fuller felt that the addition of this massive and rich territory to the roster of slave states made it less likely than ever that agreement could be reached between North and South on the abolition of slavery.

Boadicea ... Mrs Hutchinson: *Boadicea* (Boudicca): (d. AD 62) rebel queen of the Iceni, leader of the last resistance in Britain to Roman rule. *Godiva* (Godgifu): (*c*.1040–80), wife of Leofric, Earl of Mercia, rode naked through the streets of Coventry after her husband insisted that this was the only action which would persuade him to grant her requests that the people's taxation should be lightened. *Queen Emma* (d. 1052): underwent an ordeal by hot iron to prove herself chaste, according to legend. *Mrs Hutchinson*: (see notes for p. 41).

111 *This cause is your own ...*: Fuller warns women not to expect automatic support for female emancipation from those seeking the emancipation of slaves. The relationship between abolitionism and the movement for women's rights was not always cordial, despite the involvement in both causes of many prominent figures such as the Grimkés and Abby Kelley (see notes for p. 72). At the London World Anti-Slavery Convention of 1840 Lucretia Mott, Lydia Maria Child (see notes for p. 98), and other women in the American abolitionist delegation were denounced by the

British clergyman George Harvey and barred from the floor. British delegates were joined in their opposition to female representation by the 'moderate' wing of the American abolitionist movement. Against William Lloyd Garrison's insistence that abolitionism was a moral crusade which would be tainted by the hypocrisy of assigning women to an inferior sphere, more politically minded American abolitionists thought that any hint of feminism would alienate powerful groups whose support the anti-slavery movement needed.

111 *. . . why the foes of African slavery seek more freedom for women*: Fuller may be referring obliquely to abolitionists' concern at the spread of venereal disease through sexual exploitation of slave women by white men.

Five Points: nineteenth-century New York slum area, known for vice and crime.

112 *the earlier tract*: 'The Great Lawsuit'.

as was done in old-fashioned sermons: although many modern commentators, notably the influential editor Perry Miller, have pronounced *Woman* rambling and amorphous, the Fuller scholar Marie Urbanski believes that it has a very definite form: that of the sermon. The text, she says, is 'Be ye perfect' (see note to p. 8). The boundary between sermon, essay, and lecture was fluid for the male Transcendentalists: Ralph Waldo Emerson recycled one into another. Fuller had heard many of the great Unitarian preachers—William Ellery Channing, Frederic Henry Hedge, the abolitionists, Emerson himself—and might well have chosen this exalted but familiar form to fit her highly spiritual content. There is also evidence in a previously unpublished letter that she had tried writing sermons herself (letter to James Freeman Clarke, 17 April 1834).

113 *a king without a queen*: here in the sermon's final exhortation, Fuller implicitly reverts to her epigraph: 'The Earth waits for her Queen.' (See also the final poem, p. 119.)

114 *Dodona's oak*: Dodona, in Epirus in ancient Greece, site of the oldest and most important sanctuary to Zeus. The rustlings of the sacred oak of Dodona were regarded as the words of the god. The oak supposedly acquired its powers when a black dove from Thebes in Egypt landed there and ordered in a human voice that a sanctuary should be founded.

115 *Lord Edward Fitzgerald*: (1763–98), Irish politician who travelled down the Mississippi. Fuller's own first-hand observations of

squaws' burdens are recorded in the selections from her account of her travels in the West, *Summer on the Lakes in 1843*, pp. 150–203 of this volume.

115 *let them be sea-captains, if you will*: the most famous line in *Woman*, and the most poignant, in light of Fuller's own death at sea as a result of faulty captaining.

116 *maid of Saragossa ... maid of Missolonghi ... Suliote heroine*: Maria Agustín, the maid of Saragossa described by Byron in *Childe Harold* (i. 55 ff.). Agustín was a resistance fighter during the unsuccessful defence of Saragossa, the former capital of the Spanish kingdom of Aragon, against a French siege in the winter of 1808–9. This reference is a tragic foreshadowing of Fuller's own participation in the doomed defence of the Roman Republic against the French in 1849. The maid of Missolonghi is another Byronic reference: Missolonghi, in Greece, was the scene of a siege by the Turks during the war of Greek independence, and of Byron's own death in 1824. The Suliotes, a people of Greece, were defeated by the Turks in 1822, early in the war of liberation. For Emily Plater, see notes to p. 25.

117 '*... ungovernable love.*': William Wordsworth, 'Laodamia'.

A profound thinker: unidentified. This and the three paragraphs that follow are from 'The Great Lawsuit'.

118 *I stand in the sunny noon of life*: five years before her death.

119 '*Though many have suffered shipwreck ... hearts.*': unidentified. Fuller's preoccupation with metaphors of drowning is uncanny and continual. In many earlier dreams Fuller had associated water with death: in one she found herself crossing a bridge to a city on a hill, when the bridge snapped beneath her. In an 1840 dream about Emerson she was dying by the sea, and Emerson was all celestial: 'I thought I was with him on the rocks near a castellated place on the sea shore. I was dying and had that transparent spiritual feeling that I do after I have been in great pain, as if separated from the body and yet with memory enough of its pressure to make me enjoy the freedom, Mr E. was in his most angelic mood.' 'I never think of the voyage without fearing the baby will die in it', Fuller wrote of the projected crossing from Italy to America, as early as November 1849. In early 1850 she wrote: 'I am absurdly fearful about this voyage. Various little omens have combined to give me a dark feeling. Among others just now, we hear of the wreck of the ship Westmoreland ... Perhaps we shall live to laugh at these ...' Just before she

embarked, on 17 May 1850, she wrote: 'I shall embark more composedly in my merchant ship; praying, indeed fervently, that it may not be my lot to lose my babe at sea, either by unsolaced sickness, or amid the howling waves. Or that if I should, it may be brief anguish, and Ossoli, he and I go together.'

119 *The palace home of King and Queen*: this final poem, by Fuller, unifies the whole by returning to the epigraph: 'The Earth waits for her Queen.'

120 *Apuleius*: (b. *c.* AD 123) Roman author of *The Golden Ass*, quoted from Book XI.

121 *Thomas Taylor*: (1758–1835), English classical scholar and Neoplatonist.

   Lodi e preghiere a Maria [not Petrarch's title]: this is the poem which concludes Petrarch's *Canzoniere*, the collection of 366 Italian lyrics centred on his protracted and mostly unhappy love for the woman he calls Laura. At last, more than ten years after her death and more than thirty since he first saw her, Petrarch turns from the illusions and pains of memory to the Virgin Mary. The poem celebrates, in solemnly liturgical language, the powers and virtues of the Mother of God. But it is also personal: Petrarch asks the Virgin to help him abandon the fruitless obsession which has paralysed his will for most of his life and, finally, to intercede on his behalf with her Son in order that he may have the peace in death that he did not have in life. Fuller's text of Petrarch's poem contains a number of misprints, which have not been corrected.

125 *Frigga*: (old German Frija, Anglo-Saxon Frig, old Norse Frigg), goddess after whom Friday was named, wife of the supreme god of Norse myth, Odin. Like Odin, Frigg was all-wise; she protected marriage and made it fruitful. Frigg loved ornaments and jewellery: hence Fuller's reference to her as 'decked with jewels'.

   Baldur: in Norse myth, son of Odin and Frigg; god of light, whose death was brought about by the malice of the fire demon Loki.

   Lockhart's Spanish Ballads: *Ancient Spanish Ballads* (1823), anthologized by the Scottish author John Gibson Lockhart (1794–1854).

126 *Spinoza*: Baruch or Benedict Spinoza (1632–77), Dutch philosopher, an early advocate of democracy as an ideal, sometimes called its most unequivocal advocate. But with the exception of Thomas Hobbes and John Stuart Mill, none of the early demo-

cratic or liberal political philosophers, such as Locke, Rousseau, Bentham, or James Mill, envisaged that women would have any share in citizenship, and Spinoza seems to have been no different. Unlike Spinoza, Hobbes (1588–1679) held that men's supremacy over women *was* attributable to custom: to the founding of states by men rather than women and to women's subsequent subjection. Fuller's contemporary, John Stuart Mill, held likewise that forcible conquest was the basis of men's supremacy.

127 *W. E. Channing*: Ellery Channing (see notes to pp. 62 and 67), from his *Poems* (1843). Fuller is being generous here: only the year before she had been furious with her brother-in-law for his irresponsible conduct in leaving her sister Ellen in late pregnancy, while he set off on his travels.

Festus: a retelling of the Faust legend, by Philip James Bailey (1816–1902).

134 *one of the monks of the 19th century*: unidentified, but probably not meant literally. This is a fair sample of the Cult of True Womanhood (see Introduction), the background against which Fuller wrote. In *Woman*, as I argue in the Introduction, she both imitated and rejected the Cult; but she could not ignore it altogether, if she wanted to reach a readership steeped in its sanctimonious effulgences.

135 *The Memoirs of an American Lady*: (1808) by the Scottish author Anne Grant (1755–1838).

Miranda: see notes to p. 21.

137 *'Ah me! . . . tresses!'*: This and the subsequent lines are from Euripides' *Iphigenia at Aulis* (see note to p. 32).

worthless woman: Helen of Troy.

Guido's Archangel: either the thirteenth-century neo-Byzantine Italian painter Guido of Siena or, more probably, the seventeenth-century Italian painter Guido Reni.

139 *Supplicants*: sometimes called the *Suppliant Women*, another play by Euripides. Evadne is the wife of one of the seven chieftains, Kapaneos, slain in battle; the supplicants ask for the return of the heroes' bodies. Evadne throws herself on the funeral pyre with her husband. Iphis, her father, laments her death.

140 *the tragedy of his after lot*: after Orestes avenged his father Agamemnon by killing his mother Clytemnestra and her lover Aegisthus (who in their turn had slain Agamemnon for his sacrifice of Iphigenia), he was pursued by the vengeful Furies

until he sought refuge in Athens, where he was protected by the goddess Athene.

141 *Cooper*: the American novelist James Fenimore Cooper (1789–1851), best known for *The Last of the Mohicans* (1826), the second in the series of 'The Leatherstocking Tales'. Hetty Hutter and Hurry Harry March are characters in the last-written (but chronologically the first) novel of the series, *The Deerslayer* (1841).

142 *'Her prentice . . . lasses o''*: lines from Robert Burns's poem 'Green Grow the Rashes'.

Atreus' son: Agamemnon was a descendant of the house of Atreus, doomed to tragedy and bloodshed.

143 *Phrygian state*: Phrygia, in Asia Minor, here used as a synonym for Troy.

Pelasgic: in the *Iliad*, an epithet of the Zeus of Dodona (see notes to p. 114) meaning venerable and ancient. More generally used to mean the Pelasgians, the pre-Greek people inhabiting Greece, Asia Minor, and the islands of the eastern Mediterranean.

Mycenae: an ancient city in Greece, centre of the civilization which flourished between 1950 and 1100 BC, and which bears its name.

144 *Apollo Belvidere*: or Belvedere, famous Roman statue copied from the Greek.

Jeptha's daughter: the ancient Israelite king Jeptha promised that he would sacrifice to Yahweh whatever he first saw when he returned home, in return for success in battle. His daughter was the first sight that greeted him (Judges 10–12).

145 *Tennyson*: 'A Dream of Fair Women', from *Poems* (1832) of Alfred, Lord Tennyson (1809–92).

Ammon . . . Arroer . . . Arnon . . . Minneth: Ammon (Amon), Egyptian king of the gods. The others are probably gods of the Canaanites or other rival deities to Yahweh, god of the Israelites.

147 *Beatrice Cenci*: (1577–99), daughter of Francesco Cenci, suspected of sodomy, child abuse, and violence against his twelve children. She, her stepmother, and two brothers had the father murdered when they could no longer endure their virtual imprisonment in the upper rooms of the lonely castle where he had the two women confined. Beatrice was tortured, and all four were sentenced to death. The pope refused pardon, and Beatrice and Lucrezia were beheaded in September 1599; one brother was drawn and quartered, the other only imprisoned, because of his

youth. The painter Guido Reni (see notes for p. 137) and Shelley both used Beatrice Cenci as a subject.

148   *The Sacred Marriage*: poem by Fuller.

152   *Trinity and Unity*: during the eighteenth century in New England, schisms developed in the dominant Congregational Church, as a result of challenges from the radical rationalist Unitarians of Boston, who questioned all established doctrines, including that of the Trinity itself. Massachusetts was the centre of the most bitter controversies, which extended down to disputes over whether the church silver should go to the breakaway members or those who wanted to remain within the fold.

153   *Manitou islands*: probably Manitoulin, 80 miles long, in northern Lake Huron, now part of Canada.

        hamadryads: in classical mythology, spirits of particular trees.

154   *Medea's virtue*: in Greek myth, Medea, a sorceress whose magic philtres rejuvenated Aeson, father of her husband Jason.

        Manitou: in Algonquin Indian myth, a powerful and intelligent spirit. The supreme Manitou is Kitcki Manitou, the Great Spirit, father of life.

        S.: Sarah Ann Clarke, Fuller's companion for most of the voyage, sister of James Freeman Clarke, one of the editors of Fuller's posthumous *Memoirs*.

155   *Schoolcraft's Algic Researches*: Henry Rowe Schoolcraft (1793–1864), American ethnologist, appointed Indian agent to the Chippewa nation on Sault St Marie in 1822. There he married Jane D. Johnston, granddaughter of an Indian chief and daughter of an Indian trader. In 1839 he published two volumes called *Algic Researches*, which Henry Wadsworth Longfellow used as the source of the Hiawatha story. Schoolcraft's primary interest was, like Fuller's, in Indian religion and mythology.

156   *Mrs Jameson*: see p. 65, and explanatory note. Fuller had probably read her *Winter Studies and Summer Rambles in Canada* (1838).

        Cooper . . .: see note to p. 141. Uncas typifies the 'noble red man' of 'The Leatherstocking Tales'.

        Irving's books: Washington Irving (1783–1859), best known for 'The Legend of Sleepy Hollow' and 'Rip van Winkle'. In 1832 Irving travelled West, mingling with the Indians and shooting buffalo; he recorded his travels in his *Crayon Miscellanies* (1835), which included the section to which Fuller refers, entitled 'A Tour on the Prairies'.

156 *'The golden and the flame-like flowers.'*: like 'the encircling vastness' (p. 157) and the poem on p. 158, this quotation is unidentified.

160 *descendants of Madoc*: Madoc was a legendary Welsh prince who was supposed to have sailed to America in the twelfth century. It was thought that certain native tribes were descended from him and his companions. Fuller might well have come across the story in George Catlin's *Letter and Notes on the ... North American Indians* (1844), a work she cites in a passage not reproduced here, where, in an appendix, he discusses the possibility that the Mandan tribe were Madoc's descendants.

161 *Trollopian records*: Frances Milton Trollope (1780–1863), mother of the novelist Anthony Trollope, wrote a jaundiced record of her failed business venture in Cincinnati and her travels in America, *Domestic Manners of the Americans* (1832). The book caused a great outcry in America.

the Britannic fluid: bile, of Mrs Trollope's sort. The 'late French writer' is unidentified.

165 *Gothic, not Roman*: Fuller means that the settlers are vandals, like the Gothic tribes that sacked Rome.

166 *Rhesus*: in Greek myth, son of the muse Euterpe and the river-god of Thrace, Strymon. Legend said that if the horses of Rhesus drank the waters of the Xanthus, the city of Troy could never be taken.

'... still be seeking?' and (p. 168) *'The earth is full of men'*: unidentified.

168 *West*: Benjamin West (1738–1820), American painter.

169 *Those painful separations ... Atlantic coast*: Fuller may be thinking of her three brothers, Eugene, William Henry, and Arthur, who all set out for the West or South to make their fortunes, or of the friend of her youth, Sarah Clarke's brother James, who did the same. She herself had considered setting up a school in the West, but was dissuaded by her mother, who needed her help with the younger family members.

172 *Mrs Gore's novels*: Catherine Grace Frances Gore (1799–1861), prolific and popular English novelist.

173 *en revanche*: 'on the other hand'.

Apollo's darling: in Greek myth, Hyacinthus was beloved of the god Apollo, but also by the wind-gods Boreas and Zephyrus. During a discus contest between Hyacinthus and Apollo, the jealous Boreas and Zephyrus blew Apollo's discus backward, so that it struck Hyacinthus on the head and killed him. From the blood which gushed from his wound sprang up the hyacinth flower.

174 *Mariana*: the editors of the *Memoirs* took Mariana's story to be Fuller's own experience at Miss Prescott's school in Groton, confessed with 'touching truthfulness'. But Fuller's brother Arthur denied that this 'Mariana' story was true to life. In this century Perry Miller judged it 'more revealing as a psychological disclosure than as a piece of autobiography. It is one among several efforts of plain Margaret to act out the role of a beautiful and foredoomed heroine.' (Perhaps this is more revealing as a psychological disclosure about Perry Miller than about Margaret Fuller.) Whether the story really was autobiographical is debatable, especially given Fuller's own suggestion in 'The Great Lawsuit' that Miranda (see notes to p. 21) is not necessarily any more the real Margaret than Mariana, and that different characters might represent different aspects of her own personality. The story is told in the first person, by another girl, with Mariana in the third person, at a double remove. The narrator is much more like Margaret in appearance, background, and manner than is the Spanish Creole Mariana. Mariana was educated by an aunt; Margaret most certainly by a man. The rest of the Mariana narrative, after her schooldays, is clearly fictional—a standard romance in which Mariana dies of blighted love. The plot is not necessarily to be taken literally: the moral is more revealing than the melodrama.

177 *Warren Hastings*: (1732–1818), first governor-general of British India, tried by the House of Lords (hence 'the bar of Westminster Hall') on a charge of 'high crimes and misdemeanours'.

184 '. . . *met this black return*', and (p. 186) '*Whom men love not, but yet regret*': unidentified.

194 *Mrs Grant*: see note to p. 135.

   Lady Mary Montague [*sic*]: see note to p. 60.

195 *Carver*: Jonathan Carver (1710–80), American explorer of the North-West Territories. His account of his travels around the Lake Superior area was published in 1778.

   sachem: (from a Narragansett Indian word) chief of a tribe.

196 *Mackenzie*: see note to p. 106.

198 *'Still some . . . rush'*: unidentified.

202 *Butler's Analogy*: *The Analogy of Religion*, by the eighteenth-century philosopher Bishop Joseph Butler.

204 *Mrs Jameson*: see notes to pp. 65 and 156. This review, reprinted from the *New York Daily Tribune*, is included to show Fuller's continuing admiration for Jameson's willingness to speak out on the issue of prostitution—and, incidentally, to show Fuller's wry sense of humour. With Jameson, the New York Moral Reform Society, Anthony, and others, Fuller helped to construct sexuality as gender- and class-specific. She contributed to the proliferation of nineteenth-century discourses on sexuality which Michel Foucault has identified as typical of the age which we usually think of as having put piano legs into skirts. As an example of a woman who earned her own *living* by the pen, and later by writing more extensively about prostitution and female labour questions, Jameson was a positive influence on Fuller. But like Martineau, though perhaps less consciously, she was also something of an 'appeaser'. Even on behalf of queens, in her *Memoirs of Celebrated Female Sovereigns*, Jameson had been self-effacing: 'On the whole it seems indispensable that the experiments hitherto made in the way of female government have been signally unfortunate; and that women called to empire have been, in most cases, conspicuously unhappy or criminal . . .' And Jameson's style was acceptably True Womanish in her introduction to *Memoirs of the Loves of the Poets* (1829): 'These little sketches (they can pretend to no higher title) are submitted to the public with a feeling of timidity almost painful . . . to illustrate a subject . . . the influence which the beauty and virtue of women have exercised over the characters and writings of men of genius. Will it be thought unfeminine or obtrusive, if I add yet a few words?' It is this false and fluttering modesty, typical of the True Woman discourse, to which Fuller objects. Jameson's lisping manner is as annoying as the conscious dilettantism of the popular nineteenth-century novelist Caroline Lee Hentz, who had fluttered in her novel *Ernest Linwood*: 'Book? Am I writing a book? No indeed! This is only a record of my heart's life, written at random and carelessly thrown aside, sheet after sheet, sibylline leaves from the great book of Fate.'

207 [Title]: Charles Burdett, *Wrongs of American Women, First Series: The Elliott Family; or The Trials of New York Seamstresses* (New

York: E. Winchester, 1845); *The Duty of American Women to Their Country* (New York: Harpers, 1845).

207 *Mrs Stone and Miss Catherine [sic] Beecher*: possibly Lucy Stone (1818–93), an influential feminist and abolitionist speaker and organizer. The reference is somewhat dubious, however: Lucy Stone was Miss Stone (she married the feminist reformer Henry Brown Blackwell later, in 1855, but kept her maiden name), and in 1845, when Fuller's review was written, Stone was still at Oberlin College. Might 'Stone' be a misprint of 'Stowe'?— Harriet Beecher Stowe (1811–96), sister of Catharine Beecher, and already known for her *New England Sketch* (1834) and *Mayflower* (1843), both advocating that women should devote themselves to the sanctity of the home. Catharine Beecher (1800–78) was, like Fuller, the eldest of nine children, and responsible for much of her family's upbringing. She campaigned for equal education opportunities for women, but remained within the Cult of True Womanhood by resolutely opposing the vote.

natural piety: perhaps a paraphrase of Wordsworth's 'And I could wish my days to be | Bound each to each by natural piety' ('My Heart Leaps Up', 1807).

210 *nurse*: before the work of Florence Nightingale in the Crimean War and Dorothea Dix in the American Civil War, nursing was not regarded as a proper profession, or as a profession proper for ladies. In this review Fuller was being quite daring in proposing nursing as a profession for women, and later, in following her own advice by running the hospital Bene Fratelli in Rome during the revolution of 1849. As Thomas Wentworth Higginson wrote in his 1884 biography of Fuller: 'She was leading such a life as no American woman had led in this century before. During our own civil war, many women afterwards led it, and found out for themselves what it was; but by that time Margaret Fuller Ossoli had passed away.'

Mrs George Lee: Hannah F. Lee (1780–1865), a popular writer of the period.

213 *Things and Thoughts in Europe*: first published in the *New York Daily Tribune*, 3 March 1847. Following on from Fuller's developing interest in prostitution and employment restrictions among American women in the two previous pieces, this report, the tenth of her thirty-four European dispatches between 1846 and 1850, gives a good idea of her practical concern for French and English working women's lot. It makes a nice counter-

point to the sometimes high-flown rhetoric of *Woman in the Nineteenth Century*.

213 *the model prison at Pentonville*: opened in 1842, Pentonville Prison in London became the model for fifty-four new prisons built in England.

crude and hasty suggestions: Fuller may have been conscious that Charles Dickens had been attacked for over-generalizing about American prisons in his *American Notes* (1842), after his visit to the Eastern Penitentiary in Pennsylvania.

214 *puff*: exaggerated praise, as through an advertisement.

215 *Consuelo: by George Sand*: see notes to p. 46. Sand was tremendously successful in France and highly influential on the Russian writers of Dostoevsky's generation, but in the 1840s, as Henry James wrote, 'to read George Sand in America was to be a socialist, a transcendentalist, and an abolitionist'. The American writer most influenced by Sand was also the one with the shakiest moral reputation—Walt Whitman, whom Emily Dickinson refused to read because she had been told that he was shocking. Like Fuller, Whitman particularly admired *Consuelo*: 'a genuine masterpiece', he wrote, 'the most noble work George Sand has left us, the most noble in several senses, on its own ground and in all of literature'.

216 *Miss Bremer, Dumas...Andersen*: Fredrika Bremer (1801–65), Swedish novelist and social campaigner. Although her novels of this period incurred Fuller's ire for their timidity, her 1856 novel *Hertha* created an uproar because of its supposedly extreme feminism. Alexandre Dumas (Dumas *père*) (1802–70), author of *The Three Musketeers* and other popular novels. The 'Northern novelist' is probably Hans Christian Andersen, who was initially more successful as a novelist than as the author of the fairy tales for which we now remember him.

that any good thing can come out of Nazareth: John 1: 46: 'Can there any good thing come out of Nazareth?'

218 *Aglauron and Laurie*: After Fuller's thoughts on the novels of Sand, it seems appropriate to end this volume with two of her own efforts in creative literature. The first, a short story, 'Aglauron and Laurie', represents in fictionalized form the now-familiar argument, stated in *Woman*, that marriage is legalized prostitution. As proof she cites in *Woman* the phrase '*get married*'—implying that marriage is an object to be had, not a relation to be lived. Although uneducated and superficial,

the heroine of 'Aglauron and Laurie', Emily, still embodies the
female 'electrical' striving for some impossible alternative only
vaguely sensed but violently desired. She is something of a female
Werther or Byron, and it is for this portrayal that 'Aglauron and
Laurie' retains its interest, despite its overblown style.

222 *A Dialogue*: from *The Dial*, 1: 134. This final piece of writing
epitomizes Fuller's explicitness about sexuality, manifest in
'Aglauron and Laurie', as well as in *Woman* and her review
of Anna Jameson's books. Although the American critic Perry
Miller sniffed that 'her effusions are not memorable', he also
remarked on Fuller's 'startling use of a highly charged sexual
imagery' in this poem.

THE WORLD'S CLASSICS

A Select List

HANS ANDERSEN: Fairy Tales
Translated by L. W. Kingsland
Introduction by Naomi Lewis
Illustrated by Vilhelm Pedersen and Lorenz Frølich

JANE AUSTEN: Emma
Edited by James Kinsley and David Lodge

Mansfield Park
Edited by James Kinsley and John Lucas

J. M. BARRIE: Peter Pan in Kensington Gardens & Peter and Wendy
Edited by Peter Hollindale

WILLIAM BECKFORD: Vathek
Edited by Roger Lonsdale

CHARLOTTE BRONTË: Jane Eyre
Edited by Margaret Smith

THOMAS CARLYLE: The French Revolution
Edited by K. J. Fielding and David Sorensen

LEWIS CARROLL: Alice's Adventures in Wonderland
and Through the Looking Glass
Edited by Roger Lancelyn Green
Illustrated by John Tenniel

MIGUEL DE CERVANTES: Don Quixote
Translated by Charles Jarvis
Edited by E. C. Riley

GEOFFREY CHAUCER: The Canterbury Tales
Translated by David Wright

ANTON CHEKHOV: The Russian Master and Other Stories
Translated by Ronald Hingley

JOSEPH CONRAD: Victory
Edited by John Batchelor
Introduction by Tony Tanner

DANTE ALIGHIERI: The Divine Comedy
Translated by C. H. Sisson
Edited by David Higgins

VIRGIL: The Aeneid
Translated by C. Day Lewis
Edited by Jasper Griffin

HORACE WALPOLE : The Castle of Otranto
Edited by W. S. Lewis

IZAAK WALTON and CHARLES COTTON:
The Compleat Angler
Edited by John Buxton
Introduction by John Buchan

OSCAR WILDE: Complete Shorter Fiction
Edited by Isobel Murray

The Picture of Dorian Gray
Edited by Isobel Murray

VIRGINIA WOOLF: Orlando
Edited by Rachel Bowlby

ÉMILE ZOLA:
The Attack on the Mill and other stories
Translated by Douglas Parmée

A complete list of Oxford Paperbacks, including The World's Classics, OPUS, Past Masters, Oxford Authors, Oxford Shakespeare, and Oxford Paperback Reference, is available in the UK from the Arts and Reference Publicity Department (BH), Oxford University Press, Walton Street, Oxford OX2 6DP.

In the USA, complete lists are available from the Paperbacks Marketing Manager, Oxford University Press, 200 Madison Avenue, New York, NY 10016.

Oxford Paperbacks are available from all good bookshops. In case of difficulty, customers in the UK can order direct from Oxford University Press Bookshop, Freepost, 116 High Street, Oxford, OX1 4BR, enclosing full payment. Please add 10 per cent of published price for postage and packing.